ACADEMIC LIFE AND LABOUR IN THE NEW UNIVERSITY

T0300426

ACADEMIC TEACHING AND LABOUR IN THE
NEW UNIVERSITY

For my father, Alan Barcan,
Who believes in universities

Academic Life and Labour in the New University
Hope and Other Choices

RUTH BARCAN
University of Sydney, Australia

Routledge
Taylor & Francis Group

LONDON AND NEW YORK

First published 2013 by Ashgate Publishing

2 Park Square, Milton Park, Abingdon, Oxon OX14 4RN
711 Third Avenue, New York, NY 10017, USA

Routledge is an imprint of the Taylor & Francis Group, an informa business

First issued in paperback 2016

British Library Cataloguing in Publication Data
A catalogue record for this book is available from the British Library

The Library of Congress has cataloged the printed edition as follows:
A catalog record for this book is available from the Library of Congress

ISBN 978-1-4094-3621-8 (hbk)
ISBN 978-1-138-27379-5 (pbk)

Contents

Contents

Acknowledgements

A book like this is born out of countless conversations with colleagues, students and a whole host of other sympathetic listeners. I am particularly grateful for discussions about academic life over many years with Chris Fleming, Jane Goodall, Shé Mackenzie Hawke, Jay Johnston, Steven Maras, Kath McPhillips and Katrina Schlunke.

I am fortunate to have always worked in warm and generous university departments. I would like to thank my wonderful colleagues in the Department of Gender and Cultural Studies at the University of Sydney for their encouragement and support. In particular, I thank Melissa Gregg for her generous reading of a long section of this book and Elspeth Probyn and Meaghan Morris for their ongoing support of this project, for which I am deeply grateful.

Neil Jordan at Ashgate has been unfailingly cheerful, efficient and helpful and has made the hard task of writing this book much easier. Ashley Kalagian Blunt's eagle eye was of great help in polishing the manuscript. My father continues to amaze me; at 91 years of age he read the entire manuscript, made insightful comments and detected typographical errors. I am also very grateful for another family contribution; many thanks indeed to my sister Cath Barcan for her wonderful cover photo.

Several chapters have been revised from earlier publications: 'The Body of the (Humanities) Academic, Or, What is an Academic?' *Southern Review* 29(2) (1996): 128–45; 'Problems Without Solutions: Teaching Theory and the Politics of Hope.' *Continuum: Journal of Media and Cultural Studies* 16(3) (2002): 343–56; Chapter 4 originally appeared as 'The Idleness of Academics: Reflections on the Usefulness of Cultural Studies.' *Continuum: Journal of Media and Cultural Studies* 17(4) (2003): 363–77.

The cartoon in Chapter 4 – a long-time favourite of mine – is reproduced with the kind permission of Brad Veley.

The final thanks go to my family – wonderful teachers all. This book is dedicated to them and, most especially, to my father Alan Barcan, a good man, a careful scholar and a quiet and loving teacher.

Introduction: Private Feelings, Public Contexts

'… Churchill formulated accurately the mood of his countrymen and, formulating it, mobilized it by making it a public possession, a social fact, rather than a set of disconnected, unrealized private emotions'.

Clifford Geertz, 'Ideology as a Cultural System' (1973): 232

Introduction

When I am at work, silent, sinister faces glare down at me. Perhaps many people know the feeling, but these scary workplace presences are in my case a sign of privilege – part of an honoured iconography. For the grotesque faces are sandstone gargoyles, chimeras and dragons perched on the roof of a university quadrangle. A piece of colonial mimicry, they are part of an architectural iconography that ties my Australian university to the colleges of Oxford and Cambridge, and beyond that to the abbeys and monasteries of medieval Europe. In so doing, they tie it to a particular *idea* of the university: that of the university as the custodian of 'a wisdom, safe from the excesses and vagaries of individuals' (Newman 1976: 15). This is the dream of a university as solid and stable as the stone faces themselves, the embodiment and guarantor of the stability and continuity of 'deep-rooted European intellectual unity' and intellectual freedom (Dunbabin 1999: 32). As Cardinal Newman put it in his seminal tract *The Idea of a University*, a series of lectures written between 1852 and 1858 to support the establishment of a Catholic university in Dublin, universities are 'institutions which have stood the trial and received the sanction of ages' (15).

The Oxford ideal that inspired Newman[1] is, some would say, a 'liability' in the current era (Tight 2009: 7), where its lofty universal claims are contested and the social ground that made it possible has fractured. Nonetheless, this ideal 'remains an immensely strong – if slowly diminishing – influence' (Tight 2009: 7) in the British higher education system and beyond. Even in Australia, the idea of an unbroken chain from Sydney to Oxbridge[2] to medieval Europe

---

1 Newman was linked to two Oxford colleges for nearly thirty years: first as a student at Trinity College, then as a fellow and later a tutor at Oriel College.

2 This term, formed from an amalgamation of 'Oxford' and 'Cambridge', dates from the mid-nineteenth century and connotes something of the privilege of these two

is emotionally, and economically, powerful. At some Australian universities, it is made manifest architecturally, in cloisters, towers and quadrangles. In many more, it is embodied, literally, in the staff profile, for in the 1970s many Australian universities met the sudden need for an expanded academic workforce by hiring young graduates from the UK, often from Oxford and Cambridge (Hugo 2005: 329–30). The glory days of Oxbridge-in-Australia are fading fast. The newer universities of steel and glass outnumber the so-called 'sandstones',[3] and the generation of UK scholars who arrived in the 1970s will soon be retiring. Nonetheless, in the popular imagination at least, the Oxbridge model can still sometimes stand in for the broader idea and experience of university education itself, and even those students unfamiliar with, alienated by, or resistant to its histories, hierarchies and privileges might still feel something of its pull. For there is something very powerful and enticing in this vision of a world at once fanciful and venerable – of academics in caps and gowns, carillons ringing out graduations, champagne corks popping in cloisters and quadrangles, vehement discussions on lawns, and student pranks, rituals and demonstrations. But all this is not just iconography, for these symbols and practices are attached to a world of ideas and to communities of people. So these picturesque relics symbolize a more substantial invitation: to participate in lineages of thought and ideals of inquiry, and to join both a particular cohort of students and a more expansive community of former students and generations of thinkers past. This, then, is why the iconography continues to resonate despite the contemporary diversity of universities and fields of study, the variety of backgrounds of students and staff, and the crisis of faith that has prompted public debates on the identity, and the very future, of the university as an institution.

Today, gaining professional entry into this world is at once easier and more difficult than it ever was. Easier, in the sense that academia is now open to, and welcoming of, a far broader cross-section of the population than was ever the case, including women, people of colour, and people from working-class backgrounds. Harder, though, because the days of getting a permanent academic job with a good first degree are long gone, academic work is increasingly casualized, and the pool of people who might aspire to an academic job has expanded alongside substantial growth in the higher education system. In

---

institutions as a type of bloc.

3 This is the Australian 'equivalent' to the American 'Ivy League'. Sandstone refers to the material out of which a number of Australia's earlier universities, for example, the University of Sydney, were constructed, but the term 'sandstone universities' is used more broadly to denote Australia's older (i.e. pre-World War One) universities, not all of which were actually made of that stone. As only six of Australia's 39 universities are known under this term, it implies prestige and history.

contemporary Western universities, acquiring an academic job almost inevitably means acquiring a PhD, so the question of undertaking postgraduate study and the hopes for a life thereafter are thoroughly intertwined.

Perhaps some of those students who aspire to join Newman's 'assemblage of learned men' (1976: 95) are unaware of the extent to which the powerful modern idea of a university, and the types of practices it enabled, are under threat. So much of academic work is, after all, invisible – occurring in closed offices, at home, on planes, in meeting rooms and conferences – that it is still possible for outsiders, and even students, to imagine that lecturers[4] spend their days writing, teaching and discoursing eruditely with their colleagues. Di Adams reports that there is 'a mismatch between the expectations of new academics (the myths of the academy) and the reality they experience in the academic workplace' (2000: 65).

In the past, students aiming to become an academic might have doubts about their own abilities, but they would have been unlikely to have doubts about whether the university itself was a viable institution, nor if the life they might find within it would be a sustainable one. They would have been unlikely to question too deeply the value or pleasure of the life the university offers, only their own fitness to enter it. Today, though, those who are actively trying to break into it know it to be riddled with contradictions – undeniably privileged, but fraught, fractured and pressured. Newman's categorical vision of the university as 'a place of *teaching* universal *knowledge*' (1976: ix, original italics) is a far cry from the deep uncertainty or divisions around the university's mission today. As Bill Readings notes at the beginning of his incisive book *The University in Ruins*, the university is under assault from both the outside and the inside: an 'external legitimation crisis' meets an internal, intellectual, 'legitimation struggle' (1996: 1–2). Governments want many different things from universities, and universities themselves scarcely know what they are and whom they are to serve.[5] This public uncertainty has bred a certain personal and professional disquiet. According to Sue Clegg, there is, in fact, a 'crisis of faith' among academics, many of whom have 'discovered that the university life was not what they had expected or bargained for' (2003: 10). The palpability of this uncertainty can be illustrated by an excerpt from the concluding essay

---

4 I use this term in the British and Australian sense of someone who holds a (usually tenured) position at a university. It does not imply, as it can in the US, an academic without research responsibilities and/or tenure. I also use 'Professor' in the Australian sense, to refer not to all academic staff as in the US and Canada, but only to the most senior academic rank.

5 To take just one example, the *New York Review of Books*, the Humanities Initiative, and the Institute for Public Knowledge co-organized a conference in New York in 2011 titled *Who and What are Universities For?*

to a contemporary collection of essays on university pedagogy, in which the university has been transmogrified from Newman's 'universal idea' (Ker 1999: 11) into a shifting scene:

> The learning landscape is a restless place. Constantly shifting and resettling, erupting, changing, evolving. Its topography has undoubtedly been fundamentally shaped and reshaped by government, but its inhabitants continue to build on difficult terrain, supporting educational communities that are the foundations on which everything else relies. (Locker 2009: 139)

Academic Life and Labour in the New University represents the culmination of my attempts, over more than a decade, to wrestle with these big questions from inside this 'difficult terrain'. What, it asks, does it mean to enter this world today as a prospective academic, and what does it take for students and staff to work happily, ethically and usefully within it? The book explores some of the intellectual and political issues at stake, as well as some pedagogical and collegial strategies academics might deploy to allow us to thrive within it and to make of the academic profession an inheritance the next generation will want. Can we, I ask, approach the contemporary uncertainty about the nature and purpose of the university, and hence of academic life and work, from a perspective that is emotionally more mature, politically more astute, and ethically more sound than either bearing up or giving up?

Crisis? What Crisis?

Before broaching such questions, it is worth interrogating this current sense of crisis, for some might argue that claims of crisis are overstated and nostalgic. After all, one can trace laments about the decline of the university a long way back in time. Even Newman (1976), in the mid-nineteenth century, considered that the university had lost much of its authority, which he saw as having shifted to the world of journalism, where knowledge was fast-paced, eclectic, and subject to the demands of novelty, economy and fashion. The new media of periodical literature required a ceaseless supply of 'reckless originality' and 'sparkling plausibility' (14) whose temporality and temper were at odds with the systematicity, pace and order required for 'real cultivation of mind' (10). Half a century later and the term 'crisis' was already in use. In 1949, Sir Walter Moberly, a former vice-chancellor[6] of the University of Manchester and chairman of the University Grants Committee, wrote *The Crisis in the*

---

6 'Vice-chancellor' is the term used in England, Wales, Northern Ireland, Australia and some other Commonwealth countries for the administrative head of the university,

University, a controversial Christian account of the decline in moral training provided by universities and of the contemporary uncertainty about their proper role in society. Moberly was deeply disturbed by the university's failure to believe in and execute its 'former cultural task' (1949: 22): the 'creation, generation by generation in a continuous flow, of a body of men and women who share a sense of civilized values, who feel responsible for developing them, who are united by their culture, and who by the simple pressure of their existence and outlook will form and be enlightened public opinion' (Dobrée, qtd. in Moberly 1949: 22). Over-specialization, utilitarianism, prejudice and petty service provision had come to predominate, and the university was lost 'in a moral and cultural fog' (28).

This by now familiar catalogue of ills might lead us to wonder whether the current malaise is, in effect, a matter of *plus ça change*. The eminent Australian professor Denise Bradley (2011), who chaired the expert panel in a 2008 Federal Government review of the Australian tertiary education sector, is one who claims that change has been a constant part of academia – indeed of *any* workplace – for decades, and that there is in that sense nothing special about the condition of the contemporary university. 'There is nothing unusual about now. It has *always* been this way', she said in a recent keynote address (2011) to young scholars.

The higher education sector did indeed change considerably throughout the twentieth century and the idea of a university changed with it. For some, this was indubitably a good thing. In 1974, the chaplain of King's College, London noted that the 'tremendous expansion' of the British higher education sector in the 1960s meant that 'there are as many different views on the role and purpose of university life as there are different universities!' (Kingsbury 1974: 8). This, for him, was no cause for lament. On the contrary, he greeted the questioning and the diversity provoked by the rapid expansion of the sector as a strength: 'Each new university has added its own contribution to the evolving model of university life. Patterns from the past have not been overthrown; rather, they have been added to' (8).

It is undoubtedly true that both the idea of a university and the structuring of universities into national and international systems are always changing. It is also the case that the pleasures and privileges of academic life continue, even if they are rather more precarious than was once the case and are unevenly distributed across the academic workforce. But in recognizing this dynamism, we must take care not to downplay some of the very real structural and ideological changes of the last few decades, and the intimate experience of the people who have been at the forefront of those changes. One of the questions

---

who would often be called the Principal or President in Scotland, Canada, Ireland or the US.

I want to ask in this book is whether the kind of summative logic that enthused the College Chaplain (whereby each new model of the university simply *added to* rather than transformed the university as a social institution) is still operating and, if so, whether fifty years on from the boom period he describes, academics as flesh-and-blood people can actually *sustain* the role of holding onto the past while embodying the future. To ask such questions, we cannot simply accuse academics of nostalgic self-interest. Rather, we need to take seriously changes in their social role and workplace life.

Three big shifts – massification, marketization and internationalization – have underpinned and fuelled these changes. In the UK and Australia, the growth to a mass system began in earnest after World War Two and picked up pace in the 1960s. Marketization and internationalization intensified in the 1980s and 1990s. The long-term effect for academic staff of these three big shifts has been a verifiable intensification of work life. Student numbers have continued to grow but staff numbers have not: between 1991 and 1996 the increase in teaching academics in Australia was only half that of 1986 to 1991, and from 1996 to 2001 'there was no increase at all in the numbers of teaching academics' (Hugo 2005: 330). Over the decade from 1990 to 2000, the student-to-staff ratio increased from 12.9 to 18.8 (Winefield et al. 2003: 53). As a consequence, teaching loads in Australian universities rose 46.5 per cent between 1993 and 2003 (Hugo 2005: 330). The teaching role has also expanded via a substantial growth in postgraduate education. Moreover, it has been professionalized, with increased requirements for training and evaluation and an enlarged bureaucratic burden in the form of policy development and documentation. Meanwhile, other pressures have grown, in the form of a greatly expanded role for research, alongside a battery of measures for assessing its quantity and quality and the 'productivity' of individual researchers. Responding to a whole host of internal and external accountability mechanisms regarding both teaching and research now constitutes a new and substantial form of academic labour in itself. Alongside these changes, academics as individuals and departments are now also subject to a pressure towards entrepreneurialism.

My argument throughout this book is not that any of these 'improvements' is necessarily bad – indeed, a number are to be welcomed with open arms – but that the simple super-adding of requirement after requirement, task after task, has left academics unsure, confused, overburdened and – to put not too fine a point on it – wondering how much more work can be compressed into a week. While it is true that work intensification, casualization and new forms of professionalization are features of most contemporary working lives and not unique to academia, complaints about the intensification of academic work cannot be dismissed as subjective whinging, nor should the impact of work intensification and role confusion on personal wellbeing be dismissed. Workplace and organizational studies repeatedly demonstrate that academics feel themselves to be greatly under pressure (Winefield et al. 2003, Jensen and Morgan 2009) and that they suffer higher rates of mental distress than the general workforce (Ditton 2009). A detailed study of work intensification at one Australian university conducted by the National Tertiary Education Union noted how in some sections of that university 'the evidence of poor morale including fear, reports of stress, the desires for voluntary redundancy offers, and a sense of hopelessness, were [sic] quite severe' (Jensen and Morgan 2009: 58). So, the first broad argument of this book is that there is a particular *combination* of work pressures faced by academics: work intensification and role confusion combine with the longstanding conception of academic work as a vocation and the current difficulty of acquiring full-time academic work to produce an especially potent recipe for professional disquiet and occupational distress. Moreover, the sense of shared purpose and of responsibility for maintaining core values and principles that has historically characterized academic staff is likely to give rise to a quite particular form of distress associated with the erosion of such values, for example, in the shift towards a more bureaucratic and corporate identity for the university.

Such issues are true of academics as a *group*, and yet the problem is all too often met with an individualizing logic. This tendency to blame individuals flies in the face of observable structural matters, like a correlation between staff experiences of distress and institutional factors such as the wealth of a university (Winefield et al. 2003: 60). To give one example of the way individuals may find themselves blamed, a university at which I once worked underwent a major institutional restructure, forging a single new financial, operational and academic organization out of a number of geographically dispersed campuses. At every meeting I attended during the complex and painful restructure process, the standard management reproach to anyone who made a critique of the process was that they were 'resistant to change'. This is a recognizable phenomenon; Kathleen Lynch (2006: 7) describes it at work during a period of change at University College Dublin for example. Even Professor Bradley, whose experience as Chair of the national review panel gives her a uniquely sector-wide view, employed this typing of individuals as one of her rhetorical strategies aimed at dispelling the myth that the university sector had been hit harder than other work environments:

The saddest academics I know are those ... who are still telling you how well they did at school, in their undergraduate career, or in their doctorate when they are 50 or 60 ... They are often the proponents of conspiracy theories, usually toxic in the academic team, and often very discouraging to those who are early in their career. They are the ones who tell you that good people are treated badly here and that *nothing* is as good as it once was ... But when you examine their career, you often see a track record of identifying problems rather than working to find solutions, of resisting change, and of being the champion of the status quo. Sometimes too, if you know them well, you can identify their failure to deal with a particular rebuff or rejection as pivotal in their stalled career trajectory. (2011)

I acknowledge that a degree of generalization and even poetic licence is required by the genre of a public keynote address aimed at encouraging young scholars to take up the profession. Nonetheless, I am concerned about how easily such characterizations accord with popular stereotypes and, ironically, aren't academically founded, failing to reference the burgeoning literature on academic workplace wellbeing. So, while anyone who has spent a few years in academia can recognize the type Bradley describes, and while I acknowledge the truth and importance of her broader argument about the degree to which academia has been *protected* from the type of changes that have swept through industries like manufacturing, it is simply not the case that it is only an embittered few or a bypassed minority of (mostly male)[7] academics who are confused, resentful or exhausted. On the contrary, every day I see young colleagues who relish their work but are nonetheless straining, and occasionally buckling, under the pressure. Such everyday observations are, as I have said, backed by empirical studies, sometimes on a large scale (Winefield et al.'s 2003 study, for example, had almost 9,000 participants, across 17 Australian universities). This, then, is a second core plank of my analysis – attention to the way ideological, structural or intellectual critique is frequently met by strategies that individualize and pathologize those who complain – in short, that cast them as people who are failing to cope. I argue that we need to meet large-scale structural and ideological change with something more subtle than a macho, individualizing logic that implies that people are not up to the challenge. We need to resist this logic both as intellectuals and as members of a collegiate, on the grounds that it is neither an analytic of sufficient nuance nor conducive to a defensible professional or interpersonal ethics.

Certainly, doctoral graduates seem to be taking changes to the university seriously enough, since many of them are turning their backs on academia. To put it more accurately, and more critically, they are making agonizing personal risk/benefit calculations about how long to chance it in a system in which they have already invested a large portion of their young adult life but whose promises of return in the form of full-time work are – at the moment – dubious. In the 1990s, between 35–50 per cent of academics on short-term contracts left the British higher education sector each year (Bryson and Barnes 2000: 204).

---

7 Bradley characterized the 'worst' of this embittered group as being 'angry and bitter about why mother's best boy, top of his class, is not as successful as others, whom they see as less intelligent or less worthy' (2011).

Years of slogging it out on the periphery, working in serial short-term contracts that stop paying just at the point the semester ends, leaving them financially stranded for the semester breaks, have left them uncertain about the viability of academic life. So too in Australia, where the cutbacks to the university system beginning in the mid-1990s seem to have led to a demographic skewing:

> It would seem ... that the death[8] of academics aged below 40 may indicate that a significant proportion of the so-called "Generation X" (born 1967 to 1981) have been lost to academia. They are a lost generation as far as universities are concerned. It may be that the lack of opportunities in the Australian universities over the last two decades and/or a decrease in the attractiveness of academic jobs has resulted in those aged in their 40s and 50s outnumbering those in their 20s and 30s by 31.1%. (Hugo 2005: 340)

Australian and UK universities, it seems, are starting to have trouble filling permanent entry-level positions (Stevens 2004, Horsley, Martin and Woodburne 2005) in the face of what might be 'the declining attraction of academic careers' (Horsley, Martin and Woodburne 2005: 1). Some of the interviewees for Horsley et al.'s report speculated that falling doctoral applications in Australia reflect 'a view among many better students that life outside academia is more rewarding and that academic life is no longer highly valued in the community' (3). A 2011 survey of 11,710 Australian higher degree students found that the two key detractors from the perceived viability of an academic career were salaries and the availability of positions (Edwards, Bexley and Richardson 2011: 88). Salaries are particularly an issue in those disciplines likely to attract better conditions outside the academy, such as business, economics and engineering (Stevens 2004: 104). There are, in both the UK and Australia, 'real challenges to attract high quality staff members to replace those being lost' (Hugo 2005: 340).

Australia will, it seems, soon face a shortage of academics (Hugo 2005, Edwards, Bexley and Richardson 2011). Indeed, in Australia, academia is the 'second-oldest profession', second only to farmers (Hugo 2011). The imminent retirement of the baby boomers, the ageing population (which will leave a smaller proportion of people in the workforce) and government targets aimed at substantially increasing university participation over the next decade all mean that there is a predicted shortfall. The question is, will this shortfall be met by systematic recruitment of full-time staff, or by increased class sizes and increased employment of casual labour? And, moreover, will future recruitment be spread across all disciplines or will it target those disciplines perceived as most useful to the Australian economy?

---

8 This rather Freudian typographical error appears in the original. It should, of course, read 'dearth'.

The potential shortfall of academics is, in fact, why Professor Bradley was making the observations cited earlier: her comments about resistance to change were made as part of the opening address to a conference designed precisely to counter perceptions among postgraduates that academia is no longer a viable career. This conference, held at the University of Western Sydney in 2011, was funded by the Australian Federal Government. It targeted postgraduates, postdoctoral students and early career academics, and aimed to 'showcase' the potential of academia as a worthwhile career (UWS 2011). The Australian government had recognized the need for an event that would address the potential shortfall by 'deliver[ing]' graduate students 'an insight into the excitement and fulfilment provided by a rewarding career in academia' (UWS 2011).

The conference was a worthy event, and one in which I myself participated, but its very existence intrigued me, pointing as it did to the contradictory and fractured nature of contemporary academia: the contrast between the traditional allure and exclusivity of the idea of academia – the world of gargoyles and graduations – and the realities of its actual workplaces, staffed increasingly by a casualized workforce on wages that are often uncompetitive in comparison to those available in other sectors. While academic salaries are much higher in absolute terms in wealthier nations than developing ones, in terms of salary relativities *within* the nation, academics fair quite poorly in countries like the US, Australia, Canada, the UK, France and Germany (Pacheco and Rumbley 2008: 7).[9] Academics in China, South Africa, Malaysia and Colombia experience much greater percentage increases over the course of their career than those in the US, Australia, New Zealand, Japan, the UK, Germany or France (7). In the UK, academic salaries have not kept pace with either the public or the private sectors; between 1981 and 1997, UK academics' 'real purchasing power' fell by around 30 per cent (OxCHEPS 2006; cf. Shattock 2001: 28). In fact, in Australia and the UK, academic staff salaries represented the smallest proportion of total educational expenditure in any OECD country in 1995 except the Czech Republic (OxCHEPS 2006).[10] A 2005 Australian report into academic salaries likewise found that they were low in comparison to other sectors (Horsley et al. 2005).

In the US, academic salaries are higher than in Australia and the UK – sufficiently so that they represent a strong incentive for academics to migrate to

9 It is difficult to compare academic salaries on an international scale. Pacheco and Rumbley's (2008) study considers academic salaries in relation to countries' relative positions on the UN's Human Development Index.

10 In Australia in 1995, academic staff remuneration represented 29 per cent of total educational expenditure; in the UK, it was 30 per cent, compared to 39 per cent in Canada, 41 per cent in the US and 73 per cent in Belgium (OxCHEPS 2006).

the US (Stevens 2004: 111). UK academics are paid around half what their peers in the US would be paid (OxChEPS 2006). Nonetheless, the US economic woes have meant that academic salaries have fallen; in the year 2009–10, 32.6 per cent of US faculty had their salary reduced (Jaschik 2010).

The salary picture is even grimmer when one considers the inequities caused by the rise of casualization. The high salaries of so-called 'trophy professors' are offset by the cheap labour costs of casuals, especially in more marketized higher education systems. In 1992–93, 45 per cent of academic staff in the US were classified as part-time (Giroux 2002). In Australia, the proportion of teaching staff employed on a casual basis has risen from 11 per cent in 1990 to 29 per cent in 2001; by 2008, this had risen to somewhere between 40 and 50 per cent (Brown, Goodman and Yasukawa 2010: 171). The long-term trend is clear.

Meanwhile, at the time of writing, postgraduate students in the UK might likewise be struggling to be convinced of the 'exciting and rewarding careers available in academia' (UWS 2011) as they watch academics trying to cling on to their jobs in the wake of a wave of recessionary budget cuts: first in 2009–10 under a Labour Government led by Gordon Brown, then again in late 2010 under the newly elected Liberal Democrat coalition, who cut the university teaching budget by a staggering 40 per cent (BBC News 2010).[11] Unsurprisingly, these waves of cuts sparked staff redundancies, with predictions of up to 6,000 academic job losses across the country (Lipsett 2009). Universities cut courses: at one extreme, London Metropolitan University cut over 70 per cent of its courses, reducing 577 courses to 160 (Swain 2011: 7). In 2009, the decision was made to close the entire Department of Sociology at the University of Birmingham (Collins 2009) though this was rescinded after protests.

This, of course, is a moment of crisis. But it is important to recognize that the current crisis of faith has not emerged only from recent economic crises; rather, the current shockwaves are part of a collision that has been long in the making and brought to a head by the dire economic circumstances of the moment. As noted earlier, claims of crisis have been around for a good while, and many of the contemporary points of debate and division have been alive for at least a century: debates about the university and the public good; about the appropriate role for governments in funding universities; about the relationship between scholarly inquiry and vocational preparation; and about the role of research (Tight 2009: 4). These longstanding tensions have, however, been intensified by the slow transmogrification over the last decades of the twentieth century of the publically funded universities of many nations: from state-sponsored scholarly communities to something resembling transnational corporations.

---

11 Universities had been warned that the cut might even be as high as 80 per cent (Shepherd 2010).

They have moved from being the exemplars of stability and continuity to the threatened, 'restless' landscape evoked above.

Outline and Approach: Affect, Ethics, Politics

This book explores some of the human dimensions of working in this new landscape. The essays that comprise it address the question of what it is like to study, work in, or aspire to, the variegated and tumultuous scene of contemporary academia, where old ideals struggle to persist in the face of new ideologies and new economic realities. They focus on the United Kingdom and Australia, whose university systems are similar enough to make comparison possible,[12] but many of the issues canvassed are much more widespread and will be recognized in their broad lines by those who work in a range of higher education systems. Prompted by my own experiences in the Australian school and university systems, they centre on the Arts and Humanities, with a particular interest in my home discipline of Cultural Studies.

The essays making up this book are studies in ethical, affective and intellectual life in a number of university contexts. Some chapters had their genesis in the classroom, others in the corridors. Some focus on the experience of academic working life; others on student experiences; others again on pedagogical issues. Underpinning them all is the insistence that the development of more ethical, compassionate and critical forms of teaching and professional life can take place only if we actively consider the intersection of the large-scale institutional changes of the last few decades with the intellectual shifts that occurred over the same period, like the rise of transdisciplinarity and the development of a pluralist curriculum. My argument is that these large-scale institutional and intellectual shifts have produced work patterns, tacit expectations and affective relations that encourage a good many students and academics to think we are not good enough, or productive enough, or smart enough. A perspective that is at once analytical and compassionate can work to demystify these effects and

---

12 Simon Marginson notes that the first Australian universities functioned as an extension of English education into the colonies and were later 'remade by public money and national policy' based on the British, rather than European, model, which foregrounded academic autonomy (2002: 411). Denise Bradley (2011) considers Australia and the UK to be the 'closest jurisdictions'. Many policy initiatives of the late twentieth century have been shared between Australia and the UK, such as the dismantling of distinctions between vocational and university education, the introduction of a student loan scheme, and the Research Assessment Exercise (RAE), which migrated to Australia as the Excellence in Research for Australia (ERA).

to help us regain a sense of agency – but one that is not blind to the economic, political and ideological climate that also constrains us.

This book is not a lament – no simple call for a return to the good old days. First, because the good old days were good only for the happy few; second, because at least some of the changes to universities can be considered improvements; and third, because most of the changes that have occurred over the last few decades are irreversible, so lamenting is not much good. So these essays seek instead to make sense of the feelings and predicaments that arise in these new circumstances, and to see what strategies for good living, good teaching and good thinking might emerge when we refuse to disconnect feelings of worry, regret or pressure from the institutional and intellectual structures that give rise to them. The book, then, remains a critique, one that aims to connect up the big picture of the last few decades with some of the lived experiences in a contemporary Australian university.

Outline

A number of themes weave through the book: the university as a fractured and contradictory institution; the importance of an analysis that recognizes the role of structural factors in helping to create the emotional climate of particular workplaces and of professional demeanours; the vital need for a pedagogy that takes account of students' emotional experiences; and the call for an ethics of teaching, learning and research based on the open discussion of the predicaments of tertiary life rather than their concealment.

The book begins with an overview of the changes to the university in Australia and the UK in the late twentieth century. Chapter 1, *The Big Shifts: Massification, Marketization and their Consequences*, is a portrait of the rise of a mass, quasi-marketized higher education system in the UK and Australia. This survey is of necessity thematic rather than comprehensive, serving as a stage-setting manoeuvre for the chapters that follow rather than as an intervention into the fields of history of education or higher education policy, where far fuller and more nuanced accounts are of course to be found. I write as a teacher and observer rather than as a historian, and my account is indebted to scholars such as Malcolm Tight, Brian Simon, John Pratt, and indeed my own father, Alan Barcan.

Chapter 2, *The Wellbeing of Academics in the Palimpsestic University*, starts from the observation that the contemporary university is now at least three different kinds of beast simultaneously: a scholarly society, a bureaucracy and a corporation. These different institutional forms do not so much succeed each other as overlay each other in a kind of palimpsest. Each paradigm brings with it a particular set of expectations, demands and regimes of academic practice. In particular, each paradigm implies and creates particular relations to and experiences of *time*. The chapter examines what this palimpsestic configuration means for the health and wellbeing of academic staff. What do efficiency, productivity and entrepreneurialism look like in the flesh? What binds the disparate purposes and practices of the university together? It is, I argue, the body of the individual academic who tries to hold it all together.

In Chapter 3, *Pluralism and its Discontents: Teaching Critical Theory and the Politics of Hope*, I turn to a particular aspect of student experience in the Humanities, and its implications for pedagogy. The chapter explores some of the problems (practical, intellectual and political) of teaching contemporary critical theory to undergraduates. What happens to students when we routinely undo their established belief systems? Why do some students encounter critical theory as a loss while others find it empowering? The chapter argues that students' emotional responses to 'doing theory' need to be taken seriously if undergraduate teaching is to be ethically minded. It argues that we need to be deeply mindful of the importance of instilling hope when we do critique.

Chapter 4 continues the reflections on the impact of critical Humanities teaching on students, in the context of a broader public questioning of the utility of academic work in the Humanities. *The Idleness of Academics: Hopeful Reflections on the Usefulness of Cultural Studies* addresses the politically vexed question of whether Cultural Studies academics in publically funded universities feel like they are doing 'useful' work. What might 'utility' mean in the new climate of vocationalism and corporatism? The chapter examines a common public scepticism about whether academics in general (and left-wing Humanities academics in particular) are doing useful work. It also considers Cultural Studies' own brand of commitment to a notion of political and social utility, and the question of individual academics' potential personal commitment to an idea of being 'useful'. It compares these broad reflections about the usefulness or otherwise of Cultural Studies with survey responses and interview material from undergraduate students about what they find useful in Cultural Studies.

In Chapter 5, *Feeling like a Fraud: Or, The Upside of Knowing You Can Never be Good Enough*, I consider the experience of feeling like an academic fraud or imposter. This experience is commonly reported anecdotally, but because it is shameful it is rarely analysed, politicized, or de-individualized. In this chapter, I argue that this all-too-common feeling is connected to the marketization of the university and to the rise of inter- or transdisciplinarity. In the absence of widespread collegial discussion about such matters in any mode other than the confessional, it is very easy for such intellectual, pedagogic and systemic questions to be privatized, internalized and wrestled with as individual lack rather than considered as evidence of particular or changing intellectual and institutional conditions. I argue for the ethical and political importance of normalizing discussions about this experience, especially for postgraduates and early career researchers.

Moreover, I make the case that the feeling of fraudulence can be mobilized in the classroom, arguing that an ethical and intellectually honest transdisciplinarity requires us not only to rethink what it means to be an 'expert' but also to debate and communicate that as part of postgraduate research training. The chapter considers some strategies of writing and teaching that might be more intellectually and ethically rigorous than bluffing. It argues that discussing problems, opening up gaps and being aware of the limitations of our projects might in many cases be not only more intellectually honest but actually more intellectually interesting than papering over cracks and producing polished, impregnable pieces of writing.

The book's conclusion restates my belief in hope as both a political value and a personal necessity. It reaffirms the two rather contradictory truths that are posed, albeit precariously, in this book: the truth of the undoubtedly privileged nature of academic work, and that of the very real threat to the university as an institution whose role is more than merely instrumental, and the need for us to fight for its protection.

Approach

The book is neither a history nor a sociology of higher education. Rather, it is an account of living with, and teaching in, the contemporary Australian academy. Prompted as it is by my own institutional trajectory, the book emerges in the first instance from the Australian experience and uses Australia and the UK as its two points of focus. Despite the specificity of some of the examples, it is unquestionable that the underlying issues – the changing nature of the university, funding cuts, overwork, instrumentalism and productivism, the rise of transdisciplinarity, debates about funding, the dominance of 'audit culture' – face most academics. Moreover, specific policy initiatives move from country to country, the Australian uptake of the British Research Assessment Exercise being one recent example.

Each of the essays that make up this book had its genesis in an unhappy feeling-state: despair, self-doubt, worry. A number were originally published when I was in the thick of such states. Here, I rethink them in the light of what I have learnt in almost two decades of working within the academy. They represent my attempts to wrestle with the pedagogical, ethical and affective dilemmas of university life, and to think and write my way out of them. The earlier chapters – those focusing on structures and systemic changes – remain the bleakest, since this is where, I believe, academics have least sway. But once we enter the classroom, the terrain is muddier, more local, more full of messy possibility. We have more control in the classroom than in macropolitics, and that is also where we have our most human contact. So the later chapters, which focus on predicaments arising from teaching, are the most hopeful. Put together, they chart a movement – from worrying, to thinking, towards a reconfigured practice – that I hope can contribute to a professional conversation aimed at making academics less privately anguished and equipping up-and-coming academics with a conceptual repertoire and a language with which to expand this conversation.

The chapters are essays in the traditional sense: experiments in thought. Each one addresses a core human question that is thrown into the foreground by the current state of the academy – like the need for hope, or the fear that one is a fraud. They proceed in each case from my own experience, reflection and analysis, which is augmented, tested and refined by drawing on a variety of sources, including government white papers, union reports, media and pop culture sources. The analysis is situated within a cross-disciplinary academic literature drawn from Higher Education Studies, Cultural Studies, critical labour studies and feminism, among others. In addition, Chapter 3 draws on two surveys with students of Cultural Studies and some follow-up focus groups. I also make use of autobiographical and formal ethnographic accounts of academic life (e.g. Acker and Armenti 2004, Pelias 2004, Sparkes 2007) as well as anecdotes, which have an important role in feminist Cultural Studies (Gallop 2002, Morris 2006: 20–2).

Feminist Cultural Studies is, in fact, the methodological home of my transdisciplinary, mixed-methods approach, and I share many of the animating assumptions and stances of feminist methodologies more broadly. The emphasis on lived experience, for example, is absolutely central. This is not solipsism; on the contrary, it is a deeply social analytic, springing from a recognition that is found within feminism, as in other forms of identity politics, of the simultaneously emotional and political importance of articulating one's 'private discontents' and finding them to be shared (Kolodny 1980: 1). This requires a certain courage and a commitment to using troubling experiences as a prompt for critical reflection, conceptualization and action rather than seeing them as sources of shame (Reger 2001).

This emphasis on lived experience is a particularly important approach when the phenomenon under investigation is a question of wellbeing, sense of purpose and morale. Surveys about academic morale and wellbeing provide an important form of evidence, one that can counter the blithely individualizing claims, but they also have limitations. As the higher education historian David Watson notes in his book on morale in university life, they tend to repeatedly find the same thing: when asked about morale as a general condition, academics inevitably respond negatively, but when asked about their own work, they tend to respond much more positively (2009: 1–3). This discrepancy cannot, however, be disregarded as a methodological flaw or as proof that claims of a crisis in academic life are overstated. Rather, contradictions in response need to be considered as part of the very phenomenon under investigation. For the oscillation between or co-existence of different feelings and thoughts about university life – the claim that it is both enriching and oppressive – is indicative of the palimpsestic nature of the university itself.

My approach braids together three analytic imperatives: affect, ethics and politics. Affect is involved because the feminist stance I am describing requires the researcher to be true to, and responsible to, emotions, rather than seeing them as white noise to be eliminated from a critical analysis (Reger 2001). Indeed, it requires the researcher to see emotions not just as a necessary evil but as a resource for thinking with. This view is intertwined with a particular ethics, one based on strategies of openness and conversation rather than concealment. Laying one's cards on the table is, of course, never a simple process of revealing the truth; rather, it is itself a type of intellectual, affective and ethical ploy. But such *performances* of truthfulness are an important rhetorical strategy, since they are a refusal to play one of the dominant contemporary academic games, that of defensive, or to use Eve Kosofsky Sedgwick's (2003) term, 'paranoid', critical strategies. In her analysis of 'paranoid' reading strategies, Sedgwick signalled the contemporary importance of a 'hermeneutics of suspicion' (124)[13] to contemporary critical practice. Criticism has narrowed its range of possible modes, she argued, having increasingly become a game of 'unveiling' or unmasking an unpleasant hidden truth. This mode is simultaneously aggressive and defensive: aggressive, since it consists of revealing faults, flaws or sinister logics located elsewhere, and defensive, since the 'anticipatory' and 'reflexive' (130) nature of paranoia perversely protects the critic from unwelcome surprises. The 'paranoid' critic already knows a situation in advance and cannot be surprised or shocked – i.e. *affected* – by it.

A stance that insists on both the intellectual and ethical virtues of accounting truthfully for our emotions is, finally, also a political strategy because it refuses to disconnect private feelings from public contexts. The famously feminist insistence on the political nature of personal experience is a commitment to understanding emotions as, at least in part, 'social fact[s]' (Geertz 1973: 232). As the epigraph from Clifford Geertz (1973) suggests, albeit in a starker historical context than the one described in this book, mobilizing the social dimensions of our feelings can be a powerful catalyst towards action and can lift us out of individual despair or paralysis. Centralizing questions of personal experience should not be mistaken for, or allowed to drift into, mere individualism, an analysis that fails to take account of economic, social and political factors. This, then, has been my attempt: to use experience as a resource, as a prompt for thought, and as one form of evidence.

Though each essay was born of its own particular worry, collectively they trace a movement, since like all my colleagues I have had to learn to find ethical and intellectually satisfying ways of working in the new terrain brought

---

13 She draws this term from the literary critic Paul Ricoeur (Sedgwick 2003: 124).

about by the substantial intellectual and institutional changes of the last decades. They trace not just a struggle but a resolution of sorts. 'Resolution' here is not meant to imply a fixed solution – more an act of resolve or will, a determination to keep on finding ways to live, think and teach well in the academy, despite the evident problems we all face.

This is inevitably a collective endeavour. As David Watson says, morale is always both a personal and a group matter (2009: 1). Moreover, morale, as noted earlier, can be contradictory, operating differently at different registers of proximity. These contradictions are more suggestive and, ultimately, more useful than a simple diagnosis of happiness or unhappiness, and than the transformative genres, narratives and projects that might arise from the latter.

Bill Readings's name for the collective project of living in the transforming university was 'dwelling in the ruins' (1996: Ch. 11). For him, this involves 'institutional pragmatism' (168). The modern university is ruined, he says, but we must refuse both nostalgia (lamenting its loss or trying to 'rebuil[d] a ghost town' [169]) and 'bad utopianism' (178), the attempt to propose a single model that could operate as a future ideal type. Instead, we must understand what is happening, 'recognizing the University today for what it is: an institution that is losing its need to make transcendental claims for its function' (168). For Readings, dwelling effectively in the ruins is in the first instance an intellectual project, proceeding from a subtle and accurate understanding of the new situation and of the irrecoverability of the modernist university. In that sense, dwelling is an exercise in clear-seeing.

Others, though, might insist less on clear-sightedness than on the necessity of a kind of willed blindness, or perhaps a practice of seeing double. The feminist literary critic Annette Kolodny, for example, once described feminism as 'an ideology that, for many of us, helped to bridge the gap between the world as we found it and the world as we wanted it to be' (1980: 1). This, then, might be a leaping off point for another form of utopianism – a strategic form, and it too, is a foundational feminist stance. For feminist philosopher Rosi Braidotti, it is possible to practise wishful thinking not only as a bridge to the future, but also as a self-conscious and strategic way of inhabiting the present, in what she terms a 'philosophy of as if' (2011: 26): 'The practice of "as if" is a technique of strategic relocation to rescue what we need of the past so as to trace paths of transformation in our lives here and now' (27). While this is, inevitably, a form of disavowal, and hence not necessarily liberating at all, Braidotti also notes this strategy's 'potential for opening up, through successive repetitions and mimetic strategies, spaces where alternative forms of agency can be engendered' (28). It is in such a complicated and ambivalent spirit that I engage a disposition that is at once hopeful, concerned, and critical.

Cultural Studies: Home Base and Exemplary Instance

Part of this feminist approach involves recognizing the intertwining of our personal and intellectual biographies (Skeggs 1995: 194) – that is, the way we are drawn to thinkers we find compelling because they speak to our own experience, whether directly or obliquely. It also involves a certain reflexivity about the social and political dimensions of one's own intellectual formation. My own intellectual trajectory, in its movement from a liberal arts formation in a fee-free moment to a postgraduate qualification and academic career in Cultural Studies, traces one particular line through a significant moment in the evolution of the university and university life. In this book I put it to work as a window onto these changes. This is more than a pragmatic decision to stick with what I know best since, as I will shortly spell out, the Arts and Humanities have a particular symbolic importance in debates about the role of the university. Moreover, the discipline I practise, Cultural Studies, is a useful point of focus for debates about the social mission of the university.

My undergraduate education was a classic Bachelor of Arts degree in languages, English literature and ancient history, followed a few years later by a teaching diploma. After several years teaching in a senior high school, university pulled me again. I wanted to do a PhD, but I felt that I could only justify giving up useful employment if I went to study something new. 'What about this thing called "Theory" that everyone is talking about?', I naïvely asked an academic friend. He pointed me in the direction of a particular professor and thus, as easily and chancily as that, I fell into Cultural Studies, having close to no idea of what I was getting myself into. That I could embark on a study of 'Theory' in order to do more justice to my sense of the privilege of attending a publically funded university is an irony that won't be lost on those who consider Cultural Studies to be the epitome of useless self-indulgence. Clearly, it must have troubled me on some level, for the 'utility' of Cultural Studies is a theme I was later to explore with students, and to which I will return in Chapter 4.

Not that Arts itself had been self-evidently 'useful', even in the early 1980s when I began university. On the contrary, to those outside the Faculty, Arts was the dilettante's degree, a judgement so self-evident that the Bachelor of Arts was the object of a stock joke: 'BA: Please Take One', ran the graffiti above the toilet paper dispenser in the university library toilets. What was, to some, an encounter with 'the best which has been thought and said in the world' (Arnold 1869: vii) was, to others, a flimsy bit of cultural waste.

This value chasm continues to characterize public debates about the Arts and Humanities – indeed, the instrumentalist agendas of the last decades of the twentieth century have only intensified it. The Arts and Humanities have a special place at the centre of debates about higher education funding and policy. For these disciplines act as the symbolic guardians of national cultures (Readings 1996). They are central to the modern conception of nationhood itself (Readings 1996), and to universities' longstanding role as the transmitters 'of a common culture and common standards of citizenship' (Committee on Higher Education 1963: 7). The university as an institution 'pre-dates the nation state as we know it' (Sayer 1999: 83), but modern nations and modern universities are intertwined. This is the starting point of Readings's book *The University in Ruins*, which argues that the modern idea of 'culture' arose alongside the nation-state, as the 'symbolic and political counterpart to the project of integration pursued by the nation-state' (1996: 120). The modern university, he states, functioned as the 'producer, protector, and inculcator of [this] idea of national culture' (1996: 3). It was, he claims, the Germans who gave the modern university a sense of *mission* (55) – first, via Kant, and later via an idea of culture inaugurated by Humboldt, which reached its apogee, perhaps, with Schiller, for whom the university was the 'quasi-church appropriate to the national state' (40).[14] Readings argues that the idea of a national culture and the idea of the university as the inevitable disseminator of that culture have declined, as the nation-state redefines itself in the face of a newly globalized economy and itself transitions to a type of corporation. This transition has a particular impact on the Humanities, he argues, since they are the disciplines that are the most powerful symbolic guardians of national culture, and hence most seriously threatened by the decline in the idea of knowledge as culture (1996: 4–5). As knowledge-as-culture transitions to knowledge-as-commodity, the Humanities and Arts come to be regarded with 'suspicion' by governments (Keohane 1999: 59), who may see them as contributing little to the national economy or to the training of job-ready graduates, and who resent their potential resistance to marketization, along with the critical or resistive spirit they often engender.

Such suspicion of the Arts and Humanities has been evident since the 1980s at least. In the UK, the first years of Margaret Thatcher's Conservative government were driven by an explicit focus on science and technology, and on 'achieving a closer balance between supply and demand' (Secretary of State for Education and Science 1985: 8) – code for promoting the needs of business in a coordinated way across schools and higher education. The Green Paper of 1985 (the Joseph Report) made explicit the government's desire to increase the number of school students doing maths and science at A level (Secretary of State for Education and Science 1985: 7). This was a swing away from a 'demand-driven' system (Taylor 1990: 239) towards one in which the government was

---

14 Readings argues that this worked somewhat differently in the US since, he claims, American society is structured less around the idea of a single national culture than around 'the trope of the promise or contract' (1996: 33). In such a society, the university offers a means of fulfilling that promise.

determined it should set the agenda about economic needs and taxpayers' value for money. The Joseph Report expressed concern that 'the efforts by firms up and down the country to interest [school] pupils in following courses of study of particular value to business do not seem to have had sufficient effect on the choice of subject in which young people specialise' (1985: 7). There is a hint of surprise and perhaps annoyance at the seeming recalcitrance of students who insisted on *not* wanting to study what the government wanted them to study and who seemed incapable of recognizing their own best interests:

> The increased numbers of science and technology places in public sector institutions planned by the NAB [the National Advisory Body for Public Sector Higher Education] for the 1984–85 academic year have not been fully taken up. This is remarkable – given high youth unemployment and the fact that graduates in maths- and physics-based disciplines stand a better than average chance of getting jobs. (1985: 7)

In the 'increasingly centralised' (Taylor 1990: 242) university system of the 1980s, new forms of accounting were being marshalled in the contest between disciplines. The social and economic usefulness of different disciplines was argued via crude financial calculations. Interest grew in the so-called 'social rates of return' – a device simultaneously conceptual and accounting – aimed, in essence, at calculating what the government and the public were getting back for their 'investment' (Wolf 2002: 24). A 'rapidly infamous' appendix to the Joseph Green Paper, for example, attempted to set out the 'relative "social rates of return" from graduates of different disciplines' (Watson and Bowden 1999: 244). Cost per student, completion rates and labour market success were all calculated according to discipline, as well as being compared across universities and polytechnics. This rather crude exercise was followed by two brief paragraphs hinting darkly at the possibility of using such figures to calculate the 'performance' not just of the higher education sector as a whole but also of individual institutions and even departments within institutions (1985: 58). Other economic analyses of the same era (e.g. Taylor 1990) attempted to weight the relative 'success' of the disciplines via a combination of labour market measurements (graduate employment rates, graduate salaries etc.) and graduates' own perceptions of the value of their degrees.

In Australia around the same time, tuition fees gradually came to be an arena for contests about the relative worth of disciplines. In 1989, the Labor Minister for Employment, Education and Training, John Dawkins, reintroduced tuition fees, which had been abolished in 1974 by an earlier Labor Prime Minister, Gough Whitlam. Dawkins's scheme – the Higher Education Contribution Scheme (HECS) – allowed students to choose between paying fees upfront with a discount or repaying the debt through the taxation system on attainment of a particular, uniform, post-graduation salary. In that sense it was a two-tier system, since it allowed families with means to pay less. In another way, however, it was democratic, since the government charged a flat fee of $1,800 per student, irrespective of their course of study. The flat fee structure did not discriminate between the different cost structures of particular disciplines, but nor did it account for the different salaries likely to be attracted by graduates in different fields.

The link between tuition fees and fields of study was given greater force and visibility when the Liberal-National Coalition led by John Howard took power in 1996. They raised HECS charges and replaced the flat fee with a three-tier structure, in which HECS rates became discipline-specific based on the differentials in expected graduate salaries. While on the one hand this can be seen as a justice mechanism designed to reflect the very real differences in graduates' salaries, it also had the effect of normalizing a disciplinary hierarchy and reifying particular notions of value. The variable fees allowed judgements about intrinsic worth, academic standards, intellectual difficulty, social and economic utility, and the potential financial gain of graduates to become subtly commingled and conflated.

Currently, perceived national utility has unashamedly taken over as one basis for fee calculations but it, too, proves to be no straightforward beast. In early November 2011, the Australian government University Admissions Centre website explained that mathematics, science and statistics attract the lowest fees 'because these areas of study have been identified by the government as national priorities' (UAC 2011). By late November, however, maths and science were, seemingly, no longer priority areas; a mid-year budget review decided to rescind the fee discount as a revenue-saving measure (MacDonald 2011). Although maths and sciences are respected as disciplines that produce authoritative knowledge, they are nonetheless in decline in both schools and universities. Australia has a well-publicized shortage of maths and science graduates (McInnis, Hartley and Anderson 2000). But neither the economic imperative nor the general respect for maths and science as disciplines is, it seems, enough to protect them as courses of study. So, while the (perceived) economic utility of different disciplines has become an increasingly commonsensical marker of their *worth*, this does not automatically translate into student interest or government protection.

While the sciences might languish in terms of student interest, they continue to enjoy widespread public support as important and respectable contributors to the nation. The Arts and Humanities, conversely, are popular with students but have increasingly become markers of personal rather than national interest. They have suffered from a decline in public respect since their post-War boom, an era in which the Australian Prime Minister Robert Menzies (1959) could publically champion the Humanities as civilizing forces essential to the nation's geopolitical security. Their Cold War role as the guardians and guides of the nation – voices of 'sanity', 'wisdom' and 'proportion' at a time of great danger (Menzies 1959: xii) – has dissipated in favour of a widespread view of them as superfluities or luxuries.

Feminists will recognize the gendered dimensions to concepts like 'the personal' and 'the superfluous', and will not be surprised that attacks on the Arts and Humanities emerged in these terms in the hyper-masculinist climate of post-1980s economic rationalism and instrumentalism. The Arts and Humanities are feminized both in the abstract (devalued as frivolous luxuries) and, more concretely, in relation to the women who make up the bulk of enrolments in these areas. Indeed, the Joseph Report of 1985 made the gendered impact of attacks on the Arts and Humanities quite explicit, advising schools that women and children should go first as the Arts ship sank:

> Those responsible for counselling intending students (and, perhaps, particularly girls) about their subject choices should be aware that the proportion of arts places in higher education as a whole can be expected to shrink. (Secretary of State for Education and Science 1985: 9)

Similar threats face the Arts and Humanities in the current economic crisis in the UK, in which public sector spending, including in higher education, is being drastically reduced as part of the so-called stringency measures. In such a climate, the Arts and Humanities have to work to prove their social utility, and potential students – 'consumers' – have to be convinced that they represent a pathway to a good job and a decent salary. After the Liberal Democrat government led by David Cameron foreshadowed big rises in university tuition fees in 2010, there was fervent debate about the economic role of universities and the social utility of particular courses of study. A newspaper item titled 'How Only the Best Courses would Survive Budget Cuts' makes clear the slippage between quality and utility:

> Poor-quality courses will be forced to close under plans to slash state funding for degrees. Government cash for most classroom-based subjects, including arts, humanities and social sciences, could be removed as part of 80 per cent cuts to university budgets. Only courses seen as strategically important to the country would be backed by state cash, including medicine, science, technology and modern languages. (Groves and Clark 2010)

In this we hear the slippage between questions of standards ('poor-quality courses'), questions of discipline (Arts, Humanities and Social Sciences), and economic conceptions of national utility. It is evident that in government policy and public commentary alike, the Humanities have lost their civic or national functions and are perceived as a marker of preferences, interests and priorities that are purely *individual* in nature:

> If you want a Degree in Voltaire, Michelangelo, Browning, or some other artistic intellectual, by all means get one, but I don't want to pay for it. I want Doctors, Dentists, Engineers, someone who can make a difference, not quote Voltaire at me or tell me about the brushstrokes on a Rubins, I can read Browning myself, I can look at an Holbein myself, if you want degrees in fine arts, PAY FOR THEM, I will happily pay for a Doctors degree, I wont happily pay for a Degree in philosophy, it appear to you to be important, it wont heal my fibromyalgia. (Bob Brigg, 13/10/2010 readers' comment: Groves and Clark 2010, original punctuation)

The defensibility or otherwise of this quite hyperbolically individualist statement is not my point. Rather, I want to note how remarkable this argument is when one considers until how recently literature, for example, was central to the project of *collective* identity. The institutionalization of 'literature' as a university discipline was an important part of the project of nation building: 'The study of a tradition of national literature comes [in the late nineteenth and early twentieth centuries] to be the primary mode of teaching students what it is to be French, or English, or German' (Readings 1996: 16). A century later it has become a matter of contentious, indeed frivolous, personal preference.

'What is socially peripheral is often symbolically central', noted Stallybrass and White (1986: 20) in relation to medieval carnival, and perhaps the reverse can sometimes be true. Certainly, the economic marginalization of the Arts in so much higher education policy from the 1980s onwards is accompanied by a ritualistic statement of their symbolic importance. Government policy papers promoting business agendas are not complete without the ritualistic restatement of the centrality of the Arts to the cultural life of the nation. This is to be expected if one accepts Readings's argument that the modern conception of the nation-state co-evolved with and was buttressed by the cultural traditions transmitted in university Arts degrees. Even the Joseph Report, which had no qualms about foregrounding its instrumentalist agenda, was required to make this gesture, albeit it in a parenthetical aside. Its ten-line entry on 'the needs of the Humanities' (a sub-section making only some vague remarks about the need for libraries to collaborate with each other) began: 'The Government – recognising the importance of the humanities – shares the UGC's concern ... "for the health of research in the arts"' (1985: 23).[15]

---

15 The UGC is the University Grants Committee. Established in 1919, it oversaw funding arrangements for universities until its closure in 1989 (Pratt 1997: 10, Tight 2009: 24).

This was, perhaps, the nadir of the ritual defence – the point where it became mere tokenism. Certainly, Readings singles out the British failure to resist Thatcherite attacks on the Humanities as a warning to those outside the UK. He argues that the British

> could find no better argument for the humanities than vague appeals to "human richness" in a world in which leisure has already become the primary site of capitalist penetration (as Disney and the Olympics attest). (1996: 90)

The final paragraph of the Joseph Report reads:

> As mentioned above, there are other social benefits derived from higher education which are not directly associated with the education of highly qualified manpower or research. These include the cultural benefits of higher education and the preservation of the stock of knowledge. Such items are not amenable to measurement with any pretensions to objectivity but it is important that their existence should always be kept in mind. (59)

That this statement of the centrality of the Humanities comes in the final paragraph of an appendix makes it clear that it is a philosophical residue – the equivalent of putting the Humanities on reservations or in museums.

Museums come in a variety of forms, and in an overwhelmingly state-funded system private institutions can be one such form. In the UK, as in Australia, the twentieth century saw the triumph of higher education as a national, essentially *civic*, endeavour, a far cry from the privileged Oxbridge tradition. Until relatively recently, the central role played by government in higher education in Britain was widely construed as a victory for democracy, in stark contrast to the much more commercially driven and socially stratified mix of public and private institutions that characterizes the US higher education system. The 1980s, however, was a period of increasing centralization (Taylor 1990: 242), in which the Conservative government demonstrated an insistent desire to drive and direct students' choices, in stark and ironic contrast to its free market philosophy (241). In that climate, and the decades of economic rationalism that have followed it, some have come to question whether the Humanities are imperilled more by commercialism or by government instrumentalism. As we will see in Chapter 1, for some supporters of the Humanities, the preservation of the Humanities is more important than a stance against privatization. Britain's only private university – the University of Buckingham, a not-for-profit independent university founded in 1973, formally opened to students by Margaret Thatcher in 1976 – sees itself not only as a preserver of Oxbridge style teaching, but also as a force able to influence the public higher education sector (University of Buckingham n.d.[a]). They do not see themselves as a museum but rather as an active alternative to the impoverishment of the state-run system (University of Buckingham n.d.[b]). The University's website is explicit about their place in the politics of higher education:

> Buckingham was founded in 1976 by a group of Oxford academics who despaired of the way the other British universities were going. The other universities are all funded by the state, and the state is their customer, so they have to do what the state says. (n.d.[b])

The seriousness of this agenda was illustrated by the participation of Anthony O'Hear, a Philosophy professor in the Department of Education at the University of Buckingham, in a 2006 round-table interview for BBC Radio 4 on the contemporary university. In this discussion, he argued passionately for the importance of the Arts as producers of the ongoing 'conversation of mankind' and custodians of the 'most basic literature of our civilization' (Kearney 2006, Ep. 5). He acknowledged the high skills content of more practically focused degrees, but argued that 'no one could possibly pretend that [a degree in computer games design, for example] enlarges the mind in the same way that studying Homer or Aeschylus [does]'. He argued that it was the *public* system rather than the private one that diluted academic standards, since public funding meant that universities were unavoidably and inextricably mired in the agendas of meddling governments. The only way to be truly free, he argued, was to be independent.

O'Hear's claim about the role of the Arts as civilizers and guardians of a fixed cultural content was vehemently contested by other panel members. The basic literature of our civilization is, they rejoined, always changing. This, then, is the contrast theorized by Readings: between an idea of culture as an enduring tradition that reflects basic values and ties people into a unity, and which the university has a duty to inculcate and transmit; and an idea of culture as multiple and shifting, and of the university as an institution whose role is to provide skills and contribute to economic nationhood rather than to a fixed idea of national identity.

It is here that I turn to my own discipline of Cultural Studies, whose controversial and contradictory nature makes it a useful prism through which to consider the question of the changing role of the university. Cultural Studies is seen by some as evidence of the decline of the university, by others as the kind of exciting interdisciplinary project made possible by new universities, and by still others as exactly the type of critical enterprise imperilled by the move towards commercialization. Some people have see Cultural Studies as a space of hope – a way that the university's social mission might be restored (Readings 1996: 91); for others, its success prompts despair at the thought that popular culture might supplant the liberal humanist tradition, or concern and suspicion of its avowedly radical theoretical base and overtly political agenda.

Three terms – ideology, culture and politics – are at the heart of this complex entanglement. For Cultural Studies is an overtly and constitutively political enterprise. To advocates of Cultural Studies, its institutionalization in the rapidly corporatizing university 'means that it now functions as a commodity' (Rutherford 2005: 308), and its commodity status inevitably turns it away from political engagement (309). But to its critics, the political nature of Cultural Studies is *itself* an ideological corruption, a reduction of the proud tradition of liberal thought to something merely programmatic. To such critics, Cultural Studies is anti-intellectual because it is a slavish purveyor of 'feminism, political correctness and the fascism of the latest "-ism" from overseas' (Wells and Wells 1995: 86).

Regardless of where one might stand on that, following the work of Bill Readings, a number of commentators have begun to claim that the question of ideology is now in any case moot, since the university is, in fact, no longer primarily an ideological institution. Left-wing critical theory can work as well as anything else in the university, since the university no longer has a built-in ideological brief: 'The University no longer has to safeguard and propagate national culture, because the nation-state is no longer the major site at which capital reproduces itself' (Readings 1996: 13). In this account, the university is a structure that has lost its traditional intellectual *and* ideological mission, with the result that it can act as the vehicle for promoting the successful production, exchange and consumption of *any* intellectual and educational products that work in the global marketplace, regardless of their political or ideological content. That means that it remains a political institution, but not an ideological one.

Many Cultural Studies academics (e.g. Rutherford 2005) regard the bureaucratization and corporatization of the university as a political tragedy. Readings, on the other hand, appears to see it more as an *intellectual* tragedy – that is, a story whose politics lies in the degradation of meaning, purpose and identity of the university itself rather than in the downfall of any particular ideological project like Cultural Studies. This is because he reads Cultural Studies as itself demonstrating the kind of empty centre that is, paradoxically, the contemporary university's defining feature. Just as the contemporary university can encompass anything from Marxist critique to liberal humanism to events management or hospitality, so long as it does it 'excellently', so Cultural Studies can embrace anything as 'culture'.

This, then, is the second element of the complex value entanglement in which Cultural Studies is caught up and which places Cultural Studies at the heart of debates about the Humanities in the new university: the conception of culture that lies at its core. Readings claims that for Cultural Studies, culture is, ultimately, a paradoxically content-free conception. It has been 'dereferentialized' (1996: 99) and rendered internally tautological: 'Cultural forms of signifying practice proceed from culture, and culture is the ensemble of signifying practices' (99).

Cultural Studies is a discipline with a 'center of gravity' (101) rather than a centre. That doesn't mean, however, that there isn't good work that goes on under the name of Cultural Studies, nor that it is a discipline that should be critiqued wholesale (117–18). Readings sees it as 'entirely welcome' that Cultural Studies, along with other interdisciplinary movements like Women's Studies, Lesbian and Gay Studies and African-American studies, has 'signal[led] the end of "culture" as a [national] regulatory ideal' (89). At the same time, such new disciplines do, however, point to the emerging 'void' that the erosion of the idea of national culture has left in terms of the university's modern sense of social mission (89).

For Readings, the hole at the centre of Cultural Studies makes it, in fact, the discipline emblematic of and fit for the new age. Cultural Studies' non-referential definition of culture – culture is, in essence, anything that people do, think or produce within the context of some type of identifiable social context or grouping – makes it the ideal fit for the era in which the idea of culture as a canon linked to a national community is in decline. Once culture has ceased to be the 'metadisciplinary idea' (1996: 92) that drives the social mission of the university as a whole, a discipline with a non-referential core can come to 'occupy the entire field of the humanities without resistance' (99). In that sense, the institutional rise of Cultural Studies is perverse proof that culture (that is, culture in the old sense of a coherent body of valued practice recognizably expressing a national or civilizational identity) no longer matters. Culture has become, then, the intellectual equivalent of the managerial/corporate principle of 'excellence' that Readings so brilliantly sees as animating and 'unifying' the university. Excellence is, he says, an 'integrating principle' with the 'singular advantage of being entirely meaningless, or to put it more precisely, non-referential' (22).

Readings's concession about good Cultural Studies work notwithstanding, this would seem to be quite a damning intellectual, if not political, indictment of the discipline, and one that would, moreover, suggest that Cultural Studies should have an untrammelled ride to the institutional top. But in the 15 or so years since Readings's book was published, the very non-referentiality of culture has meant that Cultural Studies itself may prove unable to sustain its quasi-disciplinary force. The idea of Cultural Studies as the discipline most fit for our age may be, to paraphrase a colleague, ideationally true, but not necessarily empirically true.[16] As Ien Ang observes, Cultural Studies has, in a sense, fallen prey to its own success. Having driven a 'cultural turn' in many disciplines, it is now at risk of finding its own disciplinary claims and specificity undermined.

---

16 This insightful comment was made by Greg Hainge in a question time at the Cultural Studies Association of Australasia conference, Byron Bay, Dec. 2010.

The best way forward, suggests Ang, is for Cultural Studies to learn from other disciplines:

> This is now a very competitive marketplace indeed, and one of the challenges for cultural studies scholars today, in my view, is to give up their self-perception as being at the vanguard of cultural research, and start actively to learn from and engage with the accumulated wisdom of other disciplines, each of which has its own enabling concepts, methodological strategies, theoretical histories, and empirical horizons which can inform and enrich our research in fresh and innovative ways. (2006: 187)

Perhaps if one agrees with Readings that Cultural Studies' success arose precisely because culture is no longer the most important game for the nation-state then there is no inherent contradiction at stake. Just as the definition of culture can expand without limits once the nation-state no longer has a strong stake in it, so too, the number and name of disciplines dealing with culture can also expand 'at the point when the notion ceases to mean anything vital for the University as a whole' (Readings 1996: 91). The difficulties faced by Cultural Studies in sustaining its sense of disciplinary identity and the institutional visibility of that identity in the face of a proliferation of programmes and departments professing Humanities and Social Thought, Social and Cultural Inquiry, Comparative Cultural Studies, represent, not only an intellectual-political matter, but also a branding issue, as Ang's use of the word 'marketplace' implies.[17]

Cultural Studies' condition as 'a symptom' (Readings 1996: 102–103) of contemporary uncertainty about the university's social mission brings me to the third of the entangled issues I am highlighting here: that of politics. Cultural Studies is a useful place from which to wrestle with the perennial tension between instrumentalist and scholarly views of higher education, and with the question of the social role of the contemporary university. On the one hand, it can be a highly sophisticated and at times quite abstruse conceptual and theoretical enterprise – in that sense, a bastion of privilege moulded in the tradition of the liberal arts and remote from the pragmatism of more vocationally oriented fields. On the other, its pretensions to social and political engagement are foundational. Some Cultural Studies academics try to reconcile this contradiction by seeing themselves as examples of Antonio Gramsci's public or organic intellectual (Rutherford 2005: 298), the intellectual who is

---

17 Graeme Turner argues something a bit similar when he claims that Cultural Studies needs on the one hand to commit to maintaining its 'disciplinary future' while nonetheless serving 'as a kind of academic *lingua franca* for the new humanities, a common theoretical and methodological language which may enable those disciplines engaged in cultural research to work with each other' (2012: 12).

more theoretically informed than many traditional intellectuals, but committed to sharing that knowledge with a less privileged constituency (Frow and Morris 1993: xxiv–xxv). This tension between intellectual activity and political activism, which animates Cultural Studies discourse even today and accounts for a deal of its characteristically self-interrogatory style, makes Cultural Studies an ideal place from which to view the divisions around the purpose of the contemporary university and the privileges and responsibilities of academic life.

One of the founding fathers of Cultural Studies, Stuart Hall, reflected that the Birmingham School, where the British tradition of Cultural Studies was developed, was an attempt to produce organic intellectuals (Hall 1992: 281). Related to this question of privilege, responsibility and social engagement, then, is one final feature of Cultural Studies that makes it a useful lens from which to launch this current exploration of academic life: its interest in education as a democratic, critical enterprise. Education was 'foundational' as both a 'space of enquiry and a site of practice' (Morris 2011: 123) for the British Cultural Studies tradition out of which I write. Today, Cultural Studies raises particular classroom challenges, which are important for a book with pedagogy as one of its themes. As a politically charged, internally diverse, radically transdisciplinary field of study, (feminist) Cultural Studies raises significant classroom challenges. Its theoretical base is intellectually difficult and assumes a disciplinary formation that few undergraduates in fact actually have. It is, moreover, morally and personally confronting – challenging commonly and deeply held ideas about identity, sexuality, gender and race. It has the potential to be divisive, and yet it is also very attractive to students. The classroom is thus likely to be quite a mixed affair, where students with religious convictions sit alongside feminists or Marxists, discussing topics that are often intimate (like sexual practices) or fraught (like race).

Having emerged out of my experiences in the classroom over many years, the chapters that follow are a challenge, including to my own to my discipline of Cultural Studies, to think carefully about what we do. They suggest that we might be less emotionally punishing on our students and ourselves if we entertain a more honest and rigorous conversation about the predicaments involved in negotiating and inhabiting the 'turbulent realities of modern academia' (Smith 1999: 148). They also dare to suggest that there are times when it is good to remember that hope remains a choice.

CHAPTER 1

The Big Shifts: Massification, Marketization and their Consequences

Introduction

When I began an Arts degree in an Australian university at the age of 17 – fresh-faced, earnest and naïve (indeed, if photos are to be believed, even a wearer of pigtails) – my tutorials were held in groups of eight in the lecturer's office. After a class, it was not uncommon for my friends and me to go for a cup of coffee with the lecturer. Academic staff formed part of my social and even friendship network, since many of them were actively involved in student life, joining us in trips to the theatre, wine and cheese nights, classical toga banquets, weekend pétanque tournaments and many of the other pleasures of student life in the Arts.

Perhaps I was just lucky, and my experiences at a university in a large town may not have matched those of my peers who studied in bigger cities or in different disciplines.[1] Be that as it may, this picture of coffees and conversation, of plays and picnics, bears no resemblance to my own current life as a Humanities academic. Today, it is as much as my colleagues and I can do to schedule an annual departmental lunch, and I could count on the fingers of one hand the number of cups of coffee I have had away from the office with colleagues, let alone students, in the last five years. Conversations with students are not casual strolls to the university union after a class, but carefully scheduled

---

1 Andrew Riemer notes the 'icy, magisterial disdain' with which staff at Sydney University allegedly treated students in the late 1950s, which he found to be 'a wonderful liberation' (qtd. in A. Barcan 2011: 14). Richard Kingsbury's (1974) guide to university life for English students noted that it was easy for students and staff to classify each other as 'them', but that nonetheless many students form 'life-long friendships' with academic staff (68–9). Such factors as the size of the university, the demographics of its staff and students, and its geographical location all have an impact on the nature of the way staff and students relate. My own situation as the daughter of an academic undoubtedly played a role in my personal comfort with academics, but the ethos of sociability at my university was undoubtedly due in part to the egalitarian nature of my historically working-class home city, and it prevailed well beyond the ranks of the privileged.

appointments, often squeezed in before a lecture for maximum efficiency for both the student and me.

Efficiency and productivity have, indeed, become the hallmarks of daily professional life and the drivers of new habits – the subtle bodily register of the creeping but ultimately sweeping changes of the last few decades, which have seen great changes to the number, size, funding conditions, student population and management structure of universities. As one who has lived out this evolution from within the Australian higher education system – as an undergraduate student in a period without tuition fees, a postgraduate in the time of intellectual upheaval in the Humanities, and an employed academic in the era of cutbacks – I know these changes not only intellectually, but also as memories registered in the body, and as changes to the rhythms and habits of everyday life.

Looking back, I am in a position to make some politics out of my fond undergraduate memories, beginning with the realization that many (though by no means all) of the lecturers who joined in with students in such a leisurely fashion were male. The luxurious temporality we enjoyed and the sociality it engendered were, it now seems obvious, underpinned by a set of economic and social realities, including the hegemonic gender arrangements that allowed the predominantly male workforce time to spare. Women were less frequently or more precariously employed, and may have had had less time to spare after hours.[2]

The pleasures of my undergraduate days were politically laden in other ways. First, the level of social interaction I enjoyed was made possible because universities were much smaller. In 1980 (the year I finished high school), there was a total of 330,000 students enrolled in higher education in Australia (Marks et al. 2000: 1). By 2011, it was 1,221,008 (including international students) (Department of Industry, Innovation, Science, Research and Tertiary Education 2011). So my years of growing up in the higher education sector also track its movement from an elite to a mass system, whose student experiences cannot possibly be comparable.

I was, moreover, an undergraduate in the brief interregnum provided by the Whitlam years, when student fees had been abolished.[3] While universities

---

2 In 1988 (seven years after I began university), only 27 per cent of Australian academics were female (Hugo 2005: 334). This imbalance has yet to work its way fully through the system. Some three decades later, older women are still under-represented in Australian universities, though *overall*, women now represent more than 50 per cent of academics (334). Cambridge and – even more so – Oxford have been even more conservative: in the late 1990s only 14 per cent of tutors and 3 per cent of professors at Oxford were women (Aldrich 1996: 8).

3 Australian Prime Minister Gough Whitlam abolished university tuition fees in 1974. In 1988, they were reinstated by the Hawke Labor Government, which introduced the Higher Education Contribution Scheme (HECS). This deferred payment scheme,

had hitherto largely served the middle classes, the fee-free period I experienced meant that there were people from a wider range of backgrounds, along with many more mature-aged students than today. My classes were full of divorced women seeking new lives, middle-aged men seeking more meaningful careers, and elderly people relishing study in the Arts for its own sake. Over thirty years later I still think fondly, for example, of Mildred, a heavy smoking, red wine drinking, septuagenarian who was an active member of my university's English Society and who came with us on all our bus trips to see plays in Sydney. This to me was one of the deepest joys of university life – a breath of fresh air after high school. The constraints of school-based sociality dropped away like a heavy cloak, and many of my friendships crossed age and ethnic divides.

This was also a time when student grants, while not extravagant, were in better ratio to housing rents than they are today. As a result of this, and also of the class base of the student body, students engaged in far less part-time work than they do today when Sydney, for example, has the worst housing affordability in the English-speaking world, second only to Hong Kong (Cox and Pavletich 2011: 2). In such circumstances, campus life could flourish. Today, fees, rents and the temptations of a greatly expanded consumer culture encourage or force students to undertake paid work to a much greater extent than in my days. My long days spent almost entirely on campus – when breaks between classes were opportunities to read or chat or lie on the grass rather than infuriating obstacles to paid employment – must seem a scarcely imaginable luxury or a strange waste of time to today's Australian students, around two-thirds of whom undertake paid work off campus (Coates 2011: 3) and whose schedules are structured to allow university and work to be compressed into efficient blocks of time.[4]

How did so much change so quickly? To gesture towards the changes that underlie and motivate the essays that follow, this chapter will give an overview of this big picture, focusing on two core changes: massification and marketization. A detailed study of internationalization/globalization could of course have been included as a third major force for change, but space does not permit. Instead, I will thread a discussion of globalization through the chapters to come. (For an excellent detailed study of the impact of internationalization on higher education see Sidhu 2006). Under the rubric of massification, I consider the significant growth in the higher education sector in the twentieth

---

implemented in 1989, covered all domestic undergraduate students and some domestic postgraduate students (Smith and Frankland 2000: 7).

4 As an aside, the Australian university system has always been very accommodating of part-time university enrolment. A formal system for part-time enrolment was put in place at the University of Melbourne in the early 1900s, for example. Before that, students who worked full-time were allowed to sit exams after minimal – and occasionally zero – attendance at campus (Anderson 1990: 122).

century; under that of marketization, I explore how the idea of the university as an inevitably marketized player has become increasingly commonsensical, despite a widespread perception that this might conflict with the university's fundamentally social mission, with the ideal of disinterested knowledge and with the idea of social good. The big picture I survey in this chapter is the social, institutional and educational ground on which all the dilemmas explored in this book repose.

Massification

Massification is the somewhat inelegant but commonly used term to describe the significant expansion of the higher education system of many countries in the aftermath of World War Two. In most countries in Europe, North America, Latin America and Australasia, the development of the modern university system has been a tale of increasing participation and democratization. In many countries this expansion is the almost inevitable consequence of an expansion first of primary and then of secondary schooling (Committee on Higher Education 1963: 11). Such changes have inevitably entailed a questioning and shifting of universities' mission, their funding, and their standards.

In Britain, expansion really took off towards the close of World War Two. Malcolm Tight's (2009) history of the UK higher education sector notes three sources of expansion at this time. The first was government recognition that there would be a growing need for teachers and for science and technology graduates. This recognition helped fuel the development of technical colleges and university colleges (Tight 2009: 58–9). Immediately after the war, there was a second expansionary pressure, caused by a 'backlog' (60) of ex-servicemen and women entering universities and teacher training, assisted by targeted government assistance schemes (60). A third, more general, pressure was a substantial increase in student numbers resulting from 'the enhanced expectations of a growing population' (60).

Up till the early 1950s, there had been a slow and steady increase in student numbers. In the late 1950s and early 1960s there was a sudden boom – a 'massive institutional expansion' (Tight 2009: 61), commonly described as an 'explosion' (e.g. Kingsbury 1974: 7, Simon 1991: 225). In nine years, the number of universities doubled to 47 (Tight 2009: 65). This was not just a question of meeting existing needs, but of a deliberate, principled opening up of higher education to a greater number of people for reasons of social equity and national benefit. The so-called Robbins principle, named after the chair of the Committee on Higher Education (1961–63), whose influential report was published in 1963, is one core articulation of the newly democratic conception of the university: 'that courses of higher education should be available for all those who are qualified by ability and attainment to pursue them and who wish to do so' (Committee on Higher Education 1963: 6). This 'axiom' (1963: 8) also represented an overturning of what had till then been a hegemonic idea: that of a 'strictly limited "pool of ability"' (Simon 1991: 225). The call for expansion made in the Robbins Report was repeated later that year in a Labour Party report, which echoed the sentiment that higher education should be 'a right for all able young men and women, regardless of their families' class, income or position' (qtd. in Simon 1991: 229). Acceptance of this principle necessitated 'a rapid and continuing expansion of higher education, on a scale never before contemplated' (qtd. in Simon 1991: 229).

This expansion took place in an unexpected way, however. Though the Robbins principle was accepted by the incoming Labour government of 1964, the new government's chosen mechanism for enacting it took many by surprise. In 1965 the Secretary of State for Education, Anthony Crosland, decided to reinforce rather than dismantle the distinction between vocational/technical education and university education by creating 'a whole new higher education sector' (Tight 2009: 71) in the form of a greatly expanded polytechnic sector. Polytechnics were to be a second 'pillar' of post-school education, providing an education equal in prestige to, but different in nature from, that acquired in universities. One of the architects of the scheme, Eric Robinson, described it as 'a system with two tops' (Kearney 2006: Ep. 3). This decision, announced at Woolwich Polytechnic, the second-oldest polytechnic in Britain, was the formal instantiation of a binary policy, which was to last until 1992.[5]

Within this expansionary climate, particular attention was paid to those social groups who had hitherto faced obstacles in accessing higher education. In 1960, the Anderson Report initiated a regulation requiring local education authorities to give a grant to any student who obtained an undergraduate place (Aldrich 1996: 16, Tight 2009: 86–7). The Open University, conceived of in 1963 and opening in 1971 (Simon 1991: 265), was another important contributor, both symbolically and literally, to the process of opening up higher education. Since it allowed people to study at home part-time, it was able to accommodate new constituencies of students. According to Brian Simon, this university has had 'an astonishingly successful career' (1991: 265). Throughout the 1970s the so-called 'access' movement continued to grow, calling for the inclusion of mature, working-class and non-Anglo constituencies (Tight 2009: 74).

The drive to reduce social inequities has had some measure of success. By 1996, the number of students from ethnic minority communities obtaining a higher education qualification exceeded the national average (Aldrich 1996: 6). But social class remains an impediment. Though the numbers of people from

___
5 Crosland made it clear that he did not *invent* the binary policy, and that it had been 'developing steadily since the turn of the [twentieth] century' (qtd. in Pratt 1997: 9).

working-class backgrounds increased markedly over the twentieth century, socio-economic status still represents a significant factor in higher education participation (Tight 2009: 266–7).

The 1970s began well, with expansion across all levels of education and teacher morale high (Simon 1991: 405). A Conservative government led by Edward Heath was elected in 1970, and Margaret Thatcher served as Secretary of State for Education and Science. Thatcher's White Paper of 1972 continued the expansionist agenda, proposing an increase in full-time higher education student numbers of some 7 per cent over a ten year period (Simon 1991: 426). At the same time, it aimed to 'sharpen, and harden' the binary divide (426) by expanding the polytechnics. Its ambitions were, however, never realized: expansionary policies soon became impossible to fund in the face of economic difficulties so severe that there were five States of Emergency proclaimed in four years (406). The economic crisis of 1973 ushered in a 'wholly new perspective' (427): 'Educational expansion, on the scale that had now persisted for two decades or more, was to become a memory' (427). Between 1970 and 1973, university student numbers in fact declined by more than 50 per cent (427). Between 1974 and 1977, university budgets were cut drastically, in what was 'the worst financial crisis experienced by all universities in peacetime' (Stewart 1989: 162). For the newly established universities, the timing of these cuts couldn't have been worse.

The 1980s were dominated by the next Conservative government, elected in 1979 under Margaret Thatcher. Contradictions around the question of expansion continued. Over the nearly two decades that the Conservatives were in power (1979–97) their policy position shifted dramatically. Indeed, Watson and Bowden characterize the Tory era as a tale of two policies: "[t]hey took office with one series of policies and then suddenly and radically reversed field in the mid-1980s' (1999: 244). 'Policy A', as Watson and Bowden term it, was to cut funds drastically, to tie the universities to more pragmatic goals and to promote a more focused sector with fewer institutions (244). 'Policy B', which Watson and Bowden characterize as a 'change of heart' (245), was initiated by a 1987 White Paper recommending continued growth. Over the next decade the sector, especially postgraduate education, grew, though without overall growth in funding (245). This policy of growth without expenditure increase was achieved via a number of 'efficiency measures', including a rise in the student to staff ratio (245) and the dissolution of the binary system in 1992, which enabled the cheaper polytechnics to actively compete with the universities for students (246).

A similar picture of growth and diversification characterized post World War Two Australian higher education. One distinction, however, was that the egalitarian concern with access had manifested earlier in Australia. A number of the 'founding fathers' of Australian university education, including Henry

Parkes, had been concerned about the social exclusiveness of the new university system (Anderson 1990: 120).[6] Parkes had argued that the dedication of public money towards Australia's first university, the University of Sydney, established in 1852, should not be allowed because of the university's 'air of aristocratical predilection' (qtd. in Anderson 1990: 120). Other egalitarian characteristics of the Australian system include the earliness of its forays into distance education (122) and the central place it has always accorded to part-time education, with figures regularly showing up to one-third of undergraduates to be studying part-time (123).

As in the UK, enrolments in universities continued to rise during the early years of World War Two. This changed with the entry of Japan into the war, which made the need for manpower more urgent, and the Federal Government limited university enrolments except in certain 'restricted' fields of study (e.g. Medicine, Science and Agriculture), whose students were exempted from compulsory military service and financially supported by fee assistance and living allowances, via the Commonwealth Financial Assistance Scheme, established in 1943 (A. Barcan 1980: 288). This principle of financial assistance for those in need remained after the close of the war and was extended to all faculties (288).

As in the UK, student numbers grew suddenly after the war with the return of servicemen and women, which prompted a boost in government funding for new buildings (288). Alan Barcan sees the post-War period in Australian academia as a social and intellectual boom time:

> The years from 1944 to 1951 saw a quickening of student life in Australian universities, an immense growth in the size of universities, and an improvement in academic standards. The availability of Commonwealth government funds, the extra maturity given to student life by the presence of many ex-servicemen and women, and the idealism and enthusiasm of the immediate post-war period helped produce a flourishing academic life. (1980: 288)

Student numbers surged in the mid-1950s (Anderson 1990: 116) and concern about the social inequality in access to university was renewed (124). In 1957, the Murray Report articulated the view that Australian universities should be financed sufficiently to enable them to accept all qualified applicants (Anderson 1990: 117). This egalitarian principle, made six years before the 1963 Robbins principle, was accepted by the Martin Committee in 1964, which made the case for expansion, in part to include people from working-class backgrounds (118).

---

6 Henry (later, Sir Henry) Parkes was a 'colonial democrat' (A. Barcan 1980: 82) and middle-class liberal reformer, who argued for the necessity of state provision of education (83).

As student numbers rose, more people from working-class backgrounds entered universities, but, as in the UK, class was still a strong determinant. Moreover, the pressure of higher student numbers led to quotas being applied for popular courses and competition for places became stronger (Anderson 1990: 128). In 1974 the Labor Whitlam government abolished tuition fees in an attempt to make university entrance easier for working-class families. It also replaced competitive academic scholarships with a means-tested living allowances scheme (the Tertiary Education Assistance Scheme). Don Anderson outlines the relative failure of these measures.[7] Nonetheless these were at the very least important symbolic and psychological measures, helping to create a sense that working-class people had a right to enter university. I personally know a number of adults who credit Prime Minister Whitlam with having changed their life by allowing them to become the first member of their family to enter university, and who on that ground remain staunch 'fans' of Whitlam to this day.

In Australia, the 1960s and 70s were peak decades for equality of access, followed by a sharp reversal in the 1980s (Anderson 1990: 140). But the higher education system continued to expand. In 1988, the Labor Minister for Employment, Education and Training, John Dawkins, introduced sweeping reforms that greatly expanded the number of universities by dismantling the distinction between universities, teaching colleges and Colleges of Advanced Education (CAEs). These reforms put in place a 'Unified National System' (Commonwealth of Australia 1988), achieved via nation-wide amalgamations of CAEs with universities (or, more rarely, amalgamations between colleges to form a new university). In an unfortunate clash of directions, this expansionary policy was followed a decade afterwards by severe funding cuts under the Liberal-National government led by John Howard, whose market-based policies meant that all universities – from the newly established to the longstanding – would now be more actively competing for funds. The newly formed universities, still in the throes of establishing themselves as coherent institutional bodies out of the occasionally acrimonious amalgamations that had taken place across different geographies and organizational cultures, were, implausibly, supposed to compete on a so-called level playing field with the established universities, despite the asymmetries in prestige, facilities and financial resources.

The 1990s, then, were a time of funding cutbacks and a new, entrepreneurial, ethos in a political climate in which, as we will see in Chapter 3, 'academic

---

7 These measures, radical as they were, had relatively little impact on the social mix at universities, for a variety of reasons, including the fact that many children of poorer families would already have dropped out of the education system before the matriculation year (Anderson 1990: 129).

bashing', always something of a national sport in Australia,[8] came from the highest sources. Critics argue that such cutbacks and morale-lowering exercises were responsible for a drop in Australian higher education in OECD terms: between 1996 and 2006 (two dates roughly corresponding to the period of the Howard Coalition government), Australia dropped two places in OECD rankings – from seventh to ninth in terms of attainment among 25–34 year olds (Gillard 2009).

At the time of writing, in 2011, under a Labor government tenuously in power, the vision is once again expansionary. Responding to the 2008 Bradley Review of Higher Education, the current Federal government has set a target of 40 per cent of all 25–34 year olds to have a qualification at bachelor level or above by 2025 (Gillard 2009).

To sum up: by the early 1990s, both Australia and the UK had a greatly expanded higher education sector in which a structural distinction between technical, vocational, and university education had been dissolved. The creation of a large and variegated sector had institutionalized 'diversity' and rights of access, and in so doing put in place all the elements required for a more prominent role for the market: diversity, competition and an emphasis on consumer rights. It also set the stage for policy debates and oscillations around such questions as the relative merits of disciplinary specialization versus comprehensiveness, the desirability of a division between teaching-focused and research-focused universities, and debates about academic standards.

Since this book will focus on the pressures put on academics, many of which come in the name of accountability and standards, a few words about standards are apposite here. The term most commonly used to describe the smaller system that preceded the mass system is 'elite'. But by elite do we mean only socially elite – signalling the role of the university in the formation of a governing class, as radical critics of the university contend – and/or do we mean institutions with both the intellectual outlook and the funding base to sustain rigorous academic standards? In this question we see the intertwining of socio-political questions (the push for access), academic questions (what kind of curricula and assessment are most appropriate for a diverse student body?) and economic questions (what type of higher education can we afford to fund and where should the money come from?).

The egalitarian impact of massification has had a curious impact on academic standards. In the early days of the 'elite' system, an English university education was intellectually uncompetitive but financially and socially restrictive:

---

8 This may sound snide but I consider it a reasonably accurate characterization of the sometimes aggressive flavour of Australian egalitarianism. I am using 'bashing' in the colloquial Australian sense, to mean verbal attacks.

> Until 1945 virtually any student who could pass a relatively easy matriculation examination could go to a university if he[9] could find the money, and if he wished to do so. (Furneaux, qtd. in Tight 2009: 27)

After World War Two the situation reversed: university entrance became intellectually more challenging but socially more egalitarian (Tight 2009: 27).

The move to a mass system in the decades after World War Two inevitably shifted this picture yet again. As student numbers continued to rise and higher education institutions to proliferate, debates about standards arose. The Robbins Report of 1963 had considered it 'inevitable that some institutions will be more eminent than others' (Committee on Higher Education 1963: 9). It was, simply, 'unavoidable' (9). The writer and lecturer Kingsley Amis famously acknowledged this in a more pessimistic vein: 'more will mean worse', he stridently claimed (1960: 9). The advocates of a mass system contend that more does not mean worse, it 'means different' (Ball 1990).[10]

When discussing standards, it is hard not to fall into 'the most tedious error of all: *nostalgia*' (Wark 1993: 110, original emphasis). It seems to me that the teaching experiences I enjoyed in tutorials of eight cannot possibly be comparable with the ones my students have in classes of 25 or more. But maybe this is less a question of standards and more a question of the classroom *experience* – more about occasions to speak, to know other students, to be recognized by the tutor than about what is actually being learnt, or how well it is being learnt.

Many critics of university standards argue that the problem actually starts in *schools* and that university students arrive less well prepared than in earlier times. Some types of standards are more easily quantifiable than others: it is easier for lecturers in mathematics or physics to assess whether their students come with a working knowledge of a particular theorem or knowledge base or for language teachers to assess their incoming students' grammatical base than it is for me to know whether my students understand concepts better than they did twenty years ago.

---

9 From a feminist point of view the invisible contradiction between the masculine pronoun and the proclamation of universal access is worth noting.

10 *More Means Different* was the title of a 1990 British report (sponsored by industry, with BP playing a major role), which argued for 'a college education for everyone' (Ball 1990: 3). Seeing mass higher education as the linch-pin of continued economic growth, the report argued that there were only three possible higher education futures: a greatly expanded higher education system paid for by higher taxation; a greatly expanded system paid for by mixed means (more public investment; more economies of scale; and the introduction of student fees); or doing nothing, which would inevitably lead to 'national decline' (Horton, Foreword to Ball 1990: n.p.). They advocated the mixed funding system.

In any case, the question of standards needs to be considered in its broader social context. Perhaps we can know with some degree of certainty that (some) academic levels are not what they were, but this is not necessarily an argument against massification per se. The social benefits of education may need to be weighed against the intellectual benefits. The British economist Alison Wolf articulated this clearly in the BBC radio roundtable cited in the previous chapter. When asked 'do you think we are teaching people to think as well as we once were?' Wolf responded as follows:

> No, I don't. I think more means worse in one very simple way. If the result of it is that you spend much less per student than you used to this will have an effect. Now, you may decide that that's worth it – that more [universities] with less spent on each person is better than few with a lot spent. But to pretend that you can do this without anything happening I think is simply untrue. There is a lot of utter nonsense talked about how in the new world we can teach people much more effectively because they have to be self-directed learners and the IT revolution will change everything. Well, I'm sorry but effective learning and effective teaching are extremely expensive and they involve interaction, and the sort of education which I had ... involved an enormous amount of dedicated attention from highly educated individuals. So in *that* sense it does mean worse, though you may think the bargain is well struck. (Kearney 2006: Ep. 5)

This is no nostalgic lament, but a political analysis about the funding of teaching.

Declines in standards, then, may not necessarily be construed as a wholesale problem, when weighed against the benefits of wider participation. This is the position taken by Richard Aldrich, for example (1996: 19), who considers the trade-off in the UK between social inclusion and academic rigour to have been worthwhile. To argue this is not the same as arguing that there are no differences in academic levels over time, nor that the student and teacher experience in a mass system are the same as the type of camaraderie I enjoyed in my undergraduate days. To do so would be to buy into the faux-neutrality of the language of bureaucracy, whereby one might argue that teaching 50 per cent more students, over fewer weeks in the year in classes over three times the size represents simply an increase in 'efficiency' and not a decline in standards. This is the type of logic commonly employed by governments when implementing university budget cuts or when negotiating with teachers about salaries.

I also suggest that discussions about standards and rigour make most sense when they are situated within specified disciplinary contexts. One's thoughts about precision and rigour might be different when it relates to an engineer designing a skyscraper or a surgeon performing an operation rather than a philosophy student analysing a passage from Kant.

Any discussion about standards needs to recognize a number of things: first, the aims of higher education are neither static nor uniform, and in that sense one is rarely comparing like with like when one compares disciplines or invokes the past. Second, the contemporary instruments for determining standards – the battery of 'quality' measures – do not simply measure quality in any neat empirical sense, but actively produce the kind of things that they measure. Thus, claims that standards have improved since the introduction of 'quality' measures in the 1980s have a degree of self-referentiality to them. Third, the visible policing and publicizing of 'standards' is now intimately linked to a university's capacity to perform in the marketplace. This, then, brings us head on with the question of marketization, which is the subject of the next section.

Marketizing the University

The budgetary problem posed by massification coincided with the slow but inexorable rise of a new economic, cultural and social logic: that of marketization. Marketization and its effects is a theme that will recur throughout this book. This short overview begins by considering it paradigmatically: that is, as both an economic and a conceptual apparatus – one that in the UK and Australia is, moreover, a relatively new way of thinking and experiencing the university as an institution. This section then goes on to consider some of the operational consequences attendant on marketization: that is, how the market operates as an organizer of time, money, labour and bodies. Finally, I consider how, in the face of this deep change to the post-World War Two Anglo-Australian idea of the university, other ideals and values nonetheless persist. I argue that the contemporary university is a composite: a scholarly community, a bureaucracy and a transnational corporation. For despite the reality that the university has become a functioning player in the marketplace, with all the regimes of practice, experiences of time and divisions of labour that this entails, other ideas of the university persist. Contemporary university life, then, is characterized less by a shift into an entirely new state than by a *collision* – a lived multiplicity and ambiguity that produces conflict and confusion but also allows space for the development of new ideals.

Over the last few decades, universities in many countries have been deeply changed by the increasing enforcement and naturalization of the idea that they should be subject to some degree of marketization. This shift to market began earlier than might commonly be imagined,[11] but it was not until the 1980s that it really gained a foothold outside the US. The growth of a marketized

---

11 Lynch notes the importance of World War Two and the Cold War in beginning the commercialization of the sciences, especially in the US (2006: 2).

framework represents a significant paradigmatic shift in the UK and Australia, since distance from the market has been an important component of those countries' conception of intellectual disinterestedness.[12] This autonomy was also enabled by a freedom from direct *government* intervention, in contrast to continental Europe, where the curriculum was controlled by state education ministries. Indeed, David Smith considers European universities to have been 'completely state-controlled' (1999: 150), though the legal protection of academic freedom may actually have allowed for a stronger critical or oppositional function (Sayer 1999: 84). But in the UK and Australia, universities enjoyed an organizational freedom thanks to governments who for much of the twentieth century were prepared to fund them and to allow them intellectual autonomy out of a fundamental belief that universities were symbolically and economically important to the nation and a belief that they were best left to govern themselves.

In speaking of marketization, it is important to recognize that we are not talking simply about a distinction between public and private universities, nor about any simple narrative of the corruption of a pure scholastic enterprise by the forces of capital, but about a much more complex picture of contemporary modes of engaging with the material conditions of knowledge production and the realities of a mass system. Arguments about these questions are, fundamentally, debates about the relations between governments, universities, students and private capital, underpinned by particular conceptions of benefit, investment, contribution and responsibility.

The state has not always seen itself as responsible for a national system of education. In the UK early in the nineteenth century, the government 'could not be persuaded that [funding a national education system] would be a legitimate activity for public authorities to undertake' (Berdahl 1977 [1959]: 21). The state began to be involved in school education in a 'laissez-faire' way in 1833, when it was persuaded to give grants on an ad hoc basis to a number of societies for the construction of schools (22). University education likewise began as a complex mixture of the private and the sponsored. Oxford and Cambridge began as offshoots of the church, their activities approved by Papal Bull (Stewart 1989: 3). As they developed, they were 'endowed with land and money from influential founders' (5), and were supported by the monarchy. Henry III was 'an enthusiastic supporter' of the universities (Berdahl 1977 [1959]: 12), though the next few centuries of religious contestation in England meant that universities were both protected by the monarchy and subject to restrictions and punishments at its hand (Berdahl 1977 [1959]: 12–19, Stewart 1989: 5).

---

12 Sheila Slaughter, for example, describes pre-1980s UK academia as characterized by 'a powerful professional culture that explicitly rejected entrepreneurial initiatives and business goals' (1998: 59).

In the early nineteenth century, the alternatives to Oxford and Cambridge were privately funded (Tight 2009: 23). London University (later, the University of London), for example, was conceived of in explicit opposition to Oxford and Cambridge, and was initially financed by joint-stock capital (Stewart 1989: 10). But by the late nineteenth century the state had become 'inextricably involved in higher education funding and policy' (Tight 2009: 23). By World War Two, it had grown into the 'dominant funder' of universities (24), and something resembling a higher education 'system' could be said to exist (26–7).[13] The University Grants Committee (UGC), established in 1919 as an advisory board to government, but 'effectively in the control of the vice-chancellors' (24), oversaw funding arrangements and policy development in an arrangement in which 'the state was very much the subordinate partner in its relationship with the universities' (Salter and Tapper, qtd. in Tight 2009: 25). This was still the case when the Tories took power in 1979 (Watson and Bowden 243), and the arrangement lasted more or less unchanged until the closure of the Committee in 1989, when it was replaced by a board directly responsible to parliament. The UGC had acted as a 'buffer' between the state and individual universities (Pratt 1997: 10), so its removal represented a significant reversal of power. Along with the withdrawal of financial support that occurred in the same decade in the form of drastic budget cuts, it was clear, retrospectively, that the 'protection' afforded to the university by the nation-state had been based on an idea of national interest which, while 'long-standing' was nonetheless 'contingent' (Ryan 1998: 5).

National interest had been very evident in the first half of the twentieth century and had built the case for government funding. World War Two gave the state increased reason to intervene and increased opportunities to do so (Berdahl 1977 [1959]: 2). Robert Jackson characterizes the evolution of state funding in Britain as having involved three phases: a period of 'non-interventionist nationalization', from 1919–64; a period of 'increasingly interventionist nationalization', from 1964 and ongoing; and a period involving 'partial moves towards the re-privatization of higher education', beginning in the 1980s and continuing (1999: 94). For Jackson, universities became 'nationalized industries' on a par with steel or the railways. Though protected by statute from *direct* ministerial involvement in their particular affairs (97), they have nonetheless 'moved from a position in which they were private, grant-aided institutions trusted to develop their own idea of what they should be, to a position in which they are seen as public agencies paid to deliver the services wanted by government through processes increasingly prescribed by the state' (98).

---

13 Tight cites Silver, who says that although by 1930 all the elements of a system were in place in the UK, 'Nevertheless, commentators [at that stage] still found it difficult to *see* a "system"' (2009: 27, original italics).

Clearly, state involvement in higher education is a mixed blessing for university autonomy, but so too is market involvement. Commentators concerned about the increasing commercialization of the university often fear for the future of disinterested knowledge, seeing marketization as both an intellectual and a social ill. How, they ask, can universities continue to understand themselves and function as the producers and guarantors of disinterested knowledge? For some commentators, marketization is an unequivocal threat to these ideals; in Ramon de la Fuente's blunt formulation, 'Public policy that subjects education to the market is a bad policy' (2002: 339). Conversely, others lament the role of state control in setting educational agendas, stifling creative thought and discouraging or even quashing dissent. In particular, the state is seen to encourage instrumentalism. Here, for example, is the humanist sociologist Frank Furedi, responding to a proposed new private college of the Humanities in the UK:

> Universities face powerful pressures to subordinate higher education to a narrow instrumentalist agenda. Given the imperative of centralisation, most universities are unlikely to do anything more than go through the motions of opposing this trend. Many academics feel frustrated because this is not what they signed up for, but feel constrained by the ethos and the managerial imperative that dominates their institutions. In such circumstances, it is essential to think the unthinkable and engage in institutional innovation. Such experimentation in UK higher education [i.e. the re-introduction of private universities] is long overdue. (Furedi 2011)

This is an interesting place for a former student radical[14] to end up – supporting at least an experiment in reprivatization. It serves as a reminder that education is not a business like any other – and that for those who are cautious, critical or hostile about state authority, the value of critical thinking championed in the university, especially in the liberal humanities, may ultimately trump other questions, like those of the greater access made possible by government funding of universities. In Furedi's analysis, at the current moment the principle of intellectual autonomy free from government interference might potentially override the principle of open access enabled *by* government.

This might seem self-evident in the US, whose university system has always been characterized by a mix of funding sources and where the university 'has always had an ambiguous relation to the state' (Readings 1996: 33). Indeed, federal aid may well be construed as a 'danger' rather than a right.[15] Many of

---

14 In the late 1970s, Furedi was one of the founders of the Revolutionary Communist Tendency.

15 The Google Books blurb for Berdahl's book *British Universities and the State* (1977 [1959]) runs: 'This study of the changing relationship between the British universities

the strongest US universities were built out of the wealth of private benefactors (Keohane 1999: 54), though there has also been significant state funding of universities, especially in Michigan, North Carolina and Wisconsin (54). Americans have, it is argued, always embraced competition in higher education, and the elements of a mass, market-based system were in place there right from the beginning (Trow 1996: 26):

> Underpinning all was the spirit of competition, institutional diversity, responsiveness to markets (especially the market for students), and institutional autonomy marked by strong leadership and a diversity of sources of support. (26)

In the US, a competitive market system and institutional and academic autonomy are seen as going hand in hand. The administrative independence of universities and colleges is 'one of the hallmarks' of the US system (Keohane 1999: 59). Indeed, the American Constitution prohibits the federal government from directly managing education (Sidhu 2006: 63). Nonetheless, this shouldn't blind us to the ability of the government there, as elsewhere, to influence the universities, nor to the importance of higher education to American geopolitical and economic interests. Ravinder Sidhu claims that the US is often seen as an example of 'hands-off governance' (70), but in reality the state exercises a 'profoundly powerful role' (71) via indirect financial mechanisms like loans, scholarship, tax credits and grants (63).

But in the US, marketization is not perceived as an a priori impediment to intellectual autonomy nor to individual social mobility. So the rise of the market as the dominant paradigm for thinking about the future of the university has undoubtedly hit harder, in both practical and psychological terms, in the UK and Australia, where many universities are now neither fish nor fowl – primarily government-funded but subject to policy demands that they be increasingly self-funding, entrepreneurial, and accountable to the marketplace, while nonetheless serving government-defined national interests. In this contemporary context, in which governments are increasingly interventionist and prescriptive, moves towards marketization might be understood as contributing towards the intellectual autonomy of universities. It is nonetheless an ambiguous and somewhat circular contribution, insofar as government economic agendas align, broadly speaking, with those of business – in the sense that governments see a large part of their role as providing the contexts that enable the success of the

---

and the state offers lessons to Americans seeking to maximize the benefits and reduce the dangers of federal aid to colleges and universities'. Available at: http://books. google.com.au/books?id=cVJnBOy2-C0C&dq=offers+lessons+to+Americans+see king+to+maximize+the+benefits&source=gbs_navlinks [accessed: 3 February 2012].

free market. To that extent, government intervention and market involvement can be seen to act more in concert than in opposition.

The 1980s was the decade in which the imperative to marketize really began in earnest. In the UK, the election of the first Thatcher Conservative government in 1979 set the stage, ushering in a 'sea change' to government attitudes to higher education and the public sector more broadly (Tight 2009: 76):

> Efficiency savings, increased entrepreneurial activities, stronger institutional management and the adoption of private sector practices were the order of the day. (76)

In 1981 the Thatcher government began a staged reduction of funding for domestic undergraduate students (76) which, to its critics, constituted a veritable 'attack' on higher education (see, for example, Ryan 1998). During the eighteen years the Conservatives were in power, government expenditure on higher education grew overall, despite initial budget cuts of around 15 per cent over three years (Watson and Bowden 1999: 244). Student to staff ratios grew significantly (245). In 1989, grants to students were frozen and student loans were introduced, though grants remained for poorer students (Blake 2010). In 1992, under Secretary of State for Education and Science Kenneth Clarke, the binary system was brought to an end, thus promoting an 'undifferentiated' (Watson and Bowden 1999: 245) system in which more institutions could compete for students, the intent being to lower costs overall (Pratt 1997: 21).

But some marketizing initiatives never managed to fly politically. In 1984, Secretary of State Keith Joseph tried unsuccessfully to remove the automatic entitlement to free tuition for full-time students (Watson and Bowden 1999: 244). Likewise, the idea of a voucher system, though frequently invoked, remained a 'mirage' (249). The Conservatives even managed to avoid a 'perceived middle-class vote loser' – the seemingly inevitable principle that graduates should contribute in part to the cost of their education – for the entire period of their time in power (251).[16]

When the Tory government finally lost government in 1997 to Tony Blair's New Labour, some hoped for a return to an older educational agenda. There

---

16 The 1997 Dearing Report, which recommended that the government move from a system of full public funding to a mixed system in which students would contribute to the cost of their education, was not tabled until just after the General Election. Watson and Bowden consider this presumably deliberate timing to have been 'an extraordinary episode of political collusion' between the Conservatives and the Labour Party (1999: 243).

were some signs of this; as Power and Whitty noted in relation to New Labour's first White Paper on school education in 1997:

> ...it [was] possible to detect the promotion of renewed state involvement and investment, a confined role for markets, reference to egalitarian principles and some indication that the welfare state should provide support for education, at least from the cradle if not to the grave. (1999: 537)

They noted, however, that this was no reversion to an earlier ideology of full public responsibility for education, and that 'strands of Thatcherite thinking' continued into New Labour (538).

Indeed, the push to a more marketized system intensified under New Labour, much to the distress of those who had hoped that the end of the Tory reign would mean an ideological reversion on that score. The Dearing Report, commissioned by the Conservatives but issued in the early months of the New Labour government, noted the under-funding of the higher education sector (National Committee of Inquiry into Higher Education 1997: 2). It argued for the ongoing importance of the state rather than a fully-fledged market system (Tight 2009: 85), but proposed that funding problems should be addressed by greater contributions from the 'main beneficiaries' of higher education – that is, the students. As a result, fees of up to £1,000 were introduced in September 1998, and student grants were abolished in favour of means-tested student loans (Blake 2010). While student contribution to tuition fees does not represent a complete turn to the market, the embrace of the user-pays principle nonetheless makes it a significant step in that direction. Indeed, Malcolm Tight considers this reversal of the 1960 Anderson Report principle of mandatory student grants to be 'one of the most significant higher education policy changes in the post-war period' (2009: 86). The Dearing Report also marked another shift in the relationship between universities and government: whereas the Robbins Report had reflected the view of the academic community, the Dearing Report spoke to 'multiple audiences' and 'carried multiple agendas' (Barnett, qtd. in Tight 2009: 89).

Fees, once introduced, are only ever going to move in one direction. In 2003, the Secretary for Education and Skills Charles Clarke issued a White Paper foreshadowing a policy allowing universities to set tuition fees of up to £3,000 per annum, from 2004 on. In an interview with the *Guardian* newspaper, he described the future of higher education as 'fundamentally market-based' (Woodward and White 2003). In introducing the bill to the House of Commons, however, he stressed the opposite message, noting that 'the government will remain the major funder of higher education' (Clarke 2003).

In Australia, similar watershed structural moves towards the market occurred a little earlier than in the UK. The Dawkins reforms of 1988, which eliminated the distinction between CAEs and universities, were followed the next year by the reintroduction of fees for domestic undergraduate students in the form of the Higher Education Contribution Scheme (HECS). As noted in the Introduction, this was a loans scheme, with repayment to be made on attainment of a particular post-graduation salary, with a discount to students who could pay upfront. From that point on, it was inevitable that market logic would extend to postgraduate studies as well: from 1989 to 1994 the market emerged as 'the primary organisational principle in postgraduate coursework education' (Smith and Frankland 2000: 7). These major changes, which all took place under a Labor government, were accelerated in 1996 by a change in government from the Australian Labor Party to a Liberal-National Coalition led by Prime Minister John Howard, one of whose first policies was to significantly cut public funding to universities and to vigorously promote a more commodified, entrepreneurial and practically focused conception of the university.

At the heart of the marketization dilemma for countries in which the dominant recent tradition has been one of public funding are three questions: the nature of the personal benefits that accrue to university education; the nature of the social or national benefits that accrue; and the relationship between these two beneficiaries, the individual and the nation. How should one conceptualize and weight these different types of benefit? Rather than trace a history of this ongoing dilemma, which is too complex for my purposes here, I will extract some themes, beginning with ideas about the individual benefits accruing to university education.

Benefits to the Individual: Social Enrichment vs. Personal Enrichment

The loftiest place to start, perhaps, is the liberal humanist tradition, which focuses on the benefits of a university education to the personal, social and intellectual maturation of the student and the significance of such personal development to the social and cultural life of the nation. The life of the mind is taken to be both individually and socially significant: intellectual accomplishments are inseparable from a host of personal values and qualities. Matthew Arnold's famous characterization in *Culture and Anarchy* of an education in culture as an encounter with 'the best which has been thought and said in the world' (1869: vii) is one classic formulation. Such encounters, he believed, aided society because they were personally transformative. His concept of culture centred on its role as a personal and social 'reforming mechanism' (Bennett 1998: 94):

> For Arnold, the proper business of the study of culture consisted in identifying ideal norms of human perfection and, in holding these up as ideals to be emulated, encouraging individuals to adjust their behaviour so as to conform more closely to those norms. (94)

In similar vein, Cardinal Newman's description of the goal of a university education intertwined intellectual virtues with an idea of 'character': a university education cultivated a 'comprehensive' and 'versatile' intellect (1976: 10), disciplined by 'good sense, sobriety of thought, reasonableness, candour, self-command, and steadiness of view' (11). But for Newman such attainments were not a product only of an education in the Arts and Humanities; rather, *all* students in a university are enriched by their proximity to and contact with one another: '[Though students] cannot pursue every subject which is open to them, they will be the gainers by living among those and under those who represent the whole circle' (95). Encounters with intellectual traditions and with other scholars produce more enlightened, experienced and thoughtful individuals, and this in turn inevitably benefits society as a whole. Students will learn 'to respect, to consult, to aid each other' (95). This model of a (residential) university is thus a miniature of the idea of a harmonious society.

Newman was, of course, cognizant of the personal benefits attached to this type of cultivation. Indeed, they were one of the drivers of the Catholic University of Ireland, of which he was to be the founding Rector. A university education would give to Catholics the intellectual and personal benefits Protestants had always enjoyed, providing them with the opportunity 'to be on a level with Protestants in discipline and refinement of intellect' (1976: 9). While Newman's own emphasis was on the intertwining of personal and intellectual benefits as a goal unto themselves, he did note that for the 'ecclesiastical rulers' there was a sectarian drive behind the desire that Catholic youth might enjoy the benefits of higher education 'whatever they are' to the full, noting that Catholic leaders would consider it 'prejudicial to the interests of Religion that there should be any cultivation of mind bestowed upon Protestants which is not given to their own youth also' (9). This, then, was one particular version of the intertwining of personal benefits with a bigger social mission: that of the equalizing of personal and social opportunities for Catholics and Protestants. But Newman did not understand these social benefits in a material sense. He utterly rejected the conception of individual benefit as the maintenance or improvement of individual social standing. He began his *Idea of the University* by making it clear that he had no interest in the sort of education that aims to produce 'that antiquated variety of human nature and remnant of feudalism', the gentleman (ix). Rather, he steadfastly insisted on understanding the institution as one devoted to the formation of individual virtue and character. The university was an inculcator of truth, reason and knowledge.

This conception of social benefit – in which the cultivation of individuals enriches the whole society – is shared across disparate political and intellectual traditions. The critical pedagogy tradition, for example, while politically remote from Newman's Catholicism, nonetheless also sees the aim of university education as the development of particular intellectual capacities that enrich both the individual and society. The development of the critical spirit is understood as a social need – a fundamental tool in the development of a more just society. In that sense it is something that is good for, if not always welcomed by, the nation-state. In democratic states, the critical tradition makes publically funded universities the somewhat discomforting guests at the national table: hosted by the government whose interests they may not directly serve, but charged with the ultimately social mission of upholding the loftier principles of the democratic nation-state: freedom of inquiry, free speech, dissent. For this reason, this function of universities is typically recognized in government policy documents, though it may not always be so well respected in practice. The Dawkins White Paper of 1988, for example, even while it introduced significant moves towards the market, continued to articulate the importance of the critical tradition not just to individuals but to the nation:

> Higher education ... promotes greater understanding of culture, often at odds with majority attitudes and, in so doing, supports the development of a more just and tolerant society ... We do not want a higher education system that fails to analyse and, where necessary, criticise the society in which it operates...
> (Commonwealth of Australia 1988: 7)[17]

This principle continues to be a core value of liberal humanism. Thus, for Frank Furedi: 'The best antidote to the emergence of illiberal and authoritarian intellectual trends is a questioning and critically involved public' (Hope 2011).

One of the strongest formulations of the importance of education to social justice is in the tradition of radical pedagogy spearheaded by Paulo Freire. A Brazilian radical who worked in many sectors of education, including a stint as secretary of education in São Paulo, Freire saw education as at the heart of 'the struggle for the transformation of society' (Escobar et al. 1994: 69). He emphasized the political nature of *any* pedagogy, insisting on the need to recognize the power relations at work in any classroom, whatever the pretensions to neutral knowledge that may officially be at play (132). For Freire, 'every pedagogical act is a political act' (Torres 1994: 21). Commentators see him as in this way having espoused a 'postmodern' epistemological framework while nonetheless yoking it to the 'modernist' political values of freedom, justice, empowerment, and indeed revolutionary love (22). Freire's thought and practice have been influential well beyond the Latin American context in which he wrote and practised. Certain strands of Cultural Studies, for example, are influenced by Freirian thought. The media analyst Henry Giroux, for example, has been an

---

17 Compared to the pallid defence of the Humanities made in the Joseph Report of around the same time (Secretary of State for Science and Education 1985), Dawkins's claim of the need for universities to remain robust critics of society looks good.

advocate of critical pedagogy, and an articulate critic of the rise of corporatism, including in higher education. He argues that the development of a 'critical and productive democratic citizenry' relies upon the defence of education as a public good and 'an autonomous sphere' (Giroux 2002).

Intellectual autonomy and critical thinking have served, then, as core values for a number of educational philosophies, across sometimes quite stark differences in politics, ideology and intellectual style. Liberal humanism and critical or radical pedagogy share a certain basic postulate: that the cultivation of minds is much more than an individual matter, and that a critical, questioning mind is an important component of both a modern sensibility and a flourishing society.

This shared commitment to freedom of inquiry is one reason that people of widely different political persuasions can all be unhappy with the state of the contemporary university: they see the critical project as having been stifled by vocationalism, instrumentalism, government control and/or commercial interests. Where once universities may have been denounced by some elements of the left as socially exclusive institutions promulgating elite values for a tiny minority, now the critique has shifted. For many radical critics of the university, the problem is no longer that the university is elitist so much as that it is conformist, having been thoroughly co-opted into embodying and promulgating a new set of hegemonic values. Liberal humanists see academics as having given up on the Enlightenment project. Furedi, for example, laments the 'atmosphere of conformism' (2003: 175) that has engulfed contemporary academia, which he sees as marked by exhaustion, complacency and 'an intensely conservative imperative that is hostile to the critical questioning of society' (175). In a similar vein Desmond Ryan's retrospective analysis of the impact of Thatcherism on British higher education, written in 1998, expressed dismay at what he saw as the dampening of the critical enterprise. He argued that the rise of a mass, partially marketized, under-funded system was both intellectually and economically flattening:

> In historical perspective, British higher education between 1945 and 1980 appears as the state-sponsored workshop of the discipline of originality for an elite destined for leadership roles across those parts of the culture which gave scope to critically trained and creative minds. Today, however, as the generative source of a culture of intellectual adventurousness, of self-surpassing excellence in individual achievement, and of norm-questioning deep play, the British higher education system has been all but smashed – not by superior competition from the mindfacturing systems of other countries, but by its own former sponsor, the state. (5)

According to these critics, the university has become the servant of the state: it has been 'organizationally reconfigured to take on a politically decreed role in the economy' (Ryan 1998: 5). No longer 'producers of cultural norms', universities have become 'consumers of procedural dogmas' (5) – that is, bureaucracies. In this view, the university's bureaucratization is not an ideologically neutral overlay of extra tasks and organizational layers onto an existing base, but rather marks a fundamental shift in the university's capacity to generate views from elsewhere. Kathleen Lynch, drawing on Giroux's work, argues that even seemingly neutral operational matters are part of a neoliberal agenda, insofar as they hide educational debates behind 'a language of economic efficiency' (2006: 7).

Some see this ideological complicity as structural – the inevitable result of universities' financial dependence on economically rational, neoliberal governments. But at the sharper end of the critical-radical pedagogy spectrum, some descendants of the Freirian tradition see academics as *individually* complicit. For Peter McLaren, for example, academics are guilty of having succumbed to, and profited from, the comforts of a state-sanctioned system. They are guilty of a profound 'antiskepticism' (1994: xx) that allows the dominant capitalist order, including its new, knowledge-economy formations, to continue unchecked. He denounces 'the timid and frequently duplicitous role that university intellectuals have assumed in relation to the sociality of capital and [what the US historian Sande Cohen calls] the "catastrophe of socialized expectations"' (xix). While Denise Bradley (2011), in the address to future academics cited in the Introduction, characterized academics who criticize the current university system as resistant to change, McLaren for his part castigates the vast majority of academics as complicit *with* change. Either way, the *ad hominem* arguments make academics, as individuals and as a profession, bear the weight of the major economic, ideological and social changes of the last century.

More subtly, and without recourse to *ad hominem* arguments, a number of academics have pointed out particular disciplinary investments in liberal ideals. Tony Bennett and Ian Hunter have noted over a number of years the irony that Cultural Studies actually shares the basic mission of the liberal humanism it claims to repudiate: that of the cultivation of subjectivities and the development of a certain type of ethical sensibility (Hunter 1992, Bennett 1998), which Gary Wickham calls 'the ethical-must-be moral type of cultural studies intellectual' (2005: 73). According to Tony Bennett, some strands of Cultural Studies are 'concerned more with cultivating a certain ethical style and demeanour than with the pursuit of any practicable courses of action with specific political or policy goals in view' (1998: 25).[18]

---

18 Bill Readings likewise diagnoses a 'pietistic leftism' in much Cultural Studies work (1996: 102), which he attributes to a submerged anxiety about the lack of an automatically left-wing response to the question of cultural exclusion, since both the forces of global capitalism and their opponents might equally well be concerned about citizens (consumers) being excluded from culture.

Thus far, I have considered the question of individual benefit in traditions in which it has been viewed as inextricably tied to the enrichment of society. But of course the individual benefits attached to university study also come in much more direct and material form than the development of character, intellect, critical capacity or a certain ethical style or subjectivity: they have always included individual financial and professional benefit. The link between university education and individual benefit is in fact foundational. The medieval universities prepared students for vocations like the priesthood, medicine or law, and later the university became the pathway to a whole host of other occupations. Today, as a path to professionalization, universities are presumed to accord both a social and financial reward to students. In the US system, according to Nannerl O. Keohane, a former president of both Wellesley College and Duke University, a college degree has always been 'the most significant path' to upward mobility (1999: 48). This appears to have been so in the early years of universities in Australia as well. In his analysis of a study of the occupations of the fathers of students in the first decade of the University of Sydney, established in 1852, Don Anderson notes that at that time university education functioned as a means of 'career and social mobility upwards for a handful of young men from the middle and lower middle classes' rather than as a way of cementing the position of those who already enjoyed an established social identity (1990: 121).

As we have seen, the post-War decades were characterized by a spreading of such aspirational sentiments. In Australia, the expansionary momentum of the late 50s and the 60s was due, in part, to an emerging aspirational climate and a view of higher education as part of that picture: '[P]robably for the first time in history, a majority of citizens were coming to see more education as the chief means of advancing their life chances, or at least those of their children' (Anderson 1990: 119). So too in the UK, where the Robbins committee detected and applauded a similar sentiment in the 1960s (Committee on Higher Education 1963: 5). A 'modern community', they noted, is characterized by the spread of aspirations towards both wealth and culture (8). The Dearing Report of 1997 extended this vision both quantitatively (to encompass almost all citizens) and temporally (to last throughout a person's lifetime):

> The expansion of higher education in the last ten years has contributed greatly to the creation of a learning society, that is, a society in which people in all walks of life recognise the need to continue in education and training throughout their working lives and who see learning as enhancing the quality of life throughout all its stages. (National Committee of Inquiry 1997: 9)

An argument might be mounted that if everyone in society is a 'learner', then it is a legitimate taxpayer function to fund higher education. Nonetheless, to many commentators, the personal benefits attached to social mobility need to be borne in mind when assessing the universities' claims to be a contributor to and guardian of the social good. After all, universities originally served only a very limited population and the tension between individual and social good has existed almost since their inception. Kathleen Lynch (2006), for example, treats with some caution the traditional university claim that it is the producer and protector of disinterested knowledge. Universities have, she claims, 'traded on their Enlightenment inheritance that they are the guardians and creators of knowledge produced for the greater good of humanity in its entirety' (1). Herself no fan of commercialization, which she sees as reinvigorating the university's origins as a training-ground for the elite (2), she nonetheless draws attention to the 'hierarchical and patriarchal' history of universities (2) and to their role in 'forming the professional class of the welfare states of Europe and elsewhere' (2). She notes that

> ... the cry of the academy that its public interest functions are being undermined
> by the neo-liberal agenda can ring hollow to those who have lived for generations
> without the privilege of higher education. (2)

However sympathetic one is to critiques of marketization, then, it is worth recalling that the university's origins as a vehicle for 'higher learning for white males of the propertied classes' (Keohane 1999: 50) mean that they have never straightforwardly been 'public interest institutions' (Lynch 2006: 1) nor an unequivocal exemplum of or vehicle for social progressivism.

Nonetheless, universities have been 'quintessentially defined' as public interest institutions (Lynch 2006: 1). The concept of the social good has been one strong way to articulate what the university as an institution, and its graduates, teachers and researchers, give back to the community, or the nation, via the personal and intellectual maturation of students and the contribution of graduates and academics to the human stock of knowledge. This ideal of social service is in part a legacy of the university's essentially religious origins – both in England, where the Oxbridge colleges continued to have a 'clerical character' until the mid-nineteenth century (Green 1974: 149)[19] – and in the US, where many of the early nineteenth-century institutions were founded by religious groups (Keohane 1999: 52). Most of these institutions were sectarian, as in the

---

19 Until the passing of the University Reform Act of 1854, which took away some of the power of the colleges and the clerics, an Oxford senior common room 'was still very much like what it had been in the eighteenth century, a pleasant, masculine, clerical club...' (Green 1974: 135). Up till the end of the nineteenth century, Oxford and Cambridge remained the training grounds for church elites, among other professions (Tight 2009: 7).

Anglican colleges of Oxford and Cambridge, the Methodist, Quaker, Baptist or Presbyterian universities of the US (52), the Catholic universities of Latin America or the Catholic University of Ireland.

The intertwining of scholarly and religious life had a structural force. In the early years of the US system, for example, the university president was also the college chaplain (Keohane 1999: 51). In the UK, academics at Oxford and Cambridge had to pass religious tests and meet a celibacy rule until the passing of the University Reform Act in 1877 (Tight 2009: 6). A religious ethos filtered down into the fabric of everyday student life, for example in the rituals of daily prayers at college.

By contrast, the Australian system was established 'on a purely secular and non-sectarian basis' (Auchmuty and Jeffares 1959: 14). Auchmuty and Jeffares noted in 1959 that 'no religious test of any kind has ever existed in any Australian university' (15). The defiantly secular nature of the Australian system is illustrated by the fact that the bill introduced to parliament in 1849 to establish the University of Sydney originally included a provision explicitly preventing ministers of religion from having any part of the university's governance, though this provision was ultimately dropped (15).

In general, however, it is true to note that the intertwining of moral and social authority also infused universities in a more general way, especially in the US, where the earliest colonial universities were fundamentally oriented towards 'godliness', 'morality' and 'devotion to public good' (Keohane 1999: 50). In the UK, Oxford and Cambridge, despite their social elitism, set the pattern for an ideal of broader social involvement by offering 'extension' courses around England from the 1870s onwards, setting the mould for an ideal of service that influenced other universities and university colleges to offer adult education (Tight 2009: 7).

Religious dominance and influence slowly dissipated. University College London was founded in 1826 specifically 'to challenge the Church of England clerical monopoly of English higher education' (Jackson 1999: 93). The rise of the so-called 'civic' university-colleges in the nineteenth century continued this process, as did the later development of the 'new civics' (Tight 2009: 17).[20] Nonetheless, the essentially religious origins of the university as an institution persist today, not only in the architectural echoes of cloisters and quadrangles, but also in the moral authority accorded it by the fundamentally *social* orientation of the university as an institution, whose mission is seen as service to the broader community and indeed the world. In Chapter 2 we will see how this historical

---

20 The civic universities (also known as 'redbrick universities') were established as colleges in a number of large industrial cities in the nineteenth century and became independent universities in the first decade of the twentieth (Tight 2009: 13).

legacy and the idea of 'vocation' it sponsored continue to have an impact in the form of tacit expectations about unpaid labour.

The idea of social service has persisted long after the link between universities and churches attenuated in the UK. As Bill Readings argues, from the nineteenth century onwards, the nation-state came to fill the place of the church, and through the university's role of affirming national cultural identity, university research and teaching came to be seen as a social *mission* (1996: 90).

A structurally variegated system that differentiated between technical, vocational and scholarly education allowed space for a variety of ideas of the social benefit of post-school education to be articulated. Under the binary system, for example, universities were more able to continue to understand themselves as contributing to the social good, while polytechnics were required to be 'more responsive to social *needs* than the universities' (Booth 1999: 110, my italics). This distinction was articulated via a discourse of 'twin traditions'. This was the term used by one of Anthony Crosland's key advisors, Eric Robinson, the president of the Association of Teachers and Technical Institutions:

> We took the view that the university tradition was antagonistic. It was socially superior and antagonistic to *our* tradition, which was the service tradition. And so there should be a separate development. (Kearney 2006: Ep. 3)

The elimination of the distinction between institutions charged with vocational education and those engaged in a broader scholarly enterprise (in Australia, via the Dawkins reforms of 1988, and in the UK, via the dismantling of the binary system in 1992), meant that the idea of the university's particular mission no longer had any structural force. From that time on, debates about the proper role of higher education now had to take place *within* the university as well as across the different types of post-school education. This new structural fact not only put universities and the former CAEs or polytechnics in direct competition with each other for students, it also set the stage for a one-size-fits-all understanding of national benefit, in the form of a greater emphasis on a practical and economic conception of social good. As a result, universities were from then on less able to be sheltered from the rise of new economic orthodoxies – in particular, the rise of a user-pays principle. Bit by bit, the idea of the social good has begun to recede a little in the face of other, more instrumental, ways of conceiving the return for state funding: in particular, the question of contribution to the national economy.

Social Benefit: Higher Education as a National Economic Good

The idea of a link between the university and national economic productivity emerged in the nineteenth and twentieth centuries (Tight 2009: 25). For much of the second half of the twentieth century, individual and national benefit were not seen as mutually exclusive. Indeed, educating a society was seen as one of the major mechanisms for bringing about national economic wellbeing, rather than as a drain on the public purse. In the UK, the benefits of a university education to the nation were particularly evident post World War Two, and the expansion of universities was, as we have seen, one of many post-War revitalization strategies.

The 1960s boom period was a time in which 'governments began to value education on a quite new level' (Simon 1991: 222). The relationship of education to national economic prosperity began to be articulated in new ways: it was now seen as a form of 'investment' (222). The expansionary agenda of the Robbins Report, for example, was 'welcomed enthusiastically in all quarters' (232). The Prime Minister Douglas Home brandished a copy of the report on the television news on the day of its release as evidence of 'the government's full and enthusiastic acceptance' of the report (232).

According to Brian Simon, the call for expansion made in the Robbins Report was underpinned by two emerging perspectives. The first of these was 'human capital theory', which stressed the importance of education, especially in the areas of science and technology, to economic growth (Simon 1991: 222). The Robbins Report named this theory explicitly, and its principles were accepted by many. For example, a 1963 British Labour Party report into higher education drew on the research of the Robbins Report to argue that the 'brainpower and skill' (Simon 1991: 229) of scientists, engineers, researchers, technicians, administrators and professionals was 'a nation's primary asset' (qtd. in Simon 1991: 229). The second growing belief, according to Simon, was that policies contributing to reducing social inequalities would reduce a range of social problems (222).

Both approaches legitimated public expenditure, and in a period of economic growth they did not appear contradictory (Simon 1991: 222). Between 1960 and 1970, investment in education (including school education) increased by nearly 50 per cent (222–3). In that decade, total government spending rose from £37 million to more than £200 million, and from 1962–67 the number of full-time students increased by 63 per cent (Kingsbury 1974: 10–11). The Labour Party considered the expansion in the higher education system, including the creation of 45 new universities (Simon 1991: 230), to be 'no more and no less than a matter of national survival' (qtd. in Simon 1991: 230). This belief continued into the 1970s and 80s. Despite tough economic times and government cutbacks, belief in the economic benefits of higher and further education was 'the most consistent Conservative theme' during the two decades of Tory rule (Watson and Bowden 1999: 247).

As the twentieth century advanced, new discourses through which to conceive and express higher education's economic enrichment of the nation developed with the birth of the so-called New or Knowledge Economy. The development of computing and information technology in the late 1970s catalyzed a slow but inexorable shift from industrial to post-industrial economies in which new technologies would slowly start to move developed economies away from resources and primary industries. New Economy discourse, which 'reached its zenith' in the late 1990s (Rutherford 2005: 301), analysed and championed this shift. When it first emerged, it tended to be characterized by excitement and a vision of the future. New Economy discourse heralded the birth of a new type of economy in which ideas, images, data and creative work were to figure prominently, and in which knowledge itself was reconfigured as the *driver* of the economy (Ryan 1998: 3) – a tradeable commodity with quantifiable benefits in terms of GDP. This new, 'weightless', economy relied less on manufacturing than on 'highly educated and skilled workers selling the fruits of their knowledge' nationally and internationally (Gittins 2011). In these new 'knowledge economies', knowledge could be sold in shops (the slogan on the Blackwell's bookshop at Sheffield Hallam University reads 'The Knowledge Retailer'); traded in international markets; and produced in universities. The university could be drawn into this emerging reconceptualization of the economy in different ways. First, the knowledge produced by staff could now more readily be seen as a commodity than a gift to the store of human knowledge:

> Leaders of corporations, governments, and tertiary institutions increasingly see faculty [i.e. academic staff] work as possible intellectual property, more valuable in global markets as product or commodity than as a free contribution to an international community of scholars. (Slaughter 1998: 57)

Second, universities, as the 'central producers of technoscience, the primary product of postindustrial economies' (1998: 57), could now be understood as contributing to national wealth in new ways. Another part of the university's 'output' – graduates – could now also be imagined as part of the university's contribution to national wealth creation. Thought itself now had an obvious exchange value, and through the lens of both the knowledge economy and the liberal humanist tradition the university could be valued as a form of 'mindfacturing' (Ryan 1998: 4) that produced the kinds of thinkers needed by the knowledge economy:

> [The university] produced the producers of new, high-value, overwhelmingly abstract goods and services, the "new invisibles" of the post-imperial trading system. (1998: 4)

In this view, the university did its job best when it produced creative thinkers: those people who are so often described, ironically enough, via a cliché: that of 'thinking outside the box'. This goal of producing critical and creative thinkers was sometimes accompanied by the idea that the university could best serve this new boundary-less, limitless, non-spatial economy by producing 'job-ready graduates' and 'market-friendly disciplines' (Sidhu 2006: 14). The potential incompatibility between the ideals of critical pedagogy and those of vocationalism – between producing people who think differently and people who are ready for the workforce – was the latest incarnation of one of the most longstanding points of debate between different ideals of the university – the link between higher education and the world of work (Tight 2009: 4). It also tested governments, pitting government belief in the ability of higher education to arrest economic decline against suspicion of all that dangerously free thinking. In the Thatcher years, for example:

> [h]igher education was positively viewed as a potentially key contributor to "UK plc". Simultaneously, it was mistrusted for its apparently self-absorbed elevation of institutional autonomy over national service, its complacency, and its ideological unreliability. (Watson and Bowden 1999: 247)

The conception of knowledge as an object, and a commodity-object at that, was, of course, contested, especially within the liberal-humanist tradition. I recall a sticker on a Classics professor's office door in the mid-1980s, which said: 'Think education is expensive? Try ignorance'. This pithy critique tried to recuperate meanings of 'expense' beyond its economic meaning, at a time when costs were being calculated more in dollars than in opportunities missed, social ties weakened, or individuals left unchallenged.

But not all critics of marketization reject the basic postulate of a New Economy. Marxist analysis is, after all, founded on the task of examining changes to the nature of production and their impact on social and cultural life. Desmond Ryan (1998), for example, author of a critique of the Thatcher government's higher education policies, saw them as a failure to recognize that the economy had fundamentally changed. He claimed that the great contribution of the twentieth-century British university to the nation had been that it had generated new, often critical, perspectives on the world. He considered it a bitter political irony that the Thatcher government should have so deeply cut university funding at precisely the historical moment when the world was recognizing the crucial role of information to national economies. How, he lamented, could the Thatcher government have squandered Britain's historical legacy – its 'comparative advantages in scientific research, elite education, and quality cultural activities – design, the media, art and music' (Ryan 1998: 4)? In this analysis we see how it is possible for belief in a New Economy, a critique of privatization, and faith in the liberal humanist tradition to go hand in hand, though we have also seen that faith in a private university system can equally be compatible with liberal humanism.

Weighing up Personal and Social Benefit

The question of what the nation 'gets back' for its investment has been 'the great debate' that has accompanied the rise of state funding for universities (Tight 2009: 25). Debates about funding levels and tuition fees have centred on the weighing up of the personal benefits attendant on a university education and the benefits to society at large. While recognition of the intellectual, psychological and social maturation associated with a university education has not disappeared, 'personal benefit' has taken on an increasingly narrow tenor in much public and political discourse: as economic benefit to individuals. Thus, public debate has not only pitted economic arguments against non-economic ones (as in the familiar debate about personal cultivation versus individual economic gain), but has also pitted two essentially economic conceptions of the student against each other: that of the student as an individual agent maximizing his/her own personal life chances (i.e. a taker from the higher education system) and as a contributor to social or national wellbeing (i.e. a giver to the nation). The narrowing of the conception of personal gain to economic benefit also puts the idea of *social* good under some strain. More and more, universities are understood not just as servers of the common good or instruments of culture, national or otherwise, but also as a means of personal social and economic mobility. In June 2010, in the heated environment of the emerging economic crisis, the UK Universities Minister David Willetts stated that the cost of hundreds of thousands of university degrees was 'a burden on the taxpayer that had to be tackled' – a comment which at least one newspaper condensed in headline form into the claim that 'students "are a burden on taxpayers"' (Hough 2010).

When the Robbins Report was being written in the 1960s, the Committee expressed the optimistic view that taxpayers could and should contribute to the expansion of the system, a view enabled by a period of economic prosperity and a cautious prediction of sustained economic growth (Committee on Higher Education 1963: 208). In this climate, when the economy was strong enough to cope, individual gain and social contribution weren't seen as a zero/sum game: that is, an individual's personal and financial benefit could be understood as contributing to the wider social good, via a shared scenario of enhanced expectations. It is only right, argued the Robbins Committee, that as more people participate in higher education we should want to pay more as a society. The Robbins Report, indeed, saw the nation as the family-principle writ large:

> …we submit that it is not unreasonable to expect that the nation should be prepared to spend a higher proportion of [national income] on services such as higher education. One may buy less of services such as bus travel if one's income rises, but surely not less education. To spend more on higher education

would almost certainly be the average family's individual response. Why should it not be assumed to be true of the community of families considered collectively? (208)

A decade later, though, and a cluster of social, economic and ideological circumstances – dire economic conditions, a Conservative government with a very different worldview, the rise of economic rationalism, and the emergence of marketization as a more thoroughly social ideology – made things look a little different. Thatcher still clearly understood higher education as serving the national interest:

> To compete successfully in tomorrow's world – against Japan, Germany and the United States – we need well-educated, well-trained, creative young people. Because if education is backward today, national performance will be backward tomorrow. (Thatcher 1987a)

But the nation was not to be understood not as the family writ large; indeed, society as such didn't exist:

> [W]ho is society? There is no such thing! There are individual men and women and there are families and no government can do anything except through people and people look to themselves first. It is our duty to look after ourselves and then also to help look after our neighbour and life is a reciprocal business and people have got the entitlements too much in mind without the obligations, because there is no such thing as an entitlement unless someone has first met an obligation... (Thatcher 1987b)[21]

This, then, is an articulation of the principle of reciprocity in which the starting point and bedrock of sociality is individual responsibility. Education has gone from a 'service' (in Robbins) to something that it is a mistake to regard as an entitlement. People don't have an a priori right to expect assistance from government; that right is accrued through self-responsibility. This is a foundational principle of neoliberalism.[22]

---

21 This famous quotation has been sourced from the Thatcher archives. An edited version of the interview was published on 31 October 1987 under the title 'Aids, Education and the Year 2000!'. The remark about society caused a stir, to the point where Number 10 Downing Street issued an explanatory statement at the request of the *Sunday Times*, which published it on 10 July 1988.

22 Sheila Slaughter, in a summary of 1980s and 1990s higher education policy in Australia, the UK, Canada and the US, notes that 'none of these nations treat[s] higher education as an entitlement program' (1998: 56).

This is quite a shift from the role of government as seen in the Robbins Report. The combination of economic recessions of 1970s in the UK with the economic challenges posed by massification, alongside a new ideological climate – the rise of neoliberalism – had started to undermine the idea of mutual benefit while also reconfiguring, by narrowing, the conception of individual benefit. This involved a growing economization of the idea of return. In the 60s, the term 'investment' was used by governments to describe their own funding of universities (Simon 1991: 222). The Robbins committee were happy to consider government expenditure on higher education as an 'investment' (Committee on Higher Education 1963: 204), but also careful not to reduce investment to any crude financial calculation. First, they argued, the rate of financial return to the nation cannot be accurately measured or predicted (205). But, more fundamentally, the social gains from higher education cannot and should not be reduced to a question of money. Investments in 'human capital' (204) are fundamentally different in kind from other forms of material investment:

> Education, in short, furnishes perhaps the most conspicuous example of the importance of a social analysis of the difference between what economics call the "private" and the "social" net product of investment. (205)

They continue this argument, via a tellingly Cold War hypothetical:

> If a series of nuclear explosions were to wipe out the material equipment of the world but the educated citizens survived, it need not be long before former standards were reconstituted; but if it destroyed the educated citizens, even though it left the buildings and machines intact, a period longer than the Dark Ages might lapse before the former position was restored. Any attempt, therefore, to confine the conception of the return on educational investment to that which can be measured by earnings differentials is bound to be incomplete and runs the danger of being seriously misleading. (205)

The total social gain, then, is greater than the set of individual transactions that comprise it:

> If investment in higher education were seriously contracted, there would be a danger of a loss to the economy far greater than the measurable loss of the sum of the individual investments concerned. (205)

The Robbins committee report had made use of human capital theory with an explicit caveat: 'We must always remember, they cautioned, 'that the goal is not productivity as such but the good life that productivity makes possible' (Committee on Higher Education 1963: 204). By the time of the 1985 Green

Paper produced for the Conservative government under Secretary of State for Education and Science Keith Joseph, this suspicion of the ability of economics to capture social value had largely disappeared, except as a residual rhetorical gesture. The recognition of values that might transcend or exceed the economic was no longer a central principle, having been relegated to the final paragraph of the Appendices, after several pages of Appendices in which the economic rates of return of the various disciplines are itemized, via calculations of salary returns, costs per student per discipline, and the economic value of university research. This position clearly signals that 'culture' is no longer the guiding mission of the university, but a token residue whose value is largely symbolic. The report concludes:

> As mentioned above, there are other social benefits derived from higher education which are not directly associated with the education of highly qualified manpower or research. These include the cultural benefits of higher education and the preservation of the stock of knowledge. Such items are not amenable to measurement with any pretensions to objectivity but it is important that their existence should always be kept in mind. (Secretary of State for Science and Education 1985: 59)

Today, Australian and British governments still use the term 'investment' to discuss higher education, but one can detect some subtle changes. One shift is that the idea of an investment that might benefit the whole society is now routinely accompanied by the idea that the individual must nonetheless still be a co-investor. This conception has enabled policy shifts away from student grants to student loans. Australia led the way here, with the introduction of the HECS scheme. The UK instigated a similar policy a decade later when the student grant of £1,710 was replaced in 1997 by student loans to help pay for the new means-tested tuition fees (Alley and Smith 2004).

When a national student loan was first introduced in Australia in 1988 (for 1989) it was clearly understood and resented as a fee, though its name – HECS (the Higher Education Contribution Scheme) – was intended to suggest reciprocity rather than imposition. In 2007, the term HECS was replaced by Commonwealth-Supported Places (CPS courses). This is illustrative of a second subtle shift in the idea of investment. Rather than being seen as an imposition, fees are quietly instated as the norm, from which the government is kindly subsidizing its citizens. As the current University Admissions Centre website now puts it:

> CSP courses used to be called HECS courses – you only have to pay part of the cost of your course (a student contribution). The Australian Government pays the remainder of the cost. (UAC 2011)

A third shift in the idea of investment is that the social benefits of investment are often de-emphasized in favour of an idea of individual benefit. In neoliberalism the idea of social good is diminished in favour of a model of education as a series of private transactions (Rutherford 2005: 301). The journey of self-development is described as a trajectory of individual upward mobility often involving financial gain, rather than a narrative of social evolution. This more individualist narrative has found favour with governments, which have increasingly argued for a marketized system on the grounds that 'higher education' confers a significant private benefit' (Smith and Frankland 2000: 7) and that students are thus both able and obliged to 'invest' in their own futures. Remy Low (2013: Ch. 6) considers the idea that education serves both the national economy and personal gain to be an 'updating' of human capital theory accompanying the shift from a social liberal to a neoliberal regime.

Indeed, not only has the story of the wider good brought into being by the enhanced expectations of the populace begun to recede, even the assumption of the contribution of a university education to national economic wellbeing has been called into question. Alison Wolf, for example, has argued that although the link between higher education and individual higher income is indubitable (Wolf 2002: 23; see also Elias and Purcell 2004), the link between higher rates of education and national wealth in the form of economic growth is at best unclear. She claims that so-called 'social rates of return' analyses are flawed by the fact that people's wages are the only way of measuring how economically 'productive' they are (2002: 24). When graduate wages are used as a measure, higher education comes out well. But, Wolf argues, the use of wages as a proxy for economic productivity is a fairly dubious assumption. She argues that higher education is more useful as a signal or gauge of other things – motivation, natural ability, discipline (30) – than as a neat indicator of the economic value to societies of graduates' education. Wolf uses this conclusion to argue that governments should focus on primary and secondary rather than tertiary education. (For a similar argument in a global context, see Psacharopoulos 2006). Former Vice-Chancellor of the University of Edinburgh David Smith likewise noted the policy implications of the tenuousness of the link between higher education and national economic productivity:

> There is a clear link between being a graduate and having improved earning capacity, but there is no rigorously proven causal link between the numbers of graduates a country produces and its economic prosperity. So long as this holds, there will be increasing emphasis on the learner paying a significant proportion of the costs of higher education. (1999: 172)

Despite the rise of this individualist discourse, it remains a truism, if not necessarily a truth, that 'the accumulation of human capital' is 'a key element in economic growth and rising living standards' (Hatton and Chapman 1987: 1). In most developed nations, productivity rises coincided with a 'rise in human capital formation' (3) over the twentieth century, but the 'causal nexus' between economic growth and increased post-school training 'is far from clear' (1). Hatton and Chapman note that increases to national economic growth attributable to increased education and training have a usually forgotten economic downside: they keep people out of the paid workforce for longer (see also Wolf 2002: 23). They cite a British study from the early 1980s that estimated that the economic contribution of increased schooling was, at that time, 'almost exactly offset by later entry into the workforce' (3).[23]

Of course, in more contemporary, post-industrial, economies, cycles of employment, training, retraining and job shifts are a structural feature. In that context, the conception of a New Economy remains a strong vehicle for arguing the national significance of universities, with particular emphasis on periods of *re*training, for example by workplace in-servicing and by postgraduate university qualifications. In Australia, this pro-education discourse of 'lifelong learning' continues to have force precisely because it is needed to counterbalance Australia's traditional and ongoing economic reliance on natural resources.[24] In a nation where the mining industry is a major source of wealth, the case for the economic significance of higher education into a projected post-industrial future continually has to be re-made. Some economists continue to denounce the underfunding of Australian higher education of the last decades, arguing that there will continue to be different styles of service-based jobs: the menial and the highly skilled, and that higher education is crucial to developing jobs in the latter kind of service economy:

> [The type of jobs our children and grandchildren will have] depends on how much money and effort we put into their education and training. We've gone for the past two decades underspending on education and training at all levels, falling behind the other rich countries. If we've got any sense, we'll use part of the proceeds from the resources boom to secure our future in the global knowledge economy. (Gittins 2011)

In this account, the wellbeing of individual Australians and Australia as a nation do not tend in different directions; on the contrary, they would both be served by the same policy: that of substantial investment in higher education. Such

---

23 In later chapters I will consider this delay up close by examining how it produces agonizing personal dilemmas about how long to wait for permanent academic work.

24 The minerals boom in Australia of the early twenty-first century, fuelled in particular by the growing market in China, meant that Australia's economy survived the GFC relatively unscathed.

arguments have influenced the current policy direction of the Australian Federal Government, which is expansionary. The relation between participation in higher education, individual benefit and national benefit continues to be articulated through the ongoing acceptance of human capital theory and the premise of a knowledge economy. In 2009, the then Labor Federal Education Minister Julia Gillard, pointing to the historical underfunding of higher education during the Howard Liberal-National government from 1996 to 2007, noted:

> In an era when investment in knowledge and skills promises to be the ultimate determinant of national and individual prosperity, Australia is losing ground against our competitors … Australia has reached a critical juncture. As a nation we failed to make the boom years pay. We underinvested. We lived off the human capital accumulated in previous decades. (Gillard 2009)

Of course, most governments say this of previous political regimes.

Debates about the impacts of higher education on national wellbeing are obviously influenced by changes in the conceptualization of nationhood itself. It is not just that governments have new relations to universities; rather they have a new relation to the state itself. Governments increasingly conceive of themselves as enabling or buying rather than providing public services (Rutherford 2005: 300, Redden 2008: 10).

This has led some to claim that governments have retreated from any strong *ideological* stake in universities. The tradition of academic autonomy that has characterized the university systems of the UK, Australia and the US means that it is hard to consider the university as an ideological arm of the state in the way that state-run schools more self-evidently are. Even though the university was only ever partially or conditionally an example of what leftist sociology would once have called an Ideological State Apparatus (ISA),[25] it was nonetheless a significant contributor to the nation-state: it was, as we have noted, a vehicle for the production and reproduction of national *culture* (Readings 1996). With the rise of transnational capital, argue Readings (1996) and others (e.g. Rutherford 2005), the ideological dimensions of the university's contribution to the nation-state have diminished and the university is less and less a vehicle for the promulgation of national agendas. Governments are interested less in the content of what is taught and researched than in reducing the financial impact of funding universities and in capitalizing economically from their success and from the (argued) greater productivity of their graduates. Thus, universities are now subject to a battery of accountability measures in which intellectual content is a side issue.

---

25 The term was coined by the Marxist Louis Althusser (1971) in his classic essay 'Ideology and Ideological State Apparatuses'.

Readings (1996) was prescient in the clarity with which he grasped and articulated this shift from what he called the university of culture to the university of excellence. Content, he famously declared, is being supplanted by the notion of 'excellence'. He sees 'excellence' as an 'integrating principle' (22) rather than an ideology per se, for it 'has no content to call its own' (24). Rather, it is a 'unit of currency within a closed field' (27) – a set of measures that assume that there is a 'single standard ... in terms of which universities can be judged', irrespective of content (27). This does not make it apolitical, but it does, he argues, make it non-ideological, in the sense that it is not driven by any predetermined content (13).

Readings always made it clear that he was discussing a broad emerging trend rather than painting a picture of a transformation completed. It is therefore interesting and important to note the ways in which the content of what we research and teach, while it may not matter in the game of accountability measures and the version of 'success' and 'failure' they produce, still matters to politicians and to the public in other ways (see Chapter 3). For there remain certain contexts (e.g. international education) in which the university is still not only seen as central to the nation's economic interests, but where the state has an ideological investment to make (Sidhu 2006: 1).

To sum up, then: despite the continuity of belief for many decades in the contribution of highly educated people to national economic wellbeing, the way of conceiving the relative importance of and the balance between individual and social/national benefit has changed with the tides of economic conditions and ideological climates. A number of economic and ideological circumstances have put the idea of the university as a worthy and disinterested recipient of public funding under severe pressure. The rise of the free market as the fundamental contemporary economic form, coupled with the budgetary problem caused by the successes of massification, has brought the question of funding to the fore. Massification has made full public funding difficult to sustain economically, even while greater public participation in higher education might seem to justify public funding more evidently than in earlier times.

This, then, is the big picture of collision and conflict that lies behind the personal crises and uncertainties and the professional malaise with which I started this book. In the chapters to come, I focus on the way these contradictions play out as ambiguities, multiple demands, and uncertainties on the level of the body, which ripple across groups and communities that are divided and anxious, but also determined and occasionally creative.

CHAPTER 2

The Wellbeing of Academics in the Palimpsestic University

In the previous chapter I observed in passing that the university is now at least three different types of institution simultaneously: a scholarly community, a bureaucracy and a corporation. This chapter explores what it is like to *inhabit* this type of fractured and palimpsestic work world. Refusing the old caricature of the academic as a disembodied rationality – an egg-head in an ivory tower – it focuses instead on the academic's lived experience, exploring 'the academic body' as both victim of and vessel for the physical, intellectual and emotional work involved in making the university (seem to) cohere.

This chapter asks what it is like to live out three paradigms at once. To do so, it examines the minutiae of embodied work life to see how it is connected to larger social forces, deeper cultural logics and particular directions in higher education policy. After all, the tensions outlined in Chapter 1 about the proper nature and function of the university don't take place just as a contest of ideas; rather, they are operationalized as conflicting habits, expectations, daily rhythms and relations to others. My aim, then, is to consider what impact the contemporary conflict about the idea of the university has on the embodied wellbeing of academics. The emphasis is on the overburdened labour of 'permanent' or tenured academic staff; later chapters explore in more detail the precarious labour of the ever-increasing casual 'periphery' (Kimber 2003).

The chapter focuses on three aspects of embodied work: productivity, temporality, and stress or illness – and on the question of what it means to 'embody' an institution. With Denise Bradley's (2011) admonition about whingeing academics ringing in my ears, along with the sarcastic scoffing of online commentators around the globe,[1] I have no intention of painting a false and self-pitying account of academic work, but I do want to take seriously

---

1 As will be seen in this chapter, and again in Chapter 3, there is little public sympathy for academics. Academics' concerns about the opening of a new private university in the UK, for example, attracted little sympathy: 'Pure hyperventilation of academics … Grow up and accept that there will be many providers. You can't beat them, and cannot join them' (Calamity Jane 2011). This is, of course, part and parcel of Internet culture in general, but comments such as these nonetheless reflect widespread public antagonism towards the academic profession.

the fact that many academics feel exhausted and beleaguered. This set of experiences and feelings needs to be analysed rather than simply repudiated as the last gasp of a fading elite.

Exploring such experiences involves reprising a question that arose in the introductory chapter: in what ways, if at all, is academic work different from other industries currently undergoing structural and cultural change? Is there anything particular about academia and academic work? Is there anything about the university itself that might be undermined by requiring academics to work in the same way as in any 'other' industry? One of my conclusions is that, Bradley's (2011) caution about misplaced academic exceptionalism notwithstanding, there *is* something quite particular about the way vocationalism, bureaucracy and corporatism converge in the contemporary university and something intrinsic to the academic role as traditionally conceived that encourages particular types of embodied struggles.

To paint a complex picture of all the varieties of labour that go on in a university would take a book in itself; this chapter focuses only on the predicament of permanent academics, though it does note in places how academic labour connects to some of the 'other' white-collar labour that goes on in the palimpsestic university: that of administrators, managers and students. The labour of a whole panoply of workers – cleaners, gardeners, maintenance staff, audio-visual staff, technicians, laboratory assistants, librarians – lies, however, outside the scope of this analysis.

My theme throughout is the way academics are called upon to *embody* the fractured multiplicity that is the contemporary university. I consider the 'sacrificial labor' (Ross 2004: 192), affective labour and 'bridge work' (Myss and Shealy 1993) involved in trying to embody, represent and serve a multi-headed beast, arguing that academics feel the strain of trying to be the human glue that holds it all together. The chapter does, however, conclude on a forward-looking note, exploring some strategies and principles for living this multiplicity more happily and for ethical collegial conduct.

Two notes before I begin. The first concerns the question of generalizing about 'the body'. I began thinking about academic wellbeing in the mid-1990s, after a somewhat harrowing period working as part of a group establishing a new, radically transdisciplinary, Humanities programme at a campus of a post-1988 university located on the semi-rural fringe of Sydney. The new staff body, most of whom commuted one to two hours each way to be on campus, arrived a month or so before the first cohort of students. This was also the era when a change of government introduced drastic budget cuts, and it was the dawning of the era of widespread email use. Put together, these circumstances made a consideration of overwork and the space-time compressions of the new university inevitable, embodied and personal. While the argument had its genesis in my particular set of experiences in the New Humanities, and was originally published in that context,[2] I have no doubt that it is more widely applicable in general terms. But it is obvious that no analysis of 'the academic body' can account for all the variations of context that form, shape and influence bodily life. The nature of a given institution, as well as the age, health, family circumstances, disciplinary formation, seniority, gender and tenure status of the academic in question will clearly have their own particular corporeal impacts. So perhaps I should diligently follow Adrienne Rich's suggestion that there be a moratorium on saying 'the' body in order to prevent us from abstracting bodies (2002: 67). Rich contrasts the viscerality, immediacy and particularity of the words 'my body' with the grand claims that can be made in the name of 'the' body (67). But this chapter does not want to take up her alternative. It is true that 'my body' is more visceral, and in that particular way more true, but I want to focus on what we as an international collegiate *share*, while remaining alive to difference and particularity. So while it is true that some decades ago this essay had its genesis in my body – stressed, distressed, overburdened – and my attempts to make sense of the professional world I was encountering, this chapter is no longer about my body, which is now in another place. It is more about commonalities of experience, across differences. It is obvious that pressured academic embodiment plays out differently if one is a research scientist, a lecturer in performing arts, or a teacher of nursing. I leave each reader free to flesh out the picture with all the particulars and nuances of their own context.

The second note is that it might seem in extraordinarily bad taste to complain of the work conditions of permanent or tenured staff in contemporary academia when so many excellent scholars around the world are unable to gain permanent academic work at all and when the future of academic work looks to involve an ever-increasing casualization. Perhaps, but I would also add that it is only *within* the context of such a job market that the current work conditions I am describing make sense. The predicaments of casual and tenured academics are distinct yet overlapping; they are mutually implicated. To pre-empt the further criticism that it is in bad taste to complain about *any* type of academic labour when it remains so privileged compared to the precariousness, boredom or danger of so many workplaces, I can rejoin only by saying that this claim effectively condemns academics to silence about major changes to a fundamental social institution. To analyse lamentable change in one sector does not mean one cannot see injustices in another. Whatever self-interest, self-protection or defensiveness are at play in academic responses to a changing higher education sector, the university is nonetheless an institution

---

2 As noted in the Acknowledgements, the arguments presented in this chapter first appeared in 1996. The original article has been almost completely rewritten for this book.

that is bigger and more important than any of the individuals who work for it. Academic critiques of the contemporary university are motivated at least in part by the sincere belief that one is fighting to protect an institution that matters to society. Moreover, if it is true, as Andrew Ross has argued, that academic and artistic labour have served as a model of sacrificial labour that is 'increasingly serviceable to the new neoliberal world of labor' (2004: 193), then examining its struggles in the contemporary moment has an import well beyond the university.

Three in One: The Palimpsestic University and the Chimeric Academic

At the start of my university teaching career in the early 1990s, I was grappling to make sense of how the university at which I was working could differ so dramatically from the one at which I had done my undergraduate studies only fifteen years earlier. As far as I could understand it, the economic and ideological changes of the previous decade had produced a system struggling between its residual and emergent features, with the result that the university could best be understood, I thought, as a palimpsestic overlay of three types of institutions, each with their own exigencies, temporalities and forms of expertise: the scholarly, the bureaucratic and the corporate or commercial. The problem was not so much that the scholarly university had been replaced by the bureaucratic or commercial one, as that the university was simultaneously three different types of institution, each of which interpellated students in different ways and made different demands on academics. My impressionistic but nonetheless fiercely lived conclusion was that this was a contradiction played out on the body of the individual academic struggling to be all things to all paradigms. I still believe this to be the case.

The university is clearly a composite institution, several beasts in one. The first of these beasts is a scholarly institution, with traditions dating right back to the twelfth and thirteenth centuries. Eby and Arrowood (1940: 761) describe the medieval university in terms of three characteristics: 1) its 'corporate character' – that is, it was understood as united in one body; 2) its 'special privileges and immunities' (i.e. its autonomy); and 3) its power to grant the license to teach.

Scholarship was part and parcel of the formation of professionals in medicine, law and the church. Learning was thoroughly interlinked with the growth of Catholicism. Truth came from God, and the 'universities became the special custodians and interpreters of truth' (Eby and Arrowood 1940: 757). As the 'custodians of learning in an age in which learning was esteemed as at almost no other period in the world's history, universities enjoyed enormous prestige' (757). Nonetheless, the early medieval universities had a 'weak financial base'

(Dunbabin 1999: 42). Life as a master could often be hand to mouth, and most masters left the profession after a very few years (38).

The scholarly tradition centred on erudition, the careful preservation of traditional knowledge. Knowledge was passed on via a tradition in which the 'personal relationship between master and student was regarded as crucial' (Dunbabin 1999: 31). From the Enlightenment onwards, faith declined in the intellectual utility of erudition as the 'retrieval of the monuments of the past as an end in itself' (Ligota and Quantin 2006: 13). Descartes, for example, elaborated a distinction between scholarship, defined as the mere accumulation of learning, and science, which was to be characterized by interrogation, proof, reason and a search for certainty. From this point on, erudition would begin to be seen as 'intellectually second-rate' (2006: 17), flourishing 'as a set of procedures' rather than as a '*Denkform*' (13).

Nonetheless, the idea of tradition continued to be central. In Newman's seminal articulation of the idea of the university, the university was a vehicle for distilling and transmitting the highest and best of the cultural heritage, including in the sciences, to young people, 'and so continuing the conversation of mankind' (O'Hear, in Kearney 2006: Ep. 5). The aim of this process was

> to produce in those who come under its wing, what [Newman] calls "the true enlargement of mind" that comes through knowing one thing in depth and also being able to see it in its connection to all the other activities of human life. (O'Hear, in Kearney 2006: Ep. 5).

Other considerations – the production of knowledge, the social good – were secondary. As Anthony O'Hear summarizes Newman:

> In a way he defines the university negatively: it's *not*, in his view, a research institute; it's *not* a device for social engineering; it is *not* a device for inculcating morality (interesting, because he was a cardinal of the Catholic Church); and it's *not* an institution for training. (In Kearney 2006: Ep. 5)

The university was, rather, a place for '*teaching* universal *knowledge*' (Newman 1976: 5, original italics).

To what degree can this idea of the university as the home of the scholarly tradition thus defined still be said to hold? The answer depends a great deal on the discipline in which one works. I would struggle to claim that my primary purpose as an academic is the pursuit and dissemination of truth and knowledge. Both the terminology and the claim sound archaic. There's something especially Australian about my inability to characterize what I do this way, but there's also something of disciplinary specificity about it: I am certain that I would not hesitate were I a medical researcher. The idea of universal knowledge is undoubtedly more robust in the sciences than in the Humanities, where even the idea that we teach 'knowledge' has been undermined somewhat first by the German Idealist emphasis on teaching modalities of thought,[3] especially analytical and critical thinking, and later by the postmodern and post-structuralist critiques of epistemology, which exposed both the historicity of knowledge and the investments involved in its production. Knowledge-centred teaching is, in some progressive pedagogies, almost 'heretical' (Maton 2012). Even the very pinnacle of scholarly achievement – the PhD – is now often understood as a multifaceted process, aimed as much at research training, the mastery of research skills, and the credentialing of candidates as at producing new knowledge (Kiley 2009: 34). In Australia, governments now speak of a doctorate as contributing to the national 'innovation agenda' (35) rather than to the stock of human knowledge.

But despite the decline in status of traditional scholarly erudition (Ligota and Quantin 2006: 3), some scholars in the long-established Humanities disciplines may well still continue to think of themselves as transmitting a body of knowledge. But for academics in newer, politicized, transdisciplinary fields like Cultural Studies, it is easier to conceive of oneself in the tradition of character development (*Bildung*) – as contributing to the development of sensibilities (Bennett 1998) rather than to the stock of knowledge or the pursuit of truth. The very label 'scholar' is awkward for some, not only because of its elitist connotations but also because it implies mastery of and ties to a particular, defined, body of knowledge. But the archaic figure of the master has some residual force in the expectation – stronger in some national educational traditions than others – that academics, whether teachers or researchers or both, be experts in a defined field and share that expertise through a variety of activities, including publication, media work, public lectures and teaching.[4] But for a broader public, 'scholarly', like 'academic' itself, retains a deeply ambiguous connotation: careful, meticulous, true; or pedantic, unworldly and impractical.

Within the scholarly conception of the university there is some tension between the idea of the university as a group of researchers and of teachers. The German Idealists, whose thinking on knowledge and culture was seminal to the modern university, insisted on the university as the one scholarly institution where the two are inseparable (Readings 1996: 64). Wilhelm von Humboldt, founder of the University of Berlin, drew on the writer and philosopher Friedrich Schiller to conceive of culture as it is embodied in the university as both

---

3 Readings notes that the German Idealists were united in their belief that education – *Bildung* – consisted in helping the student learn 'the rules of thought' rather than 'the content of positive knowledge' (1996: 67). The Idealist tradition was foundational to our modern idea of the university (62).

4 I will return to the politics and tribulations of mastery in Chapter 5.

a transcendent unity (the object of investigation) and a 'developmental process' – that of character formation (*Bildung*) (Readings 1996: 66). This dual vision unites the pursuit of knowledge (objective science) and pedagogy in its fullest sense of 'subjective spiritual and moral training (cultivation)' (66). Newman, on the other hand, shared the view that the proper end of a university was personal cultivation, but saw research and teaching as such different enterprises that they required different types of specialist and different types of institution: 'To discover and to teach are distinct functions; they are also distinct gifts, and are not commonly found united in the same person' (1976: 8).

The second institutional form that gives shape to the contemporary university is that of the bureaucracy. Bureaucracy, as classically theorized by the sociologist Max Weber (1948a), is a form of 'rational administration' replacing more traditional ways of organizing work (Gornitzka, Kyvik and Larsen 1998: 23). Weber saw bureaucracy as the dominant and distinctive organizational form of advanced capitalism (1948a: 196). Bureaucracies are highly complex, rule-governed, hierarchized structures designed to manage public monies with maximum efficiency (196–8). The modern university was, to Weber, no exception. Unlike their medieval predecessors, who charged fees and classroom rental costs directly to pupils, even, in Oxford and Cambridge, bolstering their meagre livings by acting as landlords to students by establishing halls (Dunbabin 1999: 37), modern lecturers are like any other modern employees, selling their time to an employer for a salary and using premises and equipment belonging to the institution. Neither the scientist in her research lab nor the lecturer in his classroom owns or controls the facilities in which they work, procures the students, or raises their own salary. This classically modern form is, of course, the type of university with which we are all familiar. It is the medieval university – where mendicant monk lecturers poached students from each other (Dunbabin 1999: 38) or used their ethics lectures as a forum for persuading recalcitrant students to pay their fees (37) – that seems remote and fanciful to us.

In the way theorized by Weber, the last few decades have undoubtedly seen such a quantitative rise of administrative tasks as to constitute a *qualitative* shift in academic work. This growth of the administrative function is multifaceted, involving: a growth in the sheer number of staff employed by universities to do administrative work; growth in the proportion of administrative staff relative to academic staff; a rise in the number, variety and intensity of administrative tasks; the devolution of many administrative tasks onto academics; an increase in the number of administrative staff who have a university degree; and the credentialing of higher level administrative staff (via MBAs, degrees in Human Resources etc.), resulting in the creation of a structured career path specifically in university administration and management. The growth of administrative work has been accompanied by its constitution, both formally and informally, as a form of expertise in and of itself.

It is common for academics to attack bureaucratization as an inherent evil, but we do well to remember that bureaucracy was developed as an apparatus one of whose goals was to overturn feudalism, favouritism and nepotism by instituting systems designed to guarantee regularity and impartiality. As Judith Brett (1991) points out, our now routine expectations of system, procedure and ethics – the expectation, for example, that academics be highly and appropriately trained, appointed on merit, and promoted via ethical and transparent procedures – are all bureaucratic principles rather than pertaining to more traditional ways of organizing work, including the guild-like operations of scholarly communities. To that extent, Brett, like Weber, sees the bureaucratic tradition as one of the major organizational features of the modern university, rather than a late-modern corruption of it. This modern form is, however, a doubled-edged sword, having escalated in the late twentieth century to the point where its 'classical virtues' became 'perverted': 'rule-following becomes a purpose in its own right, predictability and equal treatment are turned into rigidity, and so on' (Gornitzka, Kyvik and Larsen 1998: 23). More traditional elements persist, of course, especially in older, more prestigious, universities, where the 'god-professor' may still have some sway, or more feudal modes of power and influence may persist alongside or underneath bureaucratic forms.

The third institutional form is that of the corporation, a form that is interwoven with that of the bureaucracy since large corporations are themselves bureaucratic. It is now a truism that the weakening of the nation-state as a geo-political form, the rise of marketization as a dominant economic and cultural logic, and the development of a large-scale global market in higher education, in which 'a largely uni-dimensional flow of students travel from the South and East to seek tutelage in the First World' (Sidhu 2006: viii), have all helped transform the university from a scholarly community to a global business. The discourse, values and practices of the New Economy gave extra impetus to this change, especially through the concepts of the Knowledge Economy, the Information Economy or the Experience Economy. Universities, whether public or private, are now multimillion dollar organizations, providers of educational products to a global market of discriminating customers, who seek choice, value for money and a quality product.

The marketization of the university has meant the development of private competitors in systems where they were largely unknown (such as in the UK and Australia), the development of for-profit higher education in the US (Morey 2004), and increasingly close co-operation between universities and corporations. More, though, it has resulted in 'the reconception of the University [itself] as a corporation' (Readings 1996: 10–11). This, for Bill Readings, is an epochal shift in the conception and role of the university – from being the custodian and disseminator of a national culture, to a 'transnational bureaucratic corporation' (3). This fundamental new economic reality is made manifest in a host of rhetorical and symbolic forms, such as logos, brands, slogans, mission statements and aggressive marketing campaigns (Adams 2000: 69) as well as in the rising salaries of vice-chancellors.

Students have, inevitably, been participants in the increasingly explicit commodification of education. Some have responded with a growing instrumentality: 'The mentality of the American public', asserts Nannerl Keohane, 'has shifted from an historically somewhat awed pride in our colleges and universities to a consumerist mentality' (1999: 58) in which families scrutinize universities for value for money. It was not until 1995 that I first heard a student frame his critique of a particular university subject explicitly in these terms. I still recall the moment when I overheard him complaining: 'I paid good money for this course'; 'that tutorial cost me $30'. Around the same time, the legal literalness of the consumerist model began to be evident, when the university at which I worked was forced to resolve a dispute with a student about a subject outline at the Consumer Affairs Tribunal. Over a decade later and the consumer paradigm is more deeply engrained, affecting, for example, pedagogical decisions, such as whether one can legitimately, or safely, ask students to leave a tutorial if they have not done the reading, or to leave a lecture if they continue to talk.

What, then, has happened to ideas of the academic now that the university is a deeply and complexly hybrid institution? The simple answer is that different ideas and expectations of the academic role now co-exist. Jürgen Enders notes that 'the concept of a single academic profession might be an illusion' (2000: 7). Indeed, he queries whether 'profession' is the right word to describe the academic job, noting at least three different conceptual traditions that feed into contemporary expectations of the role: 'the profession' (notably medicine and law); 'the estate' (the guild-like structures that preceded professionalization); and 'the staff' (employees of a large institution (8). Perhaps we could draw on the university's Christian origins and see the academic as some modern holy trinity, but I think a more monstrous image is apposite. So I have plumped for the chimera, the three-part monster of Homer's *Iliad*, which had a lion's head, a snake's tail, and a goat's body. Inhuman, divine in origin, and thought to be invincible, the chimera snorted out terrible fire, wreaking terror until it was eventually vanquished by Bellerophon (1951: Bk 6. ll. 179–83). In bleaker moments one might see this angry, defeated, multi-part monster, now used as a figure for foolish ideas, as an appropriate metaphor for a profession that can, it is claimed 'hardly cope with the professional tensions it has to live with, and … is endangered' (Enders 2000: 7).

My reflections about academic embodiment began, as I said earlier, in the body, but here I start my analysis with *ideas* of the academic, using the Weberian concept of the 'ideal type' (Weber 1949). This conceptual tool allows us to note how each of the three paradigms I have outlined produces its own idea and ideal of what is thinkable, sayable, or do-able as an academic. An ideal type is an 'analytical construct' that draws on, heightens, and abstracts 'certain elements of reality' in order to enable comparative analysis (Coser 1971: 223). 'Ideal' implies neither an average nor a model to be emulated (223), but refers to the use of abstractions to give a big-picture view of a complex reality. An ideal type is a 'mental construct', which 'cannot be found empirically anywhere in reality. It is a *utopia*' (Weber 1949: 90, original italics).

Ideal types, though they are abstractions, operate in the real world, exerting pulls and pressures that have a very real impact on the body. This impact will be described below, but I begin by elaborating the ideal types implied by each of the three paradigms. I do this by considering, in turn, a number of aspects of the academic's role and situation: academic labour, expertise, accountability and scrutiny, and forms of belonging.

Academic Labour in the Three Paradigms

The most significant influence on the conceptualization of academic work is that of vocation. Vocation began as a religious conception, referring either to the priestly call or the 'universal call of the gospel' (Bunderson and Thompson 2009: 32–3). With the advent of Protestantism, the idea of vocation was given wider applicability. Luther 'elevated' work into a 'divine offering' (2009: 33), believing that any faithfully executed work, no matter how humble, was a form of vocation (33). Weber saw the implication of this for capitalism, arguing that a secularized version of calling was 'embedded in the culture of capitalism' (Bunderson and Thompson 2009: 54) through the diffusion of the idea of the ennobling potential of work. Today, the idea of vocation and special talents persists in the form of 'a perceived connection between personal passions and endowments and particular domains of work' (37).

Vocationalism remains particularly strong in the university context. This is unsurprising given the university's origins as a religious institution. Vocation implies the meaningfulness of work, a privileged collectivity with whom to share it, values and goals that transcend the everyday, a tolerance of impecuniosity, and the inseparability of work and life. In the earliest medieval universities, the master lived in poverty, in close proximity with his students. In the Oxbridge model the tutor lived in college and fulfilled intellectual, organizational, religious and pastoral functions at once. His work and life could not be separated ideationally, temporally or spatially.

Though today's academic vocational model is largely secular, academic labour retains its connection to the gift, in the anthropological sense. The gift, as theorized most famously by Marcel Mauss (1990 [1923]), is a traditional mode of transaction in which the *relationship* between giver and receiver is primary, with individuals or clans bound together in webs of obligations to give, to receive and to reciprocate. In contrast to the series of seemingly voluntary transactions between individuals that characterize commodity exchange, a gift economy implies and secures the ties and obligations that bind people into a community. Vocation fits into this notion of gifted or 'sacrificial' labour (Ross 2004: 192), because it is predicated on obligation and community, and, in the case of the university, a conception of social mission. It also implies a focus on things 'above' the everyday, and hence the active embrace of, or at least willingness to tolerate, penury.

Those who adhere to this vocational model of academic work characterize the profession as unamenable to a classic modernist work-life split, and as fundamentally and constitutively inimical to the efficacy drive of bureaucratic systems:

> [Academic work is] a vocation rather than a job because, as Weber argued,[5] it's a basic orientation of one's whole life rather than simply some set of skills that one deploys when necessary. To be oriented towards the academic vocation means to *live for* the systematic construction of scientific (in the broad sense) knowledge and the creative pedagogy by which spaces for letting learn are opened. The considerations of efficacy and efficiency that dominate most of the other spheres of modern life are, *of necessity*, set aside in favor of a concern with the rigor of reason, the clarity of vision, and the mystery of intellectual encounter... (ProfPTJ 2009, original italics)

Nonetheless, the modern institutions that house this vocation are, unquestionably, bureaucratic in nature. This inevitably involves a clash of cultures. Within the logic of the bureaucracy, labour is construed very differently: regulated in law via the classic modern formulation of waged labour at an hourly rate. The administrator's work must be sufficient rather than sacrificial; dutiful rather than devoted; and effective rather than inspirational. This does not preclude an attitude of devotion, but devotion is a pleasing excess rather than a structural principle.

Some administrative work can be vocational; the proud tradition of public administration is one example of a vocational form of administrative work. Career civil (public) servants were life-long bureaucrats who had both intellectual and policy expertise, and served the state by offering policy support and advice without fear or favour. The public administrator 'stand[s] for integrity and probity against partisan interest and corruption' (Rhodes 1994: 150). In that sense, s/he is, like the academic, understood as 'a trustee of the

---

5 Weber, though he noted the bureaucratic forms in which modern academic work took place (1948a) believed in the necessarily vocational nature of the pursuit of knowledge (1948b).

public good' (150) and, again like the academic, is 'always ... thinking ahead of the community, on behalf of the community' (Parker 1989: 341). This tradition of informed, impartial advice and service was securable by dint of industrial protections offered to public servants, rather as academic autonomy was once routinely guaranteed by tenure.

Although not all administrative work is vocational, commitment may be rewarded, since effective bureaucratic functioning requires a stable staffing regime. The ideal modern bureaucrat is 'a full-time, life-time professional' (Kilcullen 1996). The bureaucracy's iconic hero is the 'organization man' of the mid-twentieth century, William H. Whyte's name for the class of devoted, but not inspirational, men who *belong to* rather than serve the organization, and who are rewarded for their loyalty by a job for life:

> They are the ones of our middle class who have left home, spiritually as well as physically, to take the vows of organization life, and it is they who are the mind and soul of our great self-perpetuating institutions. (1960: 8)

This class-based conception of different types of bureaucratic work makes the distinction between the quasi-vocational dedication of middle-tier bureaucrats and the merely functional labour of clerks.

Contemporary academics may find themselves doing administrative work of both a 'devoted' and a clerical nature. The increasing dominance of administrative logic, shared across all white-collar jobs in modern economies, has been intensified by the IT revolution, which made it possible for individual academics to carry out many clerical tasks. The proliferation of administrative functions and their increasing devolution onto academics has some democratizing force, effecting a slight rapprochement of the functions (if not the power or status) of administrative and academic staff. But the divide between administrators and academics still often works deeply and subtly, and there are also deep divisions of power and status *within* administrative functions. In the complex hierarchical structures of modern universities, administration is no simple 'Other' to academic functions. Thus, even while Di Adams's (2000) depiction of the contemporary Australian university as the site of an indignant collision between two mutually uncomprehending cultures – those of academe and of management – has an undoubted ring of truth, it is important to note that overlap and hybridization are also part of the picture.

In the corporate model, the vocational is refurbished and redirected towards serving the company or, more recently, the 'brand'. In the newer forms of corporate vocationalism, the expectation is not so much that one will be married to one's job like the organization man as that the job will allow one to express one's inner, creative self. New Economy discourse sought to undermine the modernist opposition between work and play via the conception of 'WorkPlay'

(Löfgren 2003: 245) and the expectation that work would be 'an avenue for creativity' (Sidhu 2006: 14). Though the zenith of the early New Economy 'evangelism' (Löfgren 2003: 251) has passed, the 'information workplace' in particular demands 'new kinds of commitment' (Gregg 2009: 212). As workers in an institution at once scholarly and corporate, academics are subject to the imperatives of a double vocationalism: that of the scholarly model and of the corporate model, whose demands are not the same, but which can work in concert with each other.

In each of these three paradigms, the ideal worker is a gendered type. The idea (if not the reality) of the scholar is modelled on that of the priest, a figure who is imagined to have less time for the tethers that bind ordinary mortals to the mundane world. The priest-scholar's transcendent aspirations must not be fettered by the demands of home and family. He is bound to the life of the mind, and his first loyalty is to the collegiate. So too the bureaucracy's hero – the organization man – dutifully leaves home and family for the nine to five, an enslavement in which he sacrifices his own inner freedom and creativity. The high-tech, entrepreneurial work world of the New Economy corporate whizz is also 'extremely male', perhaps even 'boyish' (Löfgren 2003: 252), and aims to mimic, replace or surpass the comforts and pleasures of home. Löfgren characterizes WorkPlay as 'a Peter Pan economy' (252). All three ideal workers, then, are modelled on a masculine ideal in which classically feminized terms – home, family, body – remain repressed or invisible. This gendering of ideals is not only an abstract philosophical matter; it is also a concrete, social fact that not everyone can be free for the Friday night drinks required by the corporate model or can work uninterrupted in the evenings as required by the scholarly model. This will remain the case so long as caring for children or relatives remains a feminized duty. So it is that professionalism is an invisibly gendered ideal – more easily achieved by those without family (or other community) responsibilities.

Expertise in the Three Paradigms

Despite the large-scale changes wrought to universities there is still, it seems, a remarkable consensus among academics around scholarly values like autonomy, impartiality and commitment (Adams 2000: 68–9). Though the scholarly tradition may be 'under siege' (Adams 1998: 421) from bureaucratic and managerial culture, traditional scholarly values are widely shared (Adams 1998) and 'remarkably stable' (Adams 2000: 68).

This is not to suggest that there is consensus around particular *intellectual* values. On the contrary, scholarly expertise differs between (and also *within*) disciplines, and different forms of expertise are valued in different types of university. Changes to the social mission and the disciplinary mix of the university have brought competing scholarly ideals. The intellectual and institutional changes of the twentieth century – the intellectual foment of postmodernism, post-structuralism and other forms of critical theory, and the abolition of the binary divide in the UK in 1992 and of CAEs in Australia in 1988 – fuelled the development of new academic and theoretical knowledge. As new fields of knowledge and practice came under the ambit of the university, they were increasingly subject to the demand to professionalize and to enrich and develop their theoretical or scholarly base. When Nursing, for example, entered Australian universities following the dissolution of CAEs, the demand for credentialing through higher degrees was almost instant. Between 1994 and 1999, the number of Australian nurse-academics with PhDs almost trebled and the proportion with a Masters increased by almost a half (Roberts and Turnbull 2002: 26). In Australia, nurse-academics are often torn between the pressure to acquire a higher degree and the pressure to 'do research' (Worrall-Carter and Snell 2003–2004: 42–3). Adding to this pressure to meet new demands is the weight of older regimes of practice. Conflicts remain even today between those academics in Nursing who look down on their 'atheoretical' colleagues and those who are scornful of the nurse who has become too remote from the hospital. The whole process of role redefinition continues to place considerable strain and anxiety on nurse-academics, who have been forced to redefine their role in workplace cultures that were often indifferent or even hostile to research and scholarship.

As the example of Nursing demonstrates, credibility is acquired differently in different fields and for different constituencies. Students may value one sort; peers another; managers another. 'Scholarliness' is often only ambivalently valued. In a Journalism department, for example, credibility with students might come from having worked in the profession, but scholarly credentialing requires a different, more theoretical, form of expertise. Similarly, I recall that when I was completing a teaching diploma, my fellow students and I were scornful of the fact that very few of the lecturers who were training us to be teachers had themselves taught in schools for any length of time.

International students likewise come with their own sets of expectations and hopes regarding the expertise of their teachers. Some students coming from more knowledge-centred educational cultures, for example, have been found to be puzzled, disillusioned and disappointed by what they perceived as a lack of scholarly expertise evinced in the more student-centred practices of progressive pedagogies (Chen, Bennett and Maton 2008).

Within a corporate logic, expertise is likewise contextually dependent. The corporatized university, in Readings's (1996) account, aspires to no a priori form of competence other than 'excellence' – whether that be in teaching, administration, or, as Readings sardonically notes, in the provision of parking facilities (24). But the semantic emptiness of 'excellence' as a governing principle does not liberate academics to be or do what they like or what they are good at. On the contrary, its free-floating nature means that at any moment one may be found deficient.

Corporate culture does, however, have its own particular forms of competence over and above its generic commitment to 'excellence'. In particular, it values certain skills, demeanours and personal styles, including the ability to deal with a greater public of 'stakeholders' beyond the student body. This facility with networking may come more easily to particular types of personality and/or to those trained in disciplines with historically strong links to external industry bodies. Corporate competence – expertise in management skills like budgeting, strategic planning, networking, recruiting or marketing – is required the more one achieves seniority. It is a seemingly inevitable component of senior academic roles, one for which academics rarely receive training. The development of a separate career path in academic management is, however, something many academics view with ambivalence.

Accountability and Scrutiny in the Three Paradigms

Each organizational form presupposes particular forms of accountability, which it enforces through its own forms of scrutiny. Under the scholarly logic, academics had a great deal of autonomy. Not only could they play a significant role in determining the nature, timing and priorities of their workload, they were also responsible for assessing the quality of scholarly work, through formal and informal peer review. Traditional scholarship was always written 'with a constituency in mind' (Ligota and Quantin 2006: 12) – originally church leaders, patrons, students or peers. Up till the late seventeenth and early eighteenth century, it was common for scholars to promote and celebrate each other's work through activities such as editing collections, preserving letters, and writing biographies (1). These tasks continue today, but as the centuries progressed, the emerging scientific method required new methods of scrutiny, including anonymous review. The inception of scientific journals over three hundred years ago instituted formal peer review as an important component of the newly crystallizing values of objectivity and impartiality (Weller 2000: 1328). Other academic genres and traditions, such as the often combative ritual forms of academic debate – seminars, conferences, rebuttals and refutations – make the embodied, emotional and occasionally personal nature of traditional academic gate-keeping quite evident.

The modernization of the university – its bureaucratization, the massive increase in state funding and control, and an ever-developing public discourse about the university's social mission – all entrained a stronger emphasis on accountability to students and to society more broadly, and a new way of understanding it. Once the state had begun to invest substantial amounts of public money into the university, it was inevitable that accountability gradually came to encompass *financial* accountability. As far back as 1974, a guide written by the Chaplain of King's College London for prospective university students noted that:

> It is hardly surprising that university life is under the microscope of public opinion. More money is being spent on educating more school-leavers than ever before. The universities have come out of the private sector into the public arena and the public have a right to know what they are getting for their money. (Kingsbury 1974: 7–8)

This seems unarguable on the level of principle, but the key question is at what level of detail such openness is required and who is best placed to judge and communicate it. Bureaucracy, unable to police scholarly *content* directly, has to content itself with imposing and policing its own systemic *values* – productivity and efficiency – and attempting to capture scholarly value through a bureaucratic notion of 'quality'. Through the mechanisms of audit culture, which will be discussed in more detail later in the chapter, academics are now subject not only to scholarly scrutiny but also to a newly metrical conception of worth.

The seeming neutrality of bureaucratic logic masks historical and contextual particularities. One example is the way the measuring of research productivity puts disproportionate strain on newly academicizing disciplines, such as Performance Studies or Nursing: 'Despite their relative newness to the tertiary system, nurse academics are judged by the same standards as other disciplines' (Roberts and Turnbull 2004: 282). The different practices, histories and trajectories of the various disciplines are rendered invisible under the seemingly neutral and seemingly reasonable call for 'quality'. This is the flattening that Readings, drawing on Foucault's (1977) account of discipline, sees as an example of normalization through surveillance (1996: 29).

The bureaucratic paradigm is not just a vehicle through which to scrutinize scholarly work; it also places its own demands on academics – reports submitted on time, familiarity with current copyright legislation, mastery of Excel spreadsheets, ability to decode budgets or process travel requisitions. Some of these tasks are purely clerical, but others presuppose particular technological expertise, for which academics may or may not receive training.

Competence within the bureaucratic framework is measured by the successful and timely completion of particular administrative tasks (reports submitted, emails answered promptly, forms filled in properly) but it can also, perhaps, be demonstrated through other markers: regular presence on campus, attendance at meetings, an empty pigeonhole, a neat office, a light on in the office, all of which indicate participation in the temporal rhythms of a bureaucracy. The importance of these latter measures differs vastly between institutions and departments. Some university departments police professionalism through such markers; others, more imbued in the scholarly tradition perhaps, might treat them with a degree of indifference or even scorn.

Thus the bureaucratic paradigm subjects academics to a double form of scrutiny – both of scholarly content, using metrical proxies for content – and of other forms of professional competence and even demeanour. Indeed, a type of *meta*-scrutiny is at play, since efficient compliance with the often technical instruments of audit culture is *itself* scrutinizable as a form of competence. So we have witnessed a shift from an era where professionalism meant that one could be trusted to one in which professionalism means that one is obliged to provide regular *evidence* of one's activity and one's competence.

The third paradigm – the commercial one – also means that academics become accountable in new ways, including to students. Within the corporate logic, the student is a discriminating purchaser endowed with consumer rights and litigatory potential. Therefore, s/he can legitimately demand a top-quality 'product'. The most obvious domain for this is student feedback on teaching, the spread of which is simultaneously the product of progressive, student-centred pedagogies and the infiltration of customer service logic into the pedagogical relation. Within such a mix, 'service' is newly scrutinizable, and so too is 'product'. The recording of lectures, for example, puts new pressures on the teacher, turning contextual embodied encounters between known persons into the dispersal of educational products to a wider audience, including people with no connection to the course or the university. In this context, the casual unscripted remark takes on a new danger, and lectures may be scrutinized not just as intellectual products but also as legal objects.

Forms of Belonging in the Three Paradigms

The university's foundational form was that of the collegiate; the university was above all a scholarly *community*. The word *universitas* initially meant any 'society of teachers and scholars', including trade guilds, and only gradually came to refer to an institution that employed those scholars (Eby and Arrowood 1940: 462). Until around the middle of the fourteenth century, universities typically had no buildings of their own (Dunbabin 1999: 35); they were, rather, 'built of men' (Pasquier, qtd. in Eby and Arrowood 1940: 762). Masters and their students were itinerant. Scholars were 'cuckoos in other birds' nests' (Dunbabin 1999: 35), ready to leave town if they were treated too badly by the local people. The university began, then, as an 'assemblage of learned men' (Newman 1976: 95), something to which one belonged. Medieval universities admitted students via a ritual of belonging called the 'oath of matriculation' (Dunbabin 1999: 41). This ritual and the tradition of 'collegiate co-operation' (Brett 1991: 515) that underpinned it proved extraordinarily durable. The University of Sydney required students to pledge allegiance in a Matriculation Ceremony right up till 1969; the university was officially *in loco parentis* until it changed it statutes in 1973 (A. Barcan 2011: 62).

The bureaucratization of the university brought with it new forms of belonging. Although we tend to think of a bureaucracy as something which one serves rather than something to which one belongs, it does rely on and create its own forms of belonging. Whyte's analysis of the proudly middling organization men participating in a newly social ethic (1960: 11) contrasts their sense of 'belongingnesss' (11) with the mere functionality of clerks (8). Whyte saw this as an emerging collectivism in stark contrast to the historical individualism of American culture (9). It was, he claimed, 'a major shift in American ideology' (9), developing as a response to the new dominance of the bureaucracy as the major institutional form. This new way of organizing work life demanded new forms of collective imagining.

Belonging in the corporate world is more strenuously required and yet more precarious. On the one hand, the logic of branding requires employees to serve the corporation but also, especially in service roles, to be seen to *embody* it. On the other hand, the corporate model offers little by way of job security, and loyalty will not necessarily be rewarded when the going gets tough. So while New Economy ideology sought to transform the image of white-collar workplaces into one of communities of belonging, this belied both the statues inequities (what Melissa Gregg vividly calls the 'entire hidden layer of unspectacular individuals' [2011: 37]) needed to support the rise of a few 'stars') and the spatial dispersal of work that accompanied the rise of new technologies.

In the newly corporatizing university, academics remain well bolstered by the tradition of the collegiate, which remains one of the strengths and joys of the academic profession. But what about students? A sense of belonging among students is likely to be stronger in the UK than in Australia, which has never had a strong tradition of living away from home in residential colleges. Australian students, unlike their British peers, typically go to university in their home town, and many continue to live at home. The exception has always been students from rural areas, who are required by Australia's vast geography and unevenly distributed population to travel long distances to study. For them, residential colleges in the Oxbridge tradition were established at older universities like Melbourne and Sydney. This collegiate tradition continues today, as do the often misogynist rituals of incorporation and belonging that accompany it, and which occasionally erupt into public scandals.

But outside of the residential colleges, how much do students feel they *belong* to something? At his bleakest, Readings is sceptical about the extent to which students can feel they 'belong' to the new, corporate, university, since consumers purchase rather than belong (1996: 11). But Readings's critique does not engage with the complexities of late-modern consumer-mediated identities, where consumption is one of the dominant forms of identity work (see, for example, Lunt and Livingstone 1992) and where communities of belonging can indeed cluster around commodity use. Though some forms of commodity mediated identity may be fleeting or superficial – moments of shared excitement or recognition – others are more enduring. Even if one believes that university life has been reduced to brand consumption (which is palpably not the case, and which is not in any case Readings's claim), it is important to think carefully about the consumption of brands and the formation of so-called 'brand communities' as 'a form of postmodern tribe' (Luedicke and Giesler 2007: 275). My guess is that a sense of belonging may have less to do with corporate identity than with the mundane organization of time, space and workloads, with its effects on the availability and quality of human interactions. The way the bureaucratic-corporate university organizes space, time and work is the aspect of corporatization that has the greatest potential to impact negatively on a sense of community and the ability to form friendships (James, Krause and Jennings 2010). Most students work long hours off-campus, their full-time lecturers have precious little time to socialize or chat with them, and casual staff are also unlikely to have much time – whether because they are juggling multiple jobs or because they have little infrastructural support, such as an office for student consultations. As one student put it to me, other students in a tutorial are just people 'I barely even knew for 13 hours of my life'.

Logics of the Palimpsest

The university, then, is a hybrid beast, but hybridity is no simple thing. When traditional and emergent institutional forms meet and overlay each other, there is an unavoidable collision of logics, purposes, values and demands, resulting in complex and dynamic modes of co-existence.

The most obvious of these is the simple story of addition. The more institutional forms a university tries to embody, the more layers of expectation are established, and academic workloads inevitably increase. Pressure builds as the logics of the newer institutional forms – the bureaucratic and the corporate – extend their reach, while academics still struggle to meet the responsibilities of the first. The privileges or freedoms associated with each discourse seem less available to the worker situated uncomfortably within all three.

The second palimpsestic logic is one of transfer or contagion. The more naturalized the university's bureaucratic and corporate functions become, the more natural it seems that academics should share in each of these functions rather than hiving them off to specialist staff. Moreover, the more power and weight that is accorded to administrative and managerial functions, the more academics themselves actively *want* to participate – not only through normalization but also as a strategic move to keep themselves alive in the game and, ironically, to try to keep scholarly goals and values in view.

A third mode of co-existence is the reconfiguration of traditional functions through a new lens. For example, the scholarly goal of the production and dissemination of knowledge takes a new turn when viewed through the lens of corporatism. In the era in which knowledge is itself a commodity, the production of commodifiable knowledge is one of the main goals of the contemporary university. So it is too simple to say that the scholarly function has been undermined by the corporate logic; rather, their co-existence produces disciplinary winners and losers. Certain forms of intellectual inquiry have been enabled and mandated by the birth of the 'knowledge economy' and the transformation of the university into a corporation, while others have been threatened or transformed.

These three logics – expansion, contagion and reconfiguration – produce new modes of paradigmatic co-existence. I am tempted to call them new 'shapes' – and certainly 'shapes' does describe well some of the structural predicaments produced by the co-habitation of different institutional forms – but it is too static a term to capture those moments when the different logics interact more dynamically. So I prefer to think of them as modes of co-existence, some of which are fluid and others more rigid.

One first mode of paradigmatic co-existence is that of interdependence. The different discourses through which the university is understood cannot always be seen as separate institutional logics in competition with one other. Though the different discourses do not all tend in the same direction, they are nonetheless all entwined and mutually dependent. The university's success as a corporation, for example, relies on the (perceived) maintenance of the scholarly function – at least as a simulacrum. The scholarly paradigm remains symbolically and economically central to the success of the corporation; it is a significant component of the university's 'brand value'. I once worked at a new university whose complex history made its long-time managers deeply ambivalent about the scholarly tradition. It was not uncommon to hear the academic profession being explicitly mocked in meetings by managers and administrators, drawing on the usual stereotypes associated with the scholarly tradition: the inability of academics to organize themselves, their lack of connection with the real world, and so on. But on symbolic, public occasions, such as opening ceremonies or graduations, the symbols of academia were needed, and tired academics in borrowed gowns were wheeled out to embody the grand tradition before students and their parents.

A second, more rigid, configuration that emerges from the unhappy co-existence of different paradigms is that of the no-win. In its struggle to meet the demands of multiple paradigms, the university can at any moment be castigated – whether for being insufficiently scholarly, inefficiently bureaucratic, or ineptly corporate. An example is the tension between the requirement to maintain scholarly goals and values and the requirement to be socially relevant and responsive to student ('consumer') and industry ('stakeholder') demands. One university response has been to establish courses in emerging areas of practice that combine theoretical knowledge and practical skills and that have strong links to industry. Here is one example of what a more traditional academic had to say about one such course – a degree in games design. Anthony O'Hear, the University of Buckingham Education professor cited in the previous chapter, was asked to respond to a description of this course by stating what he thought about closer link between universities and workplaces. Here is his reply:

> I think it's an appalling idea, because I think it overlooks a fundamental
> distinction between education and training, and I say that without in any sense
> intending to disparage training. I've no doubt that what that vice-chancellor
> fellow said about the gaming design thing does have a high skills content. But
> no one could possibly pretend that it enlarges the mind in the same way that
> studying Homer or Aeschylus is [sic], which actually are conspicuous by their
> absence in present-day universities. (In Kearney 2006: Ep. 5)

It is only to be expected that some academics will see such courses as threatening or diluting scholarly capital. Perhaps, though, universities might win points with governments for such initiatives. After all, it is governments who have repeatedly called for universities to be more relevant, less unworldly and increasingly financially self-reliant, and who have put funding policies in place to drive them in those directions. But laments about the decline of scholarly values and the rise of populism also come, ironically enough, from the very governments who have contributed to the marketization of higher education. Former Australian Higher Education minister Brendan Nelson, for example, who held his post during a time of unprecedented rhetoric about the desirability of entrepreneurialism in the sector, could nonetheless call on an older rhetoric to denounce the corruption of scholarly values:

> [Universities] pass the soul from one generation to the next, and my concern is
> that and I say to the universities, why is it, in a country where we are bleeding in
> physics and chemistry and biology and humanities and social science, why are
> we running courses in golf course management, surfboard riding, paranormal
> scepticism, aromatherapy? You can do make-up application for drag queens at
> Swinbourne [sic] [University]. (*Four Corners* 2005)

Such rhetoric (in which, to my ear at least, the chosen instances of the intellectually weak, the marketized and the popular seem to be particularly gendered practices) demonstrates the predicaments of palimpsestic overlay very clearly: universities are subject both to the utilitarian demand that they be responsive to the market and to the conservative requirement that their scholarly values not be corrupted by that same market. Required to generate more of their own funding, they must nonetheless continue to embody and pass on a national culture (the soul of one generation) and not succumb to the corrupting (and gendered) influences of the market and popular culture.

The university, clearly, is boxed in. It is hard for it to perform multiple functions to the satisfaction of all people, not only because of funding difficulties but also because there is a measure of incompatibility of goals and values in the different paradigms.

This structural impossibility is very personally and concretely lived out and embodied. If the university cannot be all things to all people, and the university is 'built of men', then it is by extension also true that each academic can, almost by definition, never be good enough. In this, an analogy with theories of gender performance is rather illuminating, since it allows us to note the very corporeal impact of conflicting ideals on academics as living human beings. Let's use the injunction for academics to be more entrepreneurial, more 'corporate', as a springboard for thinking about this. Perhaps academics wanting to accommodate this desire could start by dressing more stylishly. Jennifer Craik, in a discussion of corporate fashion, once made the passing observation that 'even academics have smartened up their dress codes as they are nudged out of the ivory tower and into liaisons with government, industry and other agencies' (1994: 11). Perhaps this is true, but it is not simple. Dress too flashily or appear on TV once too often and you are liable to find yourself condemned by your peers as a populizer rather than a scholar; show too great an interest or skill in policy matters and you have become 'One of Them'; produce research papers too slowly or in the 'wrong' fora and you might find yourself characterized as a fusty old scholar living in the past. As with gender performance, the point is, you can never permanently or definitively get it 'right'. Correct performance is contingent, externally determined, and varies with context. As a result, the individual must become his or her own self-policer, subtly regulating his or her performance if s/he wants to play the game right. Of course, becoming a self-policer does not free you from the scrutiny of outsiders (Fisher 2011: 127).

Interestingly, this logic of insufficiency, which I explore in detail in Chapter 5, runs right up to the top of the tree. Even vice-chancellors, it seems, can never be the right thing. A British Channel 4 television documentary chastized them for enjoying corporate-style benefits such as large salaries, club membership, second jobs as company directors and other perks such as so-called 'grace and favour homes' provided by the university, chauffeured cars, and so on (Gardiner 2011). And yet, in the same programme, vice-chancellors were also criticized – this time by David Willetts, the Minister of State for Universities and Science – for not being sufficiently corporately adept: 'One of the difficulties behind many of our universities is that we're promoting brilliant academics to positions of management expertise and they don't have the management expertise'. Vice-Chancellors are, in Willetts's words, 'unimpeachable' because they are appointed through the 'archaic' scholarly tradition (Gardiner 2011).

In sum, the difficult thing for academics is not so much that a new paradigm has succeeded an older one, as that several operate simultaneously, like a palimpsest. The servant of too many masters, academics must not only submit themselves to the exigencies of each regime, each with its own demands and forms of surveillance, but also to maintain life in a number of different systems simultaneously, trying to uphold the values and practices of an older regime at same time. They do this not just through personal habit or nostalgia, but because the institution and the broader society requires this of them.

In this way, all that is good about universities also becomes a burden. Academics find themselves the living bearers of tradition, struggling to reconcile the different expectations, values, procedures and rhythms of the various paradigms. In that context, the weight of the historical understanding of the university as the bastion of the cultural heritage and the promoter of the social good is not only a privilege, but also a burden that must be defended. This, then, is why I insist that there are some particularities about the academic response to substantial paradigmatic change that must not simply be dismissed as defensive professional resistance.

Living as a Chimera: The Bodily Life of the Contemporary Academic

To embody the multiple spirits of the contemporary university, one would have to be something of a monster: the scholar-bureaucrat-entrepreneur. To embody all of these to perfection is, of course, impossible, something Bill Readings captures when he claims that 'no one of us can seriously imagine him or herself as the hero of the story of the University, as the instantiation of the cultivated individual that the entire great machine works night and day to produce' (1996: 9). But we are tacitly encouraged to *try*, and so this section considers what it is like to live like this.

From the outset, it must be noted that some people revel in multiplicity. Ghassan Hage, a respected Australian scholar and teacher, spoke upliftingly at the *Scholarly Life* conference described in Chapter 1. For him, life as an academic offers an abundance of modes of being: 'I wanted to be everything', he said of his entry into academia. For Hage, living multiply involves a kind of productive friction, and academia provides an invigorating and privileged way of living multiply: 'To me, being an academic is a refusal to be captured' (2011). In this way of inhabiting the university, the multiplicity of the university allows us to experience the best of all rather than to be trapped in insufficiency.

This embodied disposition is inextricably intertwined with Hage's intellectual position as a scholar of hybrid identities, itself born in part from his own embodied and intellectual experience of migration. Feeling torn, 'being drawn by contradictory ambitions and desires' (Hage 1998: 285), is, of course, typical of the migrant experience. But, he notes, there are different ways of being and feeling hybrid: 'Even hybridity has an identity' (285).

So it is a useful caution to be reminded that a critique of multiplicity might be regressive, nostalgic and limiting. But two questions arise. First, to whom is a non-nostalgic experience of hybridity most available, and why? Second, what conditions make hybridity more likely to be experienced as multilayered coercions rather than open-ended possibilities? The answer to these inevitably involves both personal components (dispositions, values, physical energies) and structural matters: who is *structurally* more available to take up the offer of the various paradigms.

Addressing individual psychology is beyond the aim and the scope of this chapter, but it is possible to consider how institutional structures and dynamics influence, shape, mould or reward particular subjective qualities, and how these qualities are supported and enabled by aspects of our social situation (e.g. our gender) and by certain physical capacities (e.g. our physical energy and health). Accordingly, the next section turns to particular incitements and experiences produced by the palimpsestic condition. It starts with the incentive to boundless productivity and its relation to ideals of ceaseless activity, then turns to experiences of temporality as configured by the overlay of different ideas of the university. It argues that our new accountability operates not just as some general principle, but through new, concrete mechanisms of access and embodied experiences of 'reachability'.

Productivity: Ceaseless Activity and Measurable Outcomes

The big changes to the university explored in Chapter 1 – massification, marketization and the steady increase in government intervention – made it inevitable that academics would be enjoined not only to do more work but also to be *seen* to do more. Marketization, after all, requires increases in 'output' and a 'transparent' system (Rutherford 2005: 307). My analysis of productivism explores three themes: 1) work intensification as an empirical phenomenon; 2) the psychical world produced by the obsession with scrutiny; and 3) the role and goal conflict caused by the palimpsest.

Work Intensification

Academic work is not a job that involves turning up, doing your work, and going home. It has no limits – teaching can always be done differently or better;

we can always read or write more; and more events can be planned, hosted or run. Academic work is, in other words, boundless and potentially infinite, and therefore it is always a matter of *determining* and *managing* one's workload as well as simply *doing* one's work. This puts academic work squarely in a terrain where individual psychology meets collective norms.

Both qualitative changes to and a quantitative increase in academic work are consistently reported in the higher education literature (Martin 1996, Enders 2000, McInnis 2000, Winter et al. 2000, Houston et al. 2006), though of course there are national and regional differences in how well buffered academics are in terms of institutional protections and the ability to reshape their work to meet new pressures (Enders 2000). Work intensification takes a variety of forms. First, and bluntest, is the sheer increase in the number of existing scholarly tasks brought about by the under-funded expansion of the higher education sector, including the growth of postgraduate programmes. This is empirically evident, most obviously through staff-student ratios. Second, work has intensified because the academic role itself has expanded in line with the expansion of the idea of the university. Each paradigm – the scholarly, the bureaucratic and the corporate – entails its own battery of essential tasks. Third, the bureaucratization and corporatization of the university have entrained a whole set of professionalizing imperatives, some of which might be considered nuisance tasks and others of which, especially in teaching and learning, represent genuine improvements and evolution. The growth of the subject outline from a sparse one-page handout in the 1980s to a 40-page document, detailing pedagogical principles (learning objectives, assessment principles etc.) as well as some twenty-odd pages of quasi-legal documentation of university policies (e.g. on plagiarism, special consideration, special needs and so on) epitomizes the double-edged nature of professionalization as motivated simultaneously by pedagogical drives and legal contract-making and risk management. The rise of student and peer evaluation of teaching is another phenomenon that can be regarded with ambivalence as both a worthy pedagogical innovation and a contribution to managerial surveillance. A fourth source of work intensification is the explosion in knowledge itself. In the Sciences, the rate of knowledge development is formidable. In the Humanities, the intellectual developments of the late twentieth century mean that one is no longer likely to be teaching a stable canon or body of knowledge, but often a customized, transdisciplinary assemblage addressing current issues and examples. Five, increasing casualization means that the ever-increasing burden of administrative tasks and managerial roles is distributed among a decreasing pool of full-time staff (Jensen and Morgan 2009: 42). Six, the transformation of higher education into a competitive marketplace means that expansion and intensification are an explicit part of the university's commercial agenda, not just accidental by-products of its growth.

Another aspect of this intensification – again, one caused by the dominance of the bureaucratic-corporate form – is the coming into being of whole new types of work that are required but which do not actually register as work (Gregg 2009: 211). Not only do we do our work, we also do substantial forms of 'meta-work' (Fisher 2011: 127), such as asking for work (e.g. grant applications); creating and maintaining the conditions in which to *do* work (learning new software; dealing with computer problems; technical in-servicing); reporting on work (to our managers, to the government, to external stakeholders); updating our public profile; and undertaking other forms of professional development (e.g. mandatory courses on equity in the workplace, intercultural sensitivity and so on).

Of particular significance is the 'ever-diversifying array of credentialing, performance evaluation and quality assurance tasks' (Morris 2011: 126). The regime of systematic scrutiny that now characterizes academia is a double source of work intensification: first, and most significantly, because it rewards productivism and stimulates a climate of potentially competitive overwork, and second, because complying with the demands of reporting constitutes a form of labour in and of itself.

The Psychical World of Audit Culture

One of the stronger tools for analysing this new culture in its larger sociocultural context has been Michael Power's (1997) concept of the audit society. Power, who describes himself as an idiosyncratic amalgam of a financial auditor and a philosopher ('a strange philosopher-accountant' [1997 xiii]), was one of the first to see that auditing had grown from a specific accounting practice to something much bigger and deeper. Audit society is Power's term to describe the movement of auditing beyond the realm of the financial. He charts the 'audit explosion' in Britain that began in the 1980s, arguing that it represents more than just a quantitative expansion of auditing practices. It is, rather, 'the explosion of an idea' (1997: 7). Auditing has come, he argues, to have paradigmatic dimensions (9): it is now seen as a solution to many different types of problems and it has normalized new ideas of accountability and new forms of distrust. The next section investigates how three of the commonly reported qualities of this culture – its proxy, metrical and self-referential qualities – generate collective anxieties and fantasies of various forms.

Commentators have noted that in the higher education context, audit culture is necessarily reliant on the logic of the proxy (Rutherford 2005, Redden 2008: 18). Put simply, academic audit culture measures proxies because it cannot measure the real thing: first, because so much of academic work deals with intangibles like understanding, meaning and relationships (Rutherford 2005: 307), and second, because only peers are in a position to judge scholarly content.

Thus, many university auditing practices try to capture *signs* of productivity, like activity or busyness. In the words of James L. Richardson, 'The unhappy hybrid managed-market that has succeeded [the preceding scholarly academic culture] substitutes crude quantitative "performance indicators" for reasoned judgment' (2001: 111–12).

Assessing the particularities of academic expertise is beyond the direct reach bureaucratic power, which has to be wielded at one remove, for example by the quantification of 'output' or by using various metrical proxies for intellectual quality. This is a bureaucratic rationality 'characterised by the removal of the locus of power from the knowledge of practising professionals to auditors, policy-makers and statisticians, none of whom need know anything about the profession in question' (Davies 2003: 91). This is part and parcel of the widely reported 'de-professionalisation' of the academic role (Enders 2000: 10). A deep irony underpins this new regime in which trust is no longer a structural principle and a guiding ethos: that academic work has been seriously de-professionalized in the name of professionalization, bureaucratically conceived.

Despite the demotion of academic expertise, the problem of scholarly value has not fled the field. Academics, and some bureaucrats, still *want* auditing processes to do justice to the scholarly tradition. So auditing processes never remain static, but evolve continually as though just one more tweak of the system would allow it to truly and richly capture its ever-elusive objects. In the case of academic research, attempts in Australia to record and in so doing increase the *quantity* of academic research proved unsatisfactory, producing large amounts of lightweight work. So the next phase was to follow the UK in attempting to measure *quality*, despite the UK experience of the RAE, which demonstrated that attempts to capture research quality are flawed and very labour intensive, requiring teams of senior academics to give up their own research time to read and evaluate large bodies of work (Redden 2008: 12). Current efforts in the UK are focusing on the capture of *impact*, and since that word is beginning to be heard in the corridors of Australian universities, one can only assume that we are in line for the same.[6] (For a fuller account of the intricacies of various research measurement schemes in the UK and Australia, see Redden 2008).

A second characteristic of audit culture reported by critics is its metrical quality, even when applied to the most subjective or intersubjective of academic activities. When applied to teaching, for example, metrics involves the normalization and policing of particular, visible, proxies for the subtle, interpersonal, contextual sets of relations that occur in a classroom, and their conversion into numbers. I recently attended a workshop on how to apply for a

---

6 Indeed, I note with trepidation that one expert in 'research metrics' considers the Research Evaluation Framework to be 'an excellent example for other nations', naming Australia first in his list of other nations considering such a framework (Harnad 2007).

teaching excellence award. We were asked to jot down on a piece of paper what we thought the difference was between a good teacher and an outstanding one. We all came up with our various answers, of course, but the 'correct' answer was that a good teacher uses two of Stephen Brookfield's (1995) four 'lenses' for critical reflection whereas an outstanding teacher would use three or four.

It is not too long before the instruments of audit culture become not measurers but drivers of research and teaching. Evaluation systems soon begin to produce the very things they seek to monitor. This is, of course, one of their aims, but it can produce results unforeseen even by the architects of the system. Measure the quantity of research and you rapidly risk its quality, by encouraging the rapid publication of flimsy work. Omit book reviews from definitions of research or scholarship and you begin to erode one traditionally key arena for peer commentary and review, as stretched academics abandon book reviewing in favour of work that gains them or their department 'points'. Audit culture promotes a certain instrumentality: don't do anything that isn't worth writing down and that won't gain you or your department 'points'. So-called outreach or community engagement activities may be particularly at risk – done less often, or more grudgingly, or by drawing on the (strong) residual pool of academic idealism and sense of vocation. If so, this would represent an ironic result of strategies designed to enhance academics' social utility. (For more on the 'unintended but predictable' impacts of the British RAE on research cultures – including, for example, the decline of the book – see Power 1997: 100).

A third observation about bureaucratic processes aimed at measuring complex realities is that they rapidly become self-referential and externally meaningless. Readings talks about this as a principle of 'non-referential[ity]' (1996: 22), and he sees it as at the heart of the University of Excellence: 'the contemporary University of Excellence should now be understood as a bureaucratic system whose internal regulation is entirely self-interested without regard to wider ideological imperatives' (40). The Research Evaluation Framework (REF) process in the UK, which rewards research according to its intellectual or social 'impact', has to rely on proxies for these intangibles – such as citation rates, journal rankings and so on.[7] As journals now start to measure and publicize their 'impact factor', a strange irony emerges – that measures that are meant fundamentally to capture the public utility of our work produce rubrics that are intelligible only to insiders. (Who would know what it means to note that a journal has an 'impact factor' of 1.091?) Technical 'efficiencies' also contribute to the conflation of internal and external audiences. For example, in some universities data collected for internal surveillance and audit purposes, such as the amount of money earned in research grants, or current supervision loads,

---

7 See www.ref.ac.uk This scheme aims to be less costly than the quality-based RAE, and will rely more on metrics, including citation counts (Sloman 2008).

is 'efficiently' re-used on public web pages. Click on the 'Research Supervision' link on the public web page of one scholar at an Australian university, for example, and you discover:

Number of current supervisions 1

Total current UoN Masters EFTSL 0.35

This type of impenetrable rubric (which is really about how much money the academic is bringing in) is entirely congruent with Bill Readings's acerbic analysis of excellence as a 'non-referential unit of value entirely internal to the system' (1996: 39). An ironic example is that technical articles about the design of auditing instruments are themselves written by academics and, presumably, count for 'points'.

Self-referentiality is connected to the *ritual* nature of the audit process – the fact that it is a 'communal investment' in a particular set of ideas about trust (Power 1997: 4). The ritual nature of auditing processes should not be taken to imply that they are benign. On the contrary, the (pseudo) benefit of metrical strategies is that they seem to provide self-evident, standardized, publically available criteria for making judgements about worth. This was evident in the upset surrounding one Australian university's decision in late 2011 to compensate for rising infrastructure costs and a drop in international student enrolments by making some academic staff redundant, using 'research output' as the measure of performance sufficiency. Academics at that university went public to protest the vice-chancellor's plan to make academics who had not published four 'research outputs' in the previous three years redundant or take up a teaching-only role. But they found little public sympathy:

1.3 papers a year is nothing. If you can't manage that then you deserve to be let go. (young aco 2012)

It's not difficult to have book published nowadays. Not difficult to have 4 small books done in 3 years with full-time on campus and access to the world #1 digital library (don't know if it's still that level anymore). (Dawfbunny 2012)

The idea that 1.3 'outputs' a year should be 'easy' is so frustratingly wrong-headed that it seems almost redundant to unpick it. But in the name of academics everywhere who have loyally served their institution under some of its guises – teaching, administration, management, outreach – only to find themselves punished for having backed the wrong horse, I shall spell some of them out. First, the mere counting of 'outputs' evacuates the question of academic worth and quality. It is a quantitative measure whose logic comes straight out of industrial production. Second, 'outputs' is a meaningless unit of value even in purely quantitative terms since it makes a 100,000 word book, for example, equal to a 1,500 word poster presentation. It is, moreover, a unit of value that favours the sciences, where journal articles are the preferred currency, over those Humanities disciplines in which a singly-authored monograph is the pinnacle of academic achievement. It takes no account of the temporality of thought (maybe new ideas take time to form or gel), research (perhaps the academic is half-way through extensive fieldwork), writing, or publication (some elite journals in the Humanities have a two-three year lag between submission and publication). It also ignores all the other components of academic labour. Perhaps an academic was also convening a first year course with 400 students that year, or redesigning the undergraduate curriculum, or acting in a senior management role, or focusing on postgraduate supervision. Given these blunt failures it seems redundant to point out that such measures do not even pretend to do justice to other, more personal, elements affecting work life, such as whether someone was unwell, or caring for an ill relative. Even these questions – which have the effect of putting context back into numbers – do not address the more fundamental logical problem: the assumption that writing four papers make you a better academic than writing two. Perhaps it makes you twice as good. Context, subtlety and understanding – to say nothing of compassion – evaporate under the blunt tyranny of the single, summative number. 'Poor Wittgenstein, only two short books in the whole of his career', as Cummins acerbically notes (2002: 102).

As such examples indicate, numbers are condensed assumptions with very material import. They serve as a seemingly rational basis for punitive decision-making, whether by outsiders who want to claim that all academics are lazy, or by vice-chancellors who want to claim that certain staff 'aren't pulling their weight', as happened in the case just described. Their seemingly self-evident quality means that staff can be viewed simply as costs on a spreadsheet. Here is Cultural Studies professor Simon During, reflecting on how easy it is to work out whether a particular staff member 'pays their way':

> The budget I managed was determined by a formula which allocated money according to performance quantified across a number of variables. Each student, each text written by faculty, each PhD completion, each research dollar won had a money value, so that, at least in theory, it was possible to compute exactly how much each academic earned and to assess whether they were departmental profit centers. (2006: 275)

Although During presents this as a hypothetical, this ability is not just theoretical but already operationalized, and it is intensely personalized, moralized and threatening. Fifteen years later, I still recall hearing one manager at an institution I worked out saying, 'I look forward to the day when academics are paid by the number of students they teach'. Then it was merely an insult. At the time of writing, it is a concrete threat, manifesting in the form of job cuts at a number of Australian universities.

A culture of quality is, then, a culture of surveillance: metricized, ritualized and normalized. It takes place across a wide spectrum of modes of visibility – from the writing of reports, to the construction of the academic persona via the curriculum vitae, to promotions committees, academic gossip, and even joyous occasions like book launches and award nights. In classic Foucauldian disciplinary vein,[8] the subjects of this scrutiny cannot help but internalize the imperatives of this regime – in particular its injunction to ceaseless activity and visible outcomes. Such intense surveillance functions most powerfully as self-surveillance. This internalization is made even more complete by its happy conjunction with academia's historical vocationalism, which makes its subjects want to work hard and morally rewards them for doing so. A heady mix of different motivations and emotions pull together: intrinsic motivation, the desire for promotion, fear of losing one's job, the desire to *get* a full-time job, the pleasure in creating an academic persona, a commitment to social change or the advancement of knowledge, a belief in the importance of the discipline in which one works, and the traditional scholarly inseparability of research work and personal pleasure. One cannot, therefore, disentangle the complex knot of value associated with our work – the interweaving of pleasure, pain, choice, desire, social conscience, prestige, and coercion.

So it is that audit culture, despite its seeming rationality, encourages a strange new psychical world predicated on the competitive proving of merit, the generation of anxiety and fantasies of control. The proving of merit is rather infantilizing – not only in the obvious sense that perhaps nations might be able to trust their best engineers, scientists, medical researchers and philosophers to work hard – but also in terms of the psychic structures it sets in place and normalizes, which amount to the adult equivalent of keeping note of all your best work and showing it to mummy, subtly in competition with your siblings. There is something rather strange about the fact that academics are required to 'record ... every single one of their productive acts' (Savonarola, qtd. in Fisher 2011: 127). It is a repudiation of trust, not only in individuals, but in the vocational dimensions of the professions – a model that traditionally sustained not only academia, but other professions, like medicine or indeed politics.

The minute recording of one's deeds may produce moments of individual satisfaction or reassurance, but its larger impact is to bolster overwork and competitiveness and to generate a climate of anxiety. Small wonder if, in the

---

8 Foucault's influential contention, outlined in *Discipline and Punish* (1977), was that the modern form of power is characterized less by overt displays of force than by regulatory mechanisms aimed at governing life. At its deepest registers, external strictures are internalized as injunctions and restrictions, and the subject becomes increasingly self-governing.

face of the constant public injunction to be 'productive' in a system in which work is structurally boundless and potentially infinite, academics fall prey to a low-level anxiety that has trickled down to embed itself in the minutiae of actual daily labour. Scott Belsky coined the phrase 'insecurity work' to describe certain types of task whose psychological purpose or payoff is self-reassurance in the face of anxiety about creativity and productivity (2010: 104–106). Email is one obvious example. Its fragmented, trigger-and-response rhythms are perfectly suited to the channelling of low-level anxiety about 'busyness'. 'Doing email' is proof to the self and others that one is being active and productive. A colleague once sent me an email that included this observation:

> It seems to me that the only legitimate forms of academic labour are: reading and replying to emails; generating new, fresh emails; organising your inbox so it's in great shape for email; doing anything in Excel, and; attending either a LONG MEETING or a session in the library on new plagiarism detection software. Even TEACHING is becoming increasingly seen as academic fat deserving of institutional trimming – first year tutorials have dropped from 1.5 to 1 hour and the idea of actually standing up in front of students and giving a lecture is beginning to look mad – or at least narcissistic. Shorten the lecture and sit in your office, record it on an MP3 player, and post it on the internet. Then get back to your email. (Pers. comm. 2009, original emphases)

Email is also the perfect vehicle for the competitive display of overwork, as is well understood by those colleagues who take grim pleasure in sending emails at 3am so everyone knows they are working through the night. In those toxic work environments where such display is common, email is a communication vehicle in the richest sense, not only transmitting overt messages but saturated in negative affect.

Insecurity work is obviously not restricted to academics; it's clearly a widespread feature of the white-collar workplace. Two features of academic work, however, give it its own particular flavour in the university context. First, the structural boundlessness of academic work and academics' traditional autonomy in determining its limits and priorities make us especially prone to thinking we haven't done 'enough'. Second, the discourse of public accountability and the erosion of academic authority (Furedi 2003), often fed explicitly by politicians (see Chapter 3), make academics particular targets for public opprobrium and hence for self-questioning. Again, the 2011 Australian case provides plenty of examples:

> Huh? Moaning about having to publish slightly more than once a year? The whole lot of you should be sacked. (TBear 2012)

Although audit culture produces anxiety at a local level, systemically it works the other way. Anne-Marie Cummins draws on Power's (1997) account of the ritual nature of audit culture to argue that it represents a ritualized working through of the 'high and potentially ungovernable risk associated with modernity' (2002: 109). In the face of the widespread erosion of trust that characterizes modern societies, it offers a reassuringly bland guarantee of order and stability. It is, she claims, 'a social defence against anxiety' (109). Its dispassionate, impartial and metrical nature produces 'comfort' (108) via the 'obsessive collection of information' (108). Trust, which can no longer be placed in particular groups or classes of people, can now be placed in systems of accounting (109).

This points to a second set of fantasies that subtends auditing activity as an anxiety management ritual: fantasies of control. Accounting systems are driven 'at a psychic level' by 'pushes for certainty' (Cummins 2002: 106). Take the normalization of the term 'outcomes' in both pedagogical and research discourse. Outcomes are conceived in the future perfect tense – they are attempts to capture the uncertainty of the future and yoke it to the promise of productivity. This form of promise is in fact antithetical to the ethos of open-ended, curiosity-driven investigation, with its historical recognition of the importance of false starts, wrong turns, serendipity, accidents and slow progress to the development of new, original or complex ideas. Instead, researchers are asked to promise (guarantee?) that their research will be important, and to enumerate in advance what the 'outcomes' will be. As another former colleague of mine once noted rather poignantly, the word 'outcomes' has been 'robbed of its sense of contingency'.

This function of audit culture as a ritual resolution of shared social anxieties helps explain why it does not matter if the rational measuring instruments aimed at ensuring productivity are, ultimately, unwieldy, irrational wastes of money. (This is not to say they all *are* unwieldy and irrational, only to say that it doesn't matter within the logic of the system if some of them are). They are, fundamentally, signs of activity and busyness. Roderick Floud, a British vice-chancellor, wrote in 2001 of universities 'sinking' under the financial and psychological weight of an 'over-engineered' audit system that ultimately finds few flaws (2001). As Readings puts it, 'All that the system requires is for activity to take place, and the empty notion of excellence refers to nothing other than the optimal input/output ratio in matters of information' (1996: 39).

Verification systems are 'always costly' (Power 1997: 1). Bronwyn Davies notes how the redirection of money that used to *support* academics towards processes of surveillance 'somehow remains invisible, or at least is generally not spoken about, or subjected to critique' (2003: 93). An Australian example is the process of applying for research funding through the one major public funding body open to scholars in the Humanities, the Australian Research Council. Universities now invest substantial amounts of infrastructure and funding into maximizing academics' chance of success: they hire staff to train academics in grantsmanship and to read drafts; to assist with preparing budgets; to check compliance with all the application rules (font sizes, word counts etc.); and to design software to streamline submission. Workshops and in-services are run; teams and mentors established. Academics learn to become experts in each of the micro-genres associated with this scheme: the 100 word summary; the track record summary; even the keywords. From December to March, thousands of academics and administrative staff across the country are engaged in a frenzy of ARC preparation, spending their summers preparing applications that are due about two weeks into the start of the new academic year for a scheme with a 21 per cent success rate.[9] That this unwieldy machinery – replicated in every institution around the nation – arose in part from the systematization and normalization of government suspicions about work and productivity (the fear that academics may be 'wasting' time and not being sufficiently 'productive') is the ultimate irony, scarcely visible since the machinery is now so entrenched.

Such strange anomalies are comprehensible both through the type of psychoanalytically inflected analysis made by Cummins – in which the financial inefficiency of auditing processes is irrelevant since their ultimate purpose is to produce reassurance about systems themselves – as well as through the Weberian perspective on the ultimate irrationality of modernist rationalities. George Ritzer (1993), proponent of the well-known theory of the 'McDonaldization' of modern life, takes this Weberian approach. Drawing on Weber's account of modernization as hyper-rationalization, Ritzer argues that 'rational systems inevitably spawn a series of irrationalities that serve to limit, ultimately compromise, and perhaps even undermine, their rationality' (121). This is a rationality antithetical to human reason, dehumanizing in its effects (121). While Ritzer's McDonaldization thesis has rightly been critiqued for its totalizing style (Alfino et al. 1998), it nonetheless usefully draws attention to the systemic rather than idiosyncratic quality of 'the irrationality of rationality' (Ritzer 1993: 121).

A third aspect of productivism is its individualizing drive. Demands for productivity can often seem reasonable, having been so thoroughly normalized over the last few decades, but they nonetheless still have quite a stark impact. Teaching, for example, is now both subtly and unsubtly commoditized, its pedagogical drivers, rationales and values hybridizing with, or submerged beneath, the logics of service provision and quality control. Academic courses are now a form of product, and are routinely evaluated according to the business logic of 'quality control'. From both a pedagogical and a corporate perspective, student evaluation of courses might seem uncontentious, but the individualized intellectual property dimensions of high-level university teaching and the

---

9 www.arc.gov.au.ncgp.dp/DP13_selrpt.htm [accessed: 4 February 2103].

personal, embodied, nature of teaching as a set of human interactions make the evaluation of teaching much more personal, emotional and *targeted* than the more neutral, routine or industrialized forms of quality control that characterize other forms of service provision. For academic courses are *not* commodities or services emanating from distant or unidentifiable sites of production. At least in the Humanities, they are idiosyncratic and individual – designed, taught and implemented by identifiable individuals, increasingly so, as monolithic disciplines and course structures fragment into smaller and less generic units. The inextricability of the scholar's life and work sits uncomfortably with the model of service provision and quality assurance. The lecturer's 'performance style' – inseparable from his/her embodied personality – is subjected to market scrutiny under the guise of neutral product evaluation. So student evaluation can be exhilarating, but it can also be deeply and unhelpfully painful. Evaluation places the academic under the gaze of the student, academic colleagues, university administration and promotions committees, and, ultimately, under the self-scrutinizing gaze of the academic herself. The logic of product evaluation and market 'appeal' comes to exert an influence over the intellectual and pedagogical practices of the academic. An alternative to this 'product-based' evaluation, in which the student is interpellated as a discriminating purchaser of educational services rather than as a participant in learning, might be a more pedagogically driven evaluation in which, for example, students might be asked to comment about their *own* contribution and not just on the teacher's 'performance'.

Role and Goal Conflict

Palimpsestic logic makes it hard to win the productivity game. For one thing, you never know which measuring stick will be wielded at any given time. As Roger Burrows notes, a whole host of different auditing mechanisms are 'nested' together to form 'a complex data assemblage' (2012: 359) which may aggregate conflicting or incompatible perspectives or be made to serve incommensurable policy goals.

Moreover, you measure *yourself* and assess your own productivity, utility and competence using a similarly changeable yardstick. I have written two books, while working part-time, each one seven years in the making, without a government grant. You might think this might help me sleep at night – I am not costing the taxpayer more than my salary, so perhaps I am not a not unreasonable drain on public monies. Within an administrative logic I might seem like a paragon of efficiency – doing a lot on very little. From the perspective of the social good, I am 'producing' without overly burdening the taxpayer. But this isn't how the accountability game works. In not having gained a big grant I am, in fact, a lost opportunity – since the university's brand value (its status in league tables and so on) relies on how much income its researchers earn, and since governments also reward universities for having already been rewarded through grants. I am also, perhaps, worse than a lost opportunity; I may be, in fact, a parasitical drain, if not on the public purse, then on my own immediate colleagues, whose successes in attaining grants have indirectly 'bought' my department the 'empty' time I filled with writing these books. I have drawn from a subtle communal purse, whose invisible currency is time itself. So maybe I shouldn't sleep easy after all.

My point here is not to indulge some paranoid fantasy that perhaps my (in fact) generous colleagues think of me in this way. It is, rather, to note how easily paranoid fears *can* arise in such a climate, and to point out how the seemingly neutral and objective operations of audit culture and research funding and the broader context of conflicting ideas of academic work in which they are situated are, ultimately, an unwinnable game. There are, perversely, liberating elements to this, which will be canvassed at the end of this chapter.

The palimpsestic structure of the universities constantly produces such experiences of paradigmatic dissonance in the form of internal and external conflict about one's role and goals. In the face of an over-abundance of work, conflict between what we think matters and what we are asked to do, *internal* institutional inconsistency about what matters and what will be rewarded and punished, and the unpredictability of the criteria that may be wielded at any given moment, occasionally with severe consequences, it is hardly surprising if some academics suffer from anxiety and despondency.

At my most bleak, I feel like a milking cow: required to 'produce' certifiable product at reliably regular intervals. This feeling, ultimately, cannot help but reverberate at the deepest level of embodiment. The relentless focus on *output*, without regard for the processes, temporalities or engagements that *feed* us, puts input and output drastically out of balance. And what kind of body can do output without input? The body knows this bulimic rhythm to be possible only through strain: minds and imaginations are milked for ideas; bodies squeezed for energy; and time mined for effects.

Productivism, in essence, re-patterns time itself, making of it something that must be managed, mapped, controlled and rendered ever more productive. It is to the temporal dimensions of this new norm of ceaseless activity that I turn next.

Temporality: The Management and Arrangement of Time

> If the unfulfilled quest for a decent society is to remain viable in the twenty-first century, a serious-minded analysis of the temporal driving forces underlying contemporary society will have to make up a crucial element of a renewed critical theory of sociality. (Hartmut Rosa and William E. Scheuerman, *High-Speed Society* 2009: 3)

The compression and fragmentation of time in the service of maximum productivity is, of course, not unique to academia, but is typical of much white-collar work and indeed of contemporary life more generally. But the problem for academics is not just the broadly shared one of work intensification and the increased pace of life. It is also something more specific to academic work – the fact that academics are being asked to uphold different ideas of the academic role simultaneously, all predicated on different conceptions, management, arrangements and experiences of time. Academics are therefore subjected to different temporalities simultaneously. In this section I examine this collision between different types of time more closely, starting with temporality in its broadest sense, then working down through progressively smaller 'types' of time to a finer-grained analysis of the temporal textures of everyday work life.

The Temporal Orientation of Scholarly and Bureaucratic Work

The scholarly tradition has deep temporal orientations. Much contemporary scholarly work, especially in the sciences, is oriented towards the future, assuming an evolutionary conception of knowledge and motivated by a social mission yoked to ideas of progress and betterment. But the future was not always the goal of knowledge. The erudition component of early modern[10] scholarship, for example, was oriented to the past – the preserving and monumentalizing of the work of one's intellectual forebears. The monumentalizing aspect of some intellectual work today bears the traces of this, especially in the liberal Humanities, where respect for the history of ideas remains strong. Some see this monumentalizing aspect of traditional scholarship as having a submerged existential tenor:

> The desire to save past scholars and their work from oblivion may have even deeper roots, if one accepts that Western scholarship, since the Renaissance, if not much earlier, has largely been an attempt to overcome time and, ultimately, mortality itself. Scholarship is by definition endless and the inability to finish one's work before one is overtaken by illness and death has been, and will be, many a scholar's fate. (Ligota and Quantin 2006: 3)

Reading this, I recall being an undergraduate and walking past the office of a scholar who was terminally ill. From behind his closed door, late into the evenings, you could hear him typing, typing, racing against time.

Legacy is both an individual and a collective matter, and it invokes both the past and the future. 'The true test of a scholar's work is the judgment that

---

10 Ligota and Quantin, from whom I take this argument, define 'early modern' as the late seventeenth century to early eighteenth century (2006: 1).

is made not at the time his work is being done, but twenty-five or fifty years later', said the economist Milton Friedman at the time of his Nobel Prize win in 1976 (Friedman and Friedman 1998: 442). Occasionally, scholars are explicitly asked to engage in advance with the question of their own legacy. One current Australian research funding scheme aimed at senior scholars, the Australian Laureate Fellowships, asks applicants to demonstrate their 'potential to leave an enduring legacy' (Australian Research Council 2011). What a strange thing – at once immodest and subtly confronting – it is to be asked to think of oneself in the future perfect tense – to imagine one's own intellectual afterlife. Whether or not academics spend much time contemplating their own personal legacy, much scholarship is animated by a belief in the importance of transmitting a body of knowledge or an intellectual heritage to the next generation.

Only some types of work – academic work, artistic endeavour, architecture, urban planning, politics, environmental science, some family businesses – engage these big temporalities, offering people the privilege and the burden of considering their personal and collective impact on the future and their relation to the past. This connection to big goals, long-time frames and a mode of life produces a mixed picture of big-picture satisfaction combined with daily rewards, frustrations and tedium. The engagement with big temporality, while it is often challenging, offers the opportunity for work to be meaningful and connected (to others, to ideas, to the world), two features that are regularly shown to be correlated to wellbeing in a deep and broad sense if not to happiness on a more daily level. By engaging different temporalities simultaneously, academic work pits the big picture (is this a good way to be spending my life?) against the bumpier temporalities of everyday work life.

The Nature of Traditional Scholarly Time

Traditional academic time is not singular, but is comprised of at least two broad types: that of research and that of teaching. Newman saw research and teaching as fundamentally different activities requiring their own temporality and their own mode of engagement in the world (1976: 8): 'I think it must be allowed on the whole that, while teaching involves external engagements, the natural home for experiment and speculation is retirement' (8). He understood the bodily dimensions of these very different activities: 'He ... who spends his day in dispensing his existing knowledge to all comers is unlikely to have either leisure or energy to acquire new' (8). Newman saw it as a self-evident truth that research and the discovery of truth were associated with 'seclusion and quiet' (8). This is an essentially religious conception of research as a form of contemplative activity, best achieved by turning away from the world.

Newman believed that research and teaching were so different that they required their own types of institution: academies and universities respectively

(1976: 8). The debate about whether research and teaching are best conducted in separate, specialist, institutions continues today. But universities that combine them have been, until recently, able to structurally incorporate both temporalities. In many universities, the academic year was organized around a rhythm of gentle alternation between the time of scholarship and that of teaching. The annual rhythms of teaching were, originally, connected to those of the church, as evidenced by the names of the teaching terms in many of the older universities in England and Ireland: Lent Term, Trinity Term, Easter Term, or Michaelmas Term. The University of Sydney was one of the last Australian universities to give up the vestiges of the Oxbridge-inspired religious-scholarly temporality, continuing to use Lent, Trinity and Michaelmas terms up until 1988.[11]

The arrangement of terms with long breaks between them meant that over the course of a year, different types of task could be arranged into different types of time. Term time, thinking time, fieldwork time and writing time could all have their place. Moreover, even within these qualitatively different types of time, academics were granted the autonomy characteristic of vocational modalities and were trusted to regulate the intensity of their own work and organize their own priorities, a trust that was no doubt met with different levels of commitment.

The Nature of Bureaucratic-Corporate Time

Not all teaching in higher education has followed the scholarly pattern. More recent institutional forms were built on more modern, gridded, temporal patterns. In the polytechnics and CAEs, scholarly time was perceived as elitist in contrast to the more visible diligence of this gridded time. When Australian CAEs were first amalgamated with universities, these two temporalities clashed. Colleagues in a university Nursing department tell me that for some years after Nursing became a university degree, their Head of School would prowl, matron-like, along the corridors to see whose light was or wasn't on by 9am, and whose pigeonhole hadn't been emptied. By the standards of bureaucratic time, scholarly time looked slack.[12]

Administrative time, clearly, has its own rhythms and they do not easily correspond with those of scholarship. For one thing, even though bureaucratic work does have its futures – forward planning is after all a key bureaucratic

---

11 Thanks to the University of Sydney archivist Julia Mant for her assistance.

12 The connection between a certain arrangement of time and the idea of usefulness was quite direct. In the UK, polytechnics were spoken of as belonging to 'the service tradition', as opposed to the 'autonomous tradition' of universities (Pratt 1997: 9).

function – it is also significantly oriented towards the present: the effective and efficient daily running of the organization. The bureaucratization of academic work means that these more immediate temporalities of short-term planning now have a large place in academic life.

Noting Meaghan Morris's impatience about those academics who complain about administration while benefitting from the systems it makes possible (2011: 127), I should state that I recognize both the benefits of being part of a bureaucracy and the pleasures of certain forms of administrative labour. For an academic, administrative work can be a delightful alternative to, distraction from, or proxy for the labour of teaching or writing. The gentle occupational therapy of putting marks into databases, of crafting subject outlines, of choosing the best fonts or creating a course website are pleasures I know well.

But the administrative component of academic work has intensified. The sheer number and variety of administrative tasks has greatly increased at the same time as the number of administrative staff at departmental level has tended to drop in recent years (though it remains high relative to a few decades ago), owing to managerialism (which diverts administrative resources 'upwards'), funding cuts, and the subtle centrifugal drive of computing technology, which disperses administrative work outwards and allows/requires every academic to be responsible for his/her own administration. In an era when academics write up and distribute the minutes of their own meetings, draft procedural manuals, or process complex budgets, the time (not so long ago, moreover) when a head of department had a secretary who could type up a letter for him seems as outdated as the gender arrangements that underpinned it.

This picture of administrative creep is intensified still further by the university's transformation into a service industry, which has led to the infiltration of late-modern administrative time by the logic of the corporation, with its assumptions of perennial reachability. Corporatism and the rise of digital technologies have changed administrative temporalities. Servicing clients no longer only means having a desk open on workdays. It also means participating in the fast turnaround enabled by digital technologies and portable devices.

This has an effect on academics, but an even starker one on administrative staff, who are themselves increasingly subject to the demands of the palimpsest. At mid to senior levels they are expected to obey the dictates of traditional bureaucratic time (Monday to Friday, 9am–5pm), but also to keep corporate hours when required *and* to follow the rhythm of the academic's vocational tendencies – all this without the accompanying benefits of flexibility, autonomy and respect accorded to academics. In these days where mid-tier administrative staff increasingly have higher degrees, including PhDs, palimpsestic logic works against them too, and the injustice must seem stark. A 2011 survey of administrative staff in Australian universities found that workloads had intensified, staff worked a lot of unpaid overtime, and most staff were suffering 'extreme work stress' (Davies 2012).

Students, too, operate in 24/7 mode, emailing staff at any time or day of the week, expecting either that there will be a continuous virtual presence or that staff are capable enough to manage their own time as they will. This is not unreasonable; they are simply living out the dominant contemporary modern form of temporality and obeying the logic of digital technology.

The new fluid temporality ushered in by digital technologies isn't entirely unpatterned, unrhythmed or undifferentiated, and, moreover, it still buffets up against older temporalities. But it is much more overflowing than the gridded rhythms of bureaucratic time. In fact, in its boundlessness, the new temporality enabled by digital technologies produces a temporality not unlike, and compatible with, the fluid time of vocational scholarly work. But whereas research time was traditionally given some of its shape and, importantly, its *limits*, by the academic's own drives, interests and priorities, digital technology encourages a much more outwardly-directed orientation It helps generate a sense – be it expectant, fearful or hopeful – that someone else may be 'there', wanting us, *now*. Some people respond to this incipient potential presence of a host of invisible others by internalizing the feeling that a response is always required immediately, which may or may not always be true. Thus the new temporalities of digital technologies are bound up with new ideas of responsibility to others. They are also given a new spatial reach by the portability of communications devices, which make it possible for us to be contacted at home, or on the bus, or on the toilet, or while we are on holiday. Like so many workers of all kinds, academics are subject to the new temporalities, habits and subtle ethics of 'reachability' (Löfgren 2003: 239), in which students, colleagues and managers can potentially contact us at any time or place, and according to which they judge our professionalism.

The Erosion of Scholarly Time by Bureaucratic-Corporate Time

I noted in the introductory chapter how Newman, even in the mid-nineteenth century, considered the enterprise of scholarship to be under threat from the new media of his time, in particular the periodical. The trends he saw dawning have, of course, only accelerated and intensified under today's new media, where the demand for instantancity, novelty and opinion favours certain kinds of intellectual skills and endeavour – concision, wit, irony, rapidity – over others. The temporality of knowledge production has sped up so unimaginably as to render Newman's fear of the paciness of periodicals quaint.

Newman could certainly have had no inkling that the various forms of traditional academic temporality – the focused, long term or contemplative time of research and the intense, engaged time of teaching – would come to be threatened by the more domineering nature of the new, bureaucratic time, with its insistence on the exigencies of an always-urgent present. It is not just that the availability of scholarly time has been reduced by the proliferation of administrative tasks, although this is true,[13] but that the two temporalities of scholarship and administration have come increasingly to operate simultaneously: academics work nights and weekends (since their work and life are inseparable), but are expected to be increasingly visible on campus as part of the bureaucratic model. Moreover, scholarly time itself is now expected to conform to the patterns of administrative time. This is true of teaching; Readings, for example, notes that 'Much of the current furor over teaching has to do with a simple contradiction between the time it takes to teach and an administrative logic that privileges the efficient transmission of information' (1996: 19). The rise of the term 'delivery' to describe teaching is symptomatic of this failure to recognize learning as processual, cumulative and sometimes slow. It is also true of research; the scholarly enterprise is increasingly expected to mesh with corporate culture, including its demands for short-term, visible, guaranteeable 'outcomes'.

One of the most dramatic breaks in the traditional yearly rhythm that characterized the scholarly mode was the introduction of modularization (the breaking down of long courses of study into small units) and semesterization (a bureaucratic rather than traditional division of the academic year into two semesters rather than three terms). This shift, occurring over the last three decades of the twentieth century in the UK and Australia, typically took place 'without reference to academic considerations' (Lindsay, Breen and Paton-Saltzberg: 2002: 30). It was pushed in part by explicit campaigning from governments and other agencies (Morris 2000: 240).

To the bureaucratic imagination, different ways of organizing the teaching year are just 'neutral vehicles' for the delivery of knowledge (Lindsay, Breen and Paton-Saltzberg: 2002: 22). But the organization of time and space cannot ever be a neutral matter. The rise of semesterization and modularization is inextricably bound up in the university's corporatization. Since they create flexibility and enhance the capacity for choice, experimentation and customization, modularization and semesterization are congruent with the logic of consumer choice (DaCosta 1997: 163). They are part of what some see as the rise of a university degree as a component of 'lifestyle' choice as well as an investment in enhanced life chances (157). They also allow easier changing

---

13 The fact that this complaint is literally ancient – Jean Dunbabin, citing Verger, wryly notes that the first recorded complaint that administrative burdens were interfering with the proper business of teaching goes back to the thirteenth century (1999: 42) – does not mean it is untrue.

from course to course and university to university, and so promote competition within the sector and facilitate international exchange.

Roger Lindsay et al. consider modularization and semesterization to be 'amongst the most momentous changes that have affected the UK university sector during the last 20 years' (2002: 21). The pedagogical and workload impacts of these changes are many. For one thing, it is possible that modularization and semesterization shorten effective teaching time. DaCosta estimates that the doubling of revision weeks (swot vacs) and exam periods and the lack of fit in the UK between the church-based academic year (with longish breaks for Christmas, Easter and the summer) and the rational semesterized year have meant a loss of five to six teaching weeks per year (1997: 175).[14] Others estimate that the total teaching time remains about the same (Morris 2000: 240). In my experience, regardless of the nominal number of teaching weeks, semesterization shortens *effective* teaching time, by doubling the number of 'start-up' and 'wind-down' weeks, especially as the 'consumer choice' model means that students in Australian universities can drop out of or join subjects some weeks into the semester (until the end of Week 4, in my university). Shortened teaching time, when combined with continuous assessment, encourages the clumping of assignments in particular weeks, with knock-on effects for student stress and, some claim, plagiarism.

The lack of fit between school terms and university semesters presents difficulties for mature-age students with school-aged children and academic staff in the same position (DaCosta 1997: 176). The need to compress semester time may also rob staff and students of effective mid-term breaks, which in many Australian universities have been reduced from two weeks to one, with assignments typically due upon return.

In terms of classroom interactions in the Humanities, where tutorials are based on the open discussion of sometimes sensitive issues and the expression of personal opinion, a longer time-frame is an important component of encouraging students to feel comfortable enough to speak openly. Semesterization means that tutorials disperse at the very moment when they are beginning to gel, and people who were in a tutorial together may not see each other for the rest of their degree. Students in large, modularized courses (such as a Bachelor of Arts) report that though they form friendships, they have no strong sense of *cohort*. The up-side, of course, is that a dysfunctional or unsatisfying tutorial group is not bound together for an entire year, and nor are students stuck with a poor quality tutor for an entire year. Many students like the opportunities for change and variety provided by modularization, but critics

---

14 DaCosta notes that the US system has not traditionally had long Christmas or Easter breaks and so semesterization has been less troublesome (1997: 166).

argue that it is inherently inimical to the principles of sequencing and substance required for deep learning (Maskell and Robinson 2002: 96).

When contrasted to year-long subjects, semesterization doubles a lot of administrative tasks, such as those pertaining to enrolment, subject choice, room bookings, examination meetings and results processing. According to Huw Morris's survey of ten UK business schools, 'semesterisation has significantly increased costs without any accompanying benefits' (2000: 239). This inefficiency is tolerated because semesterization works hand in hand with the marketplace logic of maximizing output and diversifying product. Fragmentation (courses held night and day, at multiple campuses, offered via multiple modes of delivery) increases product range and diversity. But by doubling administrative tasks and fragmenting non-teaching time, semesterization and modularization diminish research time.

In terms of staff wellbeing, a bureaucratic relation to time brings both benefits and costs: it simultaneously rations out work, creates more work, and enshrines the right to rest. Mandatory legal limitations on the working week (for example, the 37.5 hour week according to which Australian academics are paid) are bureaucratic limits often hard-won through activism, and available only to about half the academic workforce.

The formalizing of official work time brought with it the formalizing of periods of rest. I recall the first time I ever heard about 'annual leave' – it was in the early 1990s, when I was in my first year of full-time university employment. I was informed that if I was on annual leave I needed to fill out a form. I was genuinely puzzled. I was working, it seemed, all the time: living away from home, partner and family, finishing a PhD, teaching courses for the first time, and rapidly realizing the chasm that lay between intellectual training (the PhD) and a fuller professional preparation. I was going to be back with my partner for a week during the non-teaching break, but was taking a book I had to read and review by the end of that week. Was that being on leave, I asked, without irony? 'Well, we all read', was the unenlightening reply.

Looking back, my puzzlement demonstrates how little experience of the wide workforce I had had. Having been a school student, a university student and then a school teacher in a family of schoolteachers, the only rhythms of work and rest I had ever encountered were those produced by the overlay of scholarly work on traditional church-based holiday seasons such as Easter and Christmas. As a new academic, I was working hard – working far more than the hours I was nominally being paid for – but I had no idea what it meant to negotiate bureaucratic time. In student life and school teaching, holidays, their timing, and their purpose, were not subject to negotiation, scrutiny or justification. One simply knew when they were and what they were for, and no forms needed to be filled out. But I was entering academia at a time when the basis of work-rest rhythms in scholarly time – you work when it's term time and are responsible for yourself when it's not, and you don't need to account to anyone for it – were being displaced by the forms of leave-taking that characterize administrative and industrial workplaces – formal periods agreed to by a manager, quantified, and with a clear monetary equivalent. The era I had witnessed as an undergraduate – when, for example, English academics employed in Australia could simply 'go home' for the entire long break and not be seen until term began again – was vanishing. Now, a week's absence needed to be explained.

The reason I was being quizzed on leave was that it had recently been pushed to the forefront of the university's managerial radar as the two tectonic plates of scholarly vocationalism and bureaucratic rationality began to collide for the first time on this particular front. It was the moment when new bureaucratic, monetized, relations to time were being ushered in without having yet displaced older scholarly modes, with the result that academics who were retiring at that point were double-dipping, whether inadvertently or not. They were benefiting from the advantages of both systems simultaneously: taking unaccounted-for time off over the years and then being paid at an hourly rate for accrued annual leave when they retired. It was costing the university a fortune.

Now, of course, living out the palimpsest often means the reverse. Many academics find themselves so overcommitted that they are genuinely unable to take leave. One result is that academics may sign off that they are on leave but still work (living out the devotions of the scholarly paradigm) or they may be called upon by colleagues while they are supposedly on leave (living out the demands of the corporate sector). It is not at all uncommon for people to take Long Service Leave so they can finish their book. The casual academics who have accrued no such leave, or the self-employed, manual or corporate workers who have no such entitlements will no doubt find nothing to lament here – and nor should they. But it is interesting as an example of a *reverse* temporal infiltration: the erosion of the luxuries of bureaucratic time by scholarly vocationalism.

Every now and then the trampling of scholarly time by bureaucratic time throws up something perversely satisfying – like the Time Use Survey now required of academics by the Australian government. Academics are required annually to log the hours (or parts thereof) that they spend on research, teaching and administration. The arbitrariness of this survey is revealed in the fact that new taxonomic rulings are continually required: is higher degree supervision research or teaching? Is book reviewing research or service to the discipline? Is filling out a Time Use Survey allowed to be counted as administrative work (initially yes; now no). The survey is open to corruption, since its stated purpose is to deliver more government funding to those universities who are 'found' to do more research. Its reliance on trust and honour is a perverse negation of the very drivers of audit practice. It is, in short, a piece of nonsense that is treated with flippant seriousness by most academics – since it is so evidently flawed and hence an ironic waste of time, and yet a source of important funding. This is precisely the kind of shallow compliance that typifies audit culture.

Amidst all this nonsense it is critical not to forget the preciousness of the rights and protections offered by the bureaucratic model, which were hard won and are still not available to all workers in modern economies, let alone beyond. To those workers who are rarely granted the experience of time-out at all – small business owners for example – the kind of legally protected, employer-sanctioned right to rest embodied in annual leave is a luxury beyond imagining. Likewise, casual academics, trapped in the educated 'precariat' (Standing 2011), can only dream of actually being paid to take holidays. In analysing the complexities of the ways different times mesh and overlay in the contemporary university, this fundamental fact of the protective powers of the bureaucracy should never be forgotten. As casualization increases, these protections are offered to fewer and fewer academics; for casual staff, both the traditional temporalities of scholarship and teaching *and* the protections of the bureaucratic model remain a dream. Typically employed in a never-ending series of short contracts, they lurch towards the future six months at a time – robbed of the ability to plan that future, economically, intellectually or personally, with any degree of certainty. That 60 per cent[15] of Australian academics are now employed this way is an intellectual and social catastrophe masking as 'flexibility'.

Meanwhile, pressures towards corporatization continue. The traditional temporalities of both scholarship and teaching have been challenged, distorted or threatened by corporate-style pressures towards flexibility, quantity, speed and predictability. Bulk outputs with shorter turnarounds fit the corporate demands for 'useable knowledge' (DaCosta 1997) and are more amenable to the surveillance mechanisms of audit culture. The long stretches of uninterrupted time characteristic of contemplative modes have been cut up into tiny pieces, subject to the requirement for constant, demonstrable, productivity. This has the potential to jeopardize the viability of certain types of scholarship (anthropological immersion and curiosity-driven scientific research being two examples) while also encouraging and rewarding new kinds of academic work – for example the swift response to a current issue. This new temporality is bound up in contemporary politicizations of academic work: the call for relevance, social and economic utility and so on. The ideal of research as retirement from the world that characterized Newman's vision is being replaced by that of research as a turning *towards* the world. It is also made possible by the technological innovations of the last few decades, in particular the instantaneity

---

15 May et al. arrive at this figure on a 'head count' basis (2011: 188). They cite studies indicating that over half of all undergraduate teaching in Australia is performed by casuals (188).

of online media and the physical portability of modern communication devices. Such changes simultaneously fetishize and normalize particular ideas and experiences of time.

Fetishes: Speed, Reachability, Multitasking, Synergy

Speed is a central component both of modern life and modern self-imagining. The multifaceted process that social theorists call 'social acceleration' began 'with the advent of modernity' (Rosa and Scheuerman 2009: 8). 'Speed is the hope of the West', as Paul Virilio put it (1986 [1977]: 55). At the geo-political level – in international relations, for example – speed can be a force for good, helping to break up 'closed and dogmatic identities in the domains of religion, sensuality [sic], ethnicity, gender, and nationality' (Connolly 2009: 261). William Connolly notes that in matters geo-political 'the crawl of slow time' (263) has its dangers. Speed, he notes, must be thought of as an 'ambiguous medium' (263).

In the New Economy, however, speed is not regarded ambivalently but is, in fact, one of the new business 'virtues' (Löfgren 2003: 245). Universities, as key players in this New Economy, have responded to this new virtue and the economic realities in which it is enmeshed by attempting to both speed up and compress time. For example, Australia's first private university, Bond University, opened in 1989 with a three-semester year that enables students to complete their degree in two years instead of three and which synchronizes with the rhythms of northern hemisphere universities. Bond uses this fast-tracking as a distinctive marketing point, promoting it as an active choice in a competitive employment marketplace. It will, they claim, give students an edge:

> By graduating up to a year earlier, Bond graduates are out in the workplace, earning sooner. This career head-start puts them on a promotional fast-track and many have achieved director, CEO, private practice and partnership status within 10 years of graduating from Bond. (Bond University n.d.: 6)

A number of other Australian universities have tried to follow suit with three (or even four) semesters per year, but for different reasons: either to maximize student numbers or to extract maximum labour from academics. At the time of writing, such attempts have not yet succeeded, largely because of union action.

Some academics have responded to the compression of academic time by urging that we slow down. For example, Hartman and Darab's (2012) call for 'slow scholarship' hopes to harness the affective and aesthetic pull of the Slow Food movement in opposition to the fetishization of speed. I suspect, however, that such calls will have little effect. Speed is both economically grounded (fast production and turnaround being the hallmark of the successful business) and culturally prized (speed having been so successfully 'aestheticized' in the discourses of the New Economy [Löfgren 2003: 245]).

The most common response to work intensification, and not just in universities, is, of course, simply to work longer – in the early mornings, evenings, or weekends. This is common; a survey of academics at the University of Western Sydney, for example, asked how often they worked before 8am and/or after 8pm: 51.6 per cent reported that they did this 4–5 days per week, and a further 11 per cent reported that they did this 6–7 days a week (Jensen and Morgan 2009: 13). Another strategy is to mentally reclassify certain tasks as non-work. It has become common for people to do email the night before starting work or early in the morning so as not to confuse it with the real work of the day (Gregg 2011: 46–7). Melissa Gregg calls this 'anticipatory' labour (47). It is an anxiety management strategy (48) predicated on an imaginary separation between 'real' work and 'non-work', using private time and/or the domestic sphere as its vehicles.

Such temporal strategies are enabled by the new experiences of space brought into being by new technologies – in particular the phenomenon of 'reachability'. Reachability describes not just a technical capacity or a material fact, but a new set of experiences of being in the world. Mark Fisher notes that the '"tethering" imposed by digital telecommunications is by no means always experienced as something that is straightforwardly unpleasant' (2011: 129). It is, as Gregg's (2011) study of the breaking down of the barriers between home and work makes evident, deeply ambiguous.

Digital technologies also facilitate another fetishized response to work intensification – that of multitasking. Multitasking was received with 'exuberance' in the 1990s and early 2000s (Rosen 2008: 105). It was particularly prized in corporate culture, where it began to appear on lists of desirable skills of employees (105). Contemporary technologies, from computer screens to mobile phones, are all built on, and marketed around, multitasking. Multitasking involves the rapid alternation between and 'interleaving' (Burgess 2000: 466) of often qualitatively different types of task. In one study, researchers found that workers managed a median of 65 concurrent active tasks, with some employees managing 74.4 active tasks (Bellotti et al. 2005: 103). Little wonder that multitasking has become the object of interest from a neuroscientific and experimental psychology point of view, with debates about how easily the brain can cope with multitasking and whether or not it is a 'damaging' (for example to short-term memory), stressful or 'efficient' (Brown 2010).

Multitasking has become a new habit of mind and body not only in the workplace but in everyday life, where the forms of distracted, multiple, or split attention it produces are now commonplace. Contemporary academic work, like much white-collar work, is now marked by it – both on the large scale, where research, for example, tends to proceed as multiple projects with different timelines on the go simultaneously, and on the microhabits of daily office life. Audit mechanisms that reward the rapid completion of many tasks rather than the slow elaboration of thought or writing obviously reinforce multitasking behaviour.

But as work intensity continues to grow, and doubts about the economic efficiency and personal costs of multitasking are publically debated, other ways of conceiving multiplicity have arisen. One example is the discourse of 'creative synergy', which became a buzzword at the intersection of a variety of discourses, including those of the New Economy, the New Age, the New Public Management and motivational culture. Synergy is being crafted as the new temporal virtue, to be understood as a valuable part of a creative art of modern living. According to Lori and Arnie Herz, two lawyers who have written a booklet on synergy, synergy supersedes balance as the new ideal. It differs from multitasking in that it is not based on speeding up – the rapid alternation between different types of task, which involves a constant switching between different cognitive modes. Synergy, by contrast, is understood as holistic – a true bringing together rather than a rapid 'dovetailing' (Burgess 2000: 466) of differences. Since it reconciles rather than balances differences, it is construed as both efficient and meaningful. In the way typical of both New Age and New Economy discourses, the extolling of synergy places its faith in the undoing of traditional oppositions. Its emphasis on efficiency and creativity makes it appealing both to stressed employees and to management. It is thought to offer a win-win for corporations and their staff: happier teams are more productive. Thus life-coaching for corporate 'teams' now often includes training in synergy. For Herz and Herz, synergy is about empowerment:

> The beauty of work-life synergy is that it starts and ends with us. We captain this ship. We each have the absolute power, ability and right to define what is meaningful and energizing for us and to bring that to fruition in our lives as lawyers and beyond. (2007: 11)

This neoliberalism echoes that of a whole host of empowerment and self-help genres.

In the discourse of creative synergy, the milking of time for maximum productivity has been refurbished as the most creative way to live. And perhaps it is. Herz and Herz are spot on in claiming that balance belongs to an older temporal and social order and that maximization is the name of the game today.

Certainly, practices of synergy have entered the realm of everyday embodied life. Just as it is true that 'the ideology of speed [is] materialized in seemingly trivial details of everyday office life' (Löfgren 2003: 245), so too the ideal of synergy manifests as a subterranean register of new habits, and not just in the workplace. As I write this, I am sitting in the car outside my daughter's piano teacher's house, making use of the 'wasted' time to work on this chapter. This is the tyranny and the privilege of a portable job whose currency is ideas, which may spring up at any time, anywhere, unbidden. Hearing a sound, I look up – a mother is jogging by, simultaneously pushing her toddler in a pram, exercising her dog on a leash, and listening to an iPod. There is no point in reading this either as an inventive synergy in which three, or possibly four, tasks (depending on what's playing on the iPod) are being compressed into one time and space, or as illustrative of the pressures of modern life and the tyranny of productivism. Instead, and far more simply, I find myself noting that the way academics do their work is the way, in fact, many people increasingly live their lives. Perhaps, then, academia is not that different after all.

There is a lot to be said for this championing of synergy. It seems sensible to milk time for maximum use-value, and if many of these 'uses' can feed our private selves, then well and good. This way of 'thinking multiply' allows one to devise responses that are ingenious – like meeting up with friends on the train rather than at home, thus 'adding value' to the commute and not 'wasting' precious family time on socializing, or having a supervision meeting while walking around the campus, so that one is also exercising. But this ingenuity is only *one type* of creativity – and a motivated one at that. It is a creativity that is driven, ultimately, by a single goal – maximizing time – and is thus governed from the outset by its own ends. It is the child of the New Economy's 'innovation culture' as much as the New Age's belief in having it all. Despite its seductive romanticism, it is, fundamentally, an industrial and economic model of creativity – how to get more from less. That makes it great for some tasks and goals – writing a paper more quickly, or ensuring one gets more exercise – but it lacks a theory of embodiment or a complex theory of the genesis of thought.

So when I am preparing a lecture by speaking into a tape recorder while driving to work, or listening to a work audio file while exercising on the bike, I do find myself wondering whether this is a hyper-rational squeezing of every last drop of productivity out of every wasted moment or a 'creative' response to competing needs. After all, synergy is, structurally speaking, not that dissimilar from the way work and life are inseparable in the vocational paradigm, insofar as it too presupposes the intermingling of public and private identities, of paid labour with labours of love. But synergy is not so much the overflowing of love for labour as the deliberate, strategized, maximizing of time itself. To that extent, it assumes and reproduces the idea of time itself as somehow both limited – there is never enough of it – and capacious – it can always be squeezed for one more drop of productivity or pleasure. This, then, is a temporality mined for meaning, but inimical to flow. It is perfectly suited to the neoliberal/New Age ideal of a purposeful, *controlled*, life, a 'life by design', to quote the name of one prominent life coaching programme that teaches the virtues of creative synergy. This is a refashioning of vocation to suit the times: life must be meaningful, and meaning must be actively orchestrated and directed. Clearly, this is 'both emancipatory and enslaving' (Löfgren 2003: 251). But what, I wonder, does the body make of it? Or, alternatively, what does it make of our bodies?

Rise of the Fragment, Fear of the Pause: Embodying New Temporalities

The pressure to be 'productive' and the temporal practices that have arisen as a response or solution to this pressure, such as anticipatory labour, multitasking and synergy, have rendered certain types of time increasingly unavailable. In particular, the slow, contemplative time of scholarship (be it the day spent reading or the five year writing project) threatens to disappear in the face of the smaller units of administrative or bureaucratic time – the series of tasks performed reactively, that is, as an often immediate response to unpredictable demands (phone calls, emails, enquiries, hastily-called meetings). This trigger-and-response division of time is inimical to the other kinds of thought required by teaching, reading and writing. Today, fragmentation has become a very firmly embedded part of a new phenomenal reality.

Email is a fascinating example of the way new patterns of behaviour and mental processing arise, alongside new desires, hopes, pleasures and anxieties, in response to new technologies. Most people check their email much more frequently than they realize (Renaud in Charman-Anderson 2008). The amount of interrupted time and the attention recovery time needed are also greater than commonly imagined (Jackson, Dawson and Wilson 2001, Marulanda-Carter and Jackson 2012). Moreover, people respond to an email with great rapidity: in one study, 70 per cent of users reacted within six seconds of an email arriving and 85 per cent within two minutes (Jackson, Dawson and Wilson 2001: 85). In effect, people respond to email in the same fashion they respond to a telephone call (Hair, Renaud and Ramsay 2007: 2792) – except that you might receive dozens of emails a day. This is all very well if the main purpose of your job is to answer enquiries. But what of academics?

All academics develop their own ways of living with these differently rhythmed provocations. The study of email response times cited above was undertaken in an 'office solutions'/printing business; specifically academic response patterns may be different, given academics' historically strong sense of the right to prioritize their work. Some academics may well compartmentalize, assiduously dividing their days or weeks between different types of task and disciplining themselves not to open their email before the afternoon on a research day. Me? I'm a hyper-efficient, multitasking gambler, and so I cannot help myself but interrupt my writing by regular checking of the email, 'just in case'. This I have learnt to do effectively, and so perhaps it doesn't matter, but I do recognize the effect on my mental and bodily constitution of this perennially distracted and jumpy mode of being-in-the-office, and I wonder about its invisible long-term impact on my health, on the way I think, and on other 'primordial' aspects of being, such as how outer-directed I have become, or how I may be becoming increasingly responsive, indeed reactive, to external stimuli.

What, too, of the new psychic dynamics that email has helped to generate? Some commentators highlight the intermittently rewarding nature of email (every now and then it throws up something great) and which claim that this makes it structurally just like gambling – and potentially equally habit-forming (Stafford, in Charman-Anderson 2008). Cultural theorists of network culture will no doubt wince at these assertions, and point out that every new technology is always accompanied by panic discourses about its invasiveness and its potential to corrupt the young. True enough, but my concern here is not with 'excessive connectivity' (Albury and Crawford 2012: 466) as a social or moral ill, but as a new form of rhythmicity with implications for mental processing, energy and self-orientation. Too great a focus on the discourses through which new technologies are received, understood and, eventually, assimilated into a comfortable place in the cultural imagination can prevent us from considering the differing mental, affective, bodily or psychical dimensions of particular technologies. Fisher, for example, claims that the compulsive quality of email checking indicates that it has 'hacked into libido' (2011: 129); we want and need to stay in touch. Email has become part of our contemporary modes of orientation – a way in which we constantly recreate our sense of locatedness in time, space, and re-make our webs of connection. And since email often knows no distinction between home and work, this means that work, too, is becoming fundamentally woven into white collar workers' very orientation in the world. In this way email is compatible with the *values* of scholarly vocationalism but inimical to the modes of thought that have traditionally characterized it.

Email can also hack more directly into the affect system. Certain emails have the ability to go straight to the gut, sending ripples of anxiety around the body even while the mind may be trying to reassure us that it has seen this problem before and it will all turn out all right. The ability of an email to arrive unannounced and unsolicited is one of its delights and its dangers. One email can change your day. A letter or a visitor to your office can also do the same – arrive unannounced and bring delight or dismay – but the size, speed, reach and extent of digital networks, along with the fact that the receiving device is now commonly carried everywhere on one's person, give email unparalleled access to our emotions. Moreover, the constant 'outside-in' checking put in place by audit culture is now mirrored by our own, 'inside-out' micro-checking habits, which allow us to constantly monitor if 'they' need us, or have answered us, or whether we've been awarded something, or missed out on something. Email can feed anxiety because it keeps us looped into the 'never-ending ticker of what the world thinks' (Belsky 2010: 106). In this context it becomes easy to argue, as Hair et al. have, that the stress commonly associated with email 'is self-imposed' (2007: 2792). After all, no one is forcing us to check our email every two minutes or while we are on holiday. Hair et al.'s account of the influence of self-esteem and a sense of control on how stressful workers find email sees relaxed or stressed relations to email as emanating from personality factors. Fair enough, but one must also look in the other direction – to note how a new technology like email has reconfigured everyday practice and hence *generated* patterns of response.

All this outer-directed, fragmented, busy activity is self-feeding. Predicated on the possibility and desirability of swift response, it produces a workplace culture, and a culture of thought, based upon this swiftness. This has its uplifting and enabling features. Teaching has benefited. The lecture hand-written on foolscap paper and read out to a stultified but polite audience of undergraduates year after year, without amendment, bears no resemblance to a lecture today, which may be replete with images, video and audio, updated each year, involve audience participation technologies, and be uploaded for student revision. Likewise, the speed, quantity, impact and interdisciplinary reach of our research are also undoubtedly increased. The book informed only by the contents of one university library rather than an accessible global database of scholarly resources can have only a fraction of the scope. The ideologies and technologies of speed have enabled academic conversations to cross boundaries of geography, discipline and language, and to include students, journalists and other commentators.

But there is a price to pay for this extraordinary enlivenment. Certain forms of knowledge production are more valued, more rewarded and more utilized; the journal article, for example, begins to trump the book. Certain modes of mental processing and intellectual endeavour are made rarer or more tenuous – both as culturally valued practices and as embodied experiences. For the productivist imperatives with which these exciting new forms of knowledge production and exchange are intertwined threaten not only the structural availability of other kinds of time, but also our very capacity to *experience* time in different ways. I am not arguing that focused, contemplative time is the only 'good' time; rather, I am claiming that its loss as one possible temporality among others is greatly concerning.

The correlate of the rise of the fragment is the fear of the pause. This fear occurs at all levels of temporality. On the macro level, one output must follow another in rapid succession. There must be no fallow season. The successful completion of the PhD is met with the immediate question of where it will be published. It is possible to read the audit explosion not only as the embodiment of new forms of distrust, but also, at least in part, as a political response to the fear of empty time. That is one reason auditing mechanisms don't have to be economically efficient. Their psychological job is to promote activity.

Discomfort with the pause operates at the micro level, too. The new bodily-temporal rhythms encouraged by the relentless incitement to productivity rapidly become naturalized, so that unpressured time comes to *feel* wasted, unproductive. How visceral this has become! The twenty minute gap – not long enough to 'do something, too long to "waste" – can induce anxiety. I bring something' to *do* to any occasion where there may be 'wasted' time. For me, just sitting is scarcely possible.

An academic blogger tells the story of how he was reading an academic book in his office when he was 'sprung' by a member of the administrative staff, who, seeing him reading, asked him whether he was waiting for someone (C-Dog 2009). Reading, it seems, couldn't be considered real work, not even for an academic, but it might plausibly be something one did to prevent a few minutes of wasted time. I recall a lecturer in English literature who, as late as the early 1990s, could be seen reading Wordsworth – *outside*, no less! By this time in the evolution of the Australian university, this was widely regarded as evidence of professional dereliction rather than duty.

If reading is unproductive time, how much more so is the invisible and unquantifiable labour of thinking? In the institutional and public imagination, thinking is 'unproductive time' (Rutherford 2005: 298). And yet most of us know that good ideas and solutions can often come in the pause. We know that turning away from the problem at hand can be the best way of solving it, whether by going for a walk, doing the washing up, or putting it aside for a month. Those who haven't lost the gift of undisturbed sleep might also recognize that ideas and solutions come in sleep, sometimes even in dreams. But, as in so many white-collar jobs, where mental energy is sapped by the buzz of demands and the rise of multitasking, even the pause of sleep has been robbed from many. Sleeplessness and night-time working may have gendered dimensions, as Acker and Armenti's (2004) study of female academics at two Canadian universities makes evident. The prevalence among tertiary students of insomnia and other sleep disorders associated with anxiety is likewise reported around the world (Cockcroft, Grasko and Fridjhon 2006, Gaultney 2010, Abdulghani et al. 2012), and its academic and personal impact are well noted.

The scorning of 'empty' time is both a cultural value and an embodied reality. As a society, we have, it seems, no time for time itself, only for what it can bring us or do for us. This is a mental, psychological and intellectual lived reality. It is also a political fact.

The cultural analyst Roland Barthes recognized this. In an interview in 1979, he claimed that in modern Western cultures, to be lazy is to be subversive:

Have you ever noticed that everyone always talks about the right to leisure activities but never about a right to idleness? I even wonder if there is such a thing as *doing nothing* in the modern Western world. (1985 [1979]: 341, original emphasis)

There are, of course, many ways of doing 'nothing', and in this interview, Barthes (and his translator) toyed with a range of terms for different forms of non-activity: laziness, idleness, doing nothing, boredom. He noted that some of these forms of stillness are enforced (the slow Sundays of his childhood, for example) and others are reactive – the deliberate embrace of idleness as a reaction against productivism and efficiency. Barthes was onto something. Rhythmicity is, after all, 'a crucial principle of nature' (Urry 2009: 182), and changes to deep-seated mental and bodily rhythms are subtly significant.

This is why stillness has been a staple of many spiritual and therapeutic practices. For example, the subtle significance of rhythms of pause and activity was recognised in the 1890s by the Australian actor F.M. Alexander, who founded a mode of therapeutic postural retraining known as The Alexander Technique. This technique teaches the importance of the pause in daily life – not in the sense of resting or taking chunks of time out, but in a much more micro-focused way: learning to insert a gap between stimulus and reaction. Alexander taught the importance of stopping – even for a micro-second – as a tool for breaking habitual responses. Pausing was, for him, a form of 'non-doing' that 'prevents us from running ahead of ourselves' (Drake 1996: 27). It is a particular form of conscious attention that is not concentration in the sense of focusing on one activity to the exclusion of others (29), but rather a form of mindfulness aimed at refashioning the body itself in order to ameliorate its pains and dysfunctions. Alexander called this process of pausing and noticing 'inhibition', which he meant not in the psychological sense of blocking one's feelings, but as the interruption of unreflexive, reactive or habitual patterns of embodiment. It is not an abstract assertion of agency but the building of a new bodily intelligence.

Barthes, of course, meant something far less studious, disciplined and systematic when he urged us to dare to be lazy. He did, however, allow himself a momentary flirtation with Eastern concepts of stillness, which he associated with the loss of the self. Being 'dispossessed of [one's] consistency as a subject' would, he claimed, 'be true idleness. To be able, at certain moments, to no longer have to say "I"' (1985 [1979]: 342). He thought it unlikely that Westerners could achieve such stillness: 'These days, idleness probably consists not in doing nothing, since we're incapable of that, but in cutting time up as often as possible, in diversifying it' (341).

Today, cut-up time is, to my mind, part of the problem rather than the solution – whether it be the casual employee's fragmented and precarious future cut-up into three month blocks, or the tenured academic's mental world, abuzz with a host of fragmented imperatives. Certainly, doing one thing at a time – especially for a long period of time – has none of the sexiness of speed, multitasking or synergy. Christine Rosen opens her critique of multitasking with a piece of advice given by Lord Chesterfield to his son in the 1740s. It sounds, to the modern ear, rather fusty:

> There is time enough for everything in the course of the day, if you do but one thing at once, but there is not time enough in the year, if you will do two things at a time ... This steady and undissipated attention to one object, is a sure mark of a superior genius; as hurry, bustle, and agitation, are the never-failing symptoms of a weak and frivolous mind. (Qtd. in Rosen 2008: 105)

There is, however, a contemporary revival of interest in attentiveness as part of a strategy of survival and resistance in the face of social acceleration. There has arisen both a popular and scientific interest in the mental (if not necessarily intellectual) benefits of certain modes of contemplation. Mindfulness is enjoying a boom. But the boom is double-edged, for even stillness can be recuperated, as the current corporate interest in meditative practice may attest.

Branded: Embodying the University

In classic waged labour, we sell our time to the employer. But of course workers often do more than this – they may treat their job as a vocation and put their heart and soul into it; they may sacrifice their physical health to it; or they may be required to embody the company in some way. This is especially so in the 'culturalized' (Sidhu 2006: 15) industries of the New Economy, which place particular importance on symbolic elements like iconography, imagery and branding (14). Part of the logic of branding is not just that institutions and corporations brand themselves, but that their workers are invited or sometimes compelled to identify themselves with that brand – to represent and embody it.In some occupations, embodying the brand means little more than not putting it into disrepute: adopting a professional tone of voice, being courteous and displaying a certain dispassionate friendliness to customers. In others, embodiment goes further. Sales personnel in the fashion and beauty industries, for example, carry out a form of 'aesthetic labour' (Warhurst et al., in Pettinger 2004: 177) that involves their dress, demeanour and even beauty.

Now that the university is, at least in part, a global corporation, academics have some obligation to embody their university's brand. The palimpsest works well for the university here; the vocational and the corporate models can work together. The ancient idea of the university as a collegiate can be made to map very nicely onto the modern idea of the corporation as a community all pulling together. To explore this further, and to connect it to my theme of embodiment, I take a step back to think about the idea of the corporate body.

The Corporate Body

Universities always were corporations in the old sense of the world. The word 'corporate' derives from 'corpus', or body; the term 'corporate body' is really a tautology. The archaic meaning was 'united into one body'. In the sixteenth century, 'corporate' used to mean 'having a body' or 'embodied', or 'pertaining to or affecting the body'. An obsolete meaning is 'large of body; corpulent'. 'Corporate', in sum, could mean pertaining to the body, large of body, or united into one body.[16]

The idea of incorporation has a religious dimension to it. In the Catholic tradition, the Eucharist is a double incorporation: one incorporated Christ through eating the transubstantiated wafer, an act that simultaneously incorporated one into the body of Christ (the church). Transubstantiation turns symbols into concrete realities, and makes them deeply corporeal: 'Alone among all the Sacraments, which never went any farther than the surface of the body, the Eucharist penetrated all the way into man's bowels' (Camporesi 1989: 229). The viscerality of this metaphor-made-flesh is evident in a quotation from the eighteenth-century theologian Fulgenzio Cuniliati:

> We become living limbs which are truly joined to Christ, our Head. Indeed, in a way, we become one with Him: we become the limbs of His body, of His flesh, of His bones ... by eating His divine flesh with His bones, we become, through this conjunction, even more specifically the limbs of His divine body... [T]he Eucharist ... brings Jesus Himself inside our chest. (Qtd. in Camporesi 1989: 229)

The food does not transform itself into the person; the person spiritually turns into the food (Cuniliati, qtd. in Camporesi 1989: 230). In the process, the congregation are momentarily united into one body.

Some of the religious logic of incorporation persists subtly in the imaginary space of the modern corporation. The corporation is at once very concrete (a hierarchical collection of individuals), and abstract (a legal fiction, enjoying some of the legal rights of personhood) (Mander 1992: 133).[17]

---

16 These meanings are all sourced from the *Oxford English Dictionary*.

17 A corporation is regarded under the US Constitution as a 'person' entitled to 'due process' under the Fourteenth Amendment. It is a person, but not a citizen (McQueen 2001: 25–6).

On a material level, the wellbeing of the employee and that of the corporation are mutually interlinked, even if they are not coterminous. As the employee is part of a bigger unity, his/her health and wellbeing become not only a private good but also a requirement of the corporation. Nonetheless, a principle of classical organizational theory was 'the subordination of individual interest to the common good' (Fayol, qtd. in Stoner et al. 1994: 37–8), and there comes a point at which the maximization of corporate profit and the wellbeing of the employee must eventually and necessarily collide.

Contemporary corporations aim to find a synergy between the wellbeing of the employee and that of the corporation, and to bring the whole person within the ambit of corporate life. Services and programmes such as employer-sponsored counselling, stress reduction seminars and corporate fitness programmes blur the dividing lines between private and work domains and are one of the signals that corporations in the New Economy recognize the employee's body as central to their success.

The University as a Corporate Body and a Brand Community

The concept of a 'brand community' alluded to earlier is helpful in thinking about the particular types of belonging found in the university. The phrase is normally used of the consumers of brands; it refers to 'a form of postmodern tribe that connects consumers on the basis of a trademark' (Luedicke and Giesler 2007: 275) – but it can usefully be extended to think about the type of work employees do on behalf of the brand. In this, I am drawing on Adam Arvidsson's (2005) account of the way consumers add real but invisible economic value to a brand through their affective labour – that is, the way they use, discuss and feel deeply about particular brands. This 'immaterial labour' (2005: 239) is, he argues, of real economic significance in contributing to a commodity or corporation's 'brand value'.[18]

According to Muniz and O'Guinn, brand communities have three properties: 1) 'consciousness of kind' – i.e. a sense of connections between members and difference from others not in the community; 2) rituals and traditions, which 'perpetuate the community's shared history, culture and consciousness'; and 3) 'a sense of duty or obligation to the community as a whole' (qtd. in Luedicke and Giesler 2007: 277). As a corporation in both the ancient and modern senses, the university shares in all these elements of the brand community.

I have already noted how a sense of connection – to each other and to a profession with a long and noble history – helps keep academic vocationalism alive and provides a significant economic boon to the university through gifted

---

18 Melissa Gregg notes how feminist scholarship has long recognized the existence and political significance of various forms of affective labour (2009: 211).

labour (Ross 2004, Redden 2008, Gregg 2009). The second aspect of this definition – rituals and traditions – is equally important to the university brand in the culturalized world of the New Economy.

Academics are frequently called upon to embody the university in traditional scholarly mode: to wear the gown, speak the speak, and to produce knowledge in the right genres on demand, whether that be in class, in the media, or as a public showpiece (as in Open Day lectures). We are required to produce the spectacle of academia on public occasions when a traditional idea of the university is required. Graduations are a classic example of the rituals and traditions that bind a brand community together. Each graduation spectacle requires a crowd of dons donned suitably in order to provide the colour and movement necessary to the culminating moment of a student's experience in the traditional university. In some circumstances – when one knows the students – it is a pleasure, and wearing those heavy robes makes one feel the weight of history, quite literally. Graduation is a ritual not only of completion, but also of incorporation, and it is a source of great joy and pride to many.

In modern times there is always something fanciful about this ritual – almost everyone in the room is dressed in borrowed robes, and the 'community' into which one is being incorporated is too vast and diverse to be meaningful as a social entity. There can be something quite dismal about participating in a graduation when one scarcely knows one's fellow colleagues on the stage, let alone the students processing before one. The increase in student numbers and the fragmented curriculum make it less and less likely that you will have taught the students, or taught them for long. Increasingly, students are not being incorporated into a community of people who know each other and share much in common, so much as into a modern network with an old name ('alumni'). A report into the experience of first year students at Australian universities makes this evident, recording that there has been a 'significant decline' in the number of students who believe that at least one lecturer knows them by name: 58 per cent in 2009, down from 66 per cent in 2004 (James, Krause and Jennings 2010: 35).

As the expansion of the university sector continues apace, the element of simulacrum grows. When as an undergraduate I made the speech on behalf of the graduates at my own university, I could turn towards a stage on which were seated academics with whom I had enjoyed close relationships in a number of ways: language tutors who had taught me for six hours of classes a week for three years and then one-on-one work for a further Honours year; English tutors in whose office I had attended tutorials with only five or six other students; and other academics with whom I had socialized in clubs and societies and even outside the university. Today, I count myself lucky if I have the same student in a class of 25 or more for two semesters running. Still and all, many of us continue to have a sentimental stake in inviting students to partake in the traditional rituals of incorporation, and I often wear the priestly gowns with pride.

The third element of Muniz and O'Guinn's definition of a brand community – the sense of duty to the community as a whole – is an effective tool for mobilizing staff. Before one university Open Day many years ago (which was held on a Sunday), academics were exhorted in the following terms to participate:

> Open Day for some of you is just another thing that you have to do!!!! Yes, we are all tired, overworked ad [sic] overstaffed!!! [sic] BUT The University is no longer in a PRODUCER driven environment where we dictate what the community needs from higher education – but in a MARKET driven environment where we are now actively competing for students with other institutions and TAFE. We need to actively recruit to secure our future as a quality provider of higher education. … HAVE A GOOD DAY AND HAPPY RECRUITING

Here, the academic is called to entrepreneurial arms, a call that translates, as is typical of service industries,[19] into an individual bodily requirement, finishing with the decree to be happy.

So, following Arvidsson (2005), we might read the labour invested by academics to hold the palimpsestic university together as a form of under-valued emotional labour, an example of what Andrew Ross calls 'sacrificial labor' (2004: 192). But what happens when the sacrifice becomes too great and the cracks begin to show?

Faltering Embodiment: Academic Stress and Illness

Academic stress is real. One major report, which drew on nearly 9,000 responses, begins by citing thirteen other studies from around the world over a twenty year period, all of which found that academic stress caused by increased workloads and lack of support has become 'a cause for concern' (Winefield et al. 2003: 52). (See also Abouserie 1996, Davies and Bansel 2005).

The previous sections outlined some of the reasons that workers in a traditionally privileged occupation should be suffering such ill effects – notably the work intensification associated with palimpsestic overlay – but I want to extend this analysis by considering some of the psychological and emotional ramifications of the palimpsest, by returning to the question of vocationalism.

I have already cited Bill Readings's claim that no one could legitimately imagine himself as embodying the spirit of the contemporary university – 'as

---

19 See Melissa Gregg's account of the way service industry jobs 'rely on the *emotional* lives of employees for company benefit' (2009: 211, original emphasis).

the instantiation of the cultivated individual that the entire great machine works night and day to produce' (1996: 9). Readings was referring to abstract ideas of the academic, pointing out that there is no singular ideal type that could personify the new hybrid university. But the claim is equally true of real-life bodies: it is very hard to live up to the rigours of three paradigms at once.

To this struggle we need to add the fact that academics are fighting not just to manage as individuals, but to preserve something they believe in – trying to be the human bridge or glue binding the hybrid university together. This is the 'double-edged sword' (Bunderson and Thompson 2009: 32) of vocationalism, which typically entails a willingness to sacrifice pay and personal time (42), and hence renders one vulnerable to exploitation by managers (43).[20] Vocationalism is 'both binding and ennobling' (32). It has the potential to produce resentment or anger; those possessed by a sense of calling want their management to 'take its moral duty as seriously as they do' (43–4). They may be equally hard on themselves, seeing giving up or under-performing as a 'moral failure' (41).

Vocationalism has deep ontological dimensions. A sense of calling means that one sees oneself as, fundamentally, a particular type of person (Bunderson and Thompson 2009: 39). Vocation is 'central to an individual's personal myth' (Bogart 1994: 12). In the light of this, it is unsurprising that there is a high correlation between vocationalism and wellbeing. Perceived purpose in life, meaningful work and a measure of control in the workplace are all correlated with good health (Wilkinson and Marmot 2003: 18) and psychological wellbeing (Treadgold 1999). There are 'significant' negative correlations between being engaged in meaningful work and depression (Treadgold 1999: 92) and, to a lesser extent, stress (97).

So the repeated finding that academics have a faltering sense of mission (Enders 2000: 10) – or rather, that they see a widening gap between what they consider to be the core of their work and the work they spend most of their time doing – has significant implications for psychological, emotional and physical wellbeing. Paradigmatic dissonance – a significant gap between one's sense of mission and the realities of one's working life – undermines the 'cognitive unity and clarity of self-concept' that are important components of professional psychological wellbeing (Treadgold 1999: 88). Hard work is tiring, but a thwarted sense of purpose is demoralizing.[21]

---

20 This discussion of vocationalism comes from a study of zoo-keeping, but I consider its salient points about the experience of feeling a 'calling' to be eminently applicable to academia.

21 This distinction is evident in the anecdotal reports cited in the Introduction claiming that when academics are asked about the state of university life in general, they are usually demoralized and pessimistic. When asked about their own research, however, they tend to be much cheerier (Watson 2009: 1–3). Enders noted nearly

It is possible that this distress is transitional. Those who enter the university system now may come with a different set of expectations. As the university moves towards a more fully corporatized identity, new staff will enter it without having experienced, either as students or staff, an earlier regime. Perhaps they will bring with them neither nostalgia nor a preservationist ethos. It remains to be seen what forms of critique they will elaborate.

Is vocationalism, perhaps, dying out, to be replaced by a new, more pragmatic, ethos? In the mid-1980s, Bellah et al. considered the idea of calling to be a historical remnant, restricted to 'a few economically marginal but symbolically significant instances' (2008 [1985]: 66). Perhaps it was, then, but now a cluster of interrelated discourses have reinvigorated the idea of vocation – among them the neoliberal insistence on agentic self-management, the psychological understanding of life as a journey of self-actualization and self-expression, the New Age and consumerist insistence on fulfilment, and the New Economy discourse of work as an avenue for creativity, control and freedom. All these have contributed to a climate in which the idea of a calling might be seen to be moving back from the margins to the mainstream of white-collar work – ironically in a world where jobs are more precarious. The new corporatism is replete with the stylistics of transcendentalism. Mission statements speak of igniting passions, stirring souls and questing: 'At Company X we strive to serve our customers with integrity at every touchpoint to enhance the customer experience', insists the screensaver on the company computer. This call to community is a corporate version of the 'consciousness of kind' identified by Muniz and O'Guinn as a component of brand communities (qtd. in Luedicke and Giesler 2007: 277). In the university context, this corporate vocationalism does not replace so much as overlay the 'powerful sense of kinship' (Bunderson and Thompson 2009: 39) associated with traditional vocationalism. As a result, academics are subject to a double dose of vocationalism.

One logical bodily result of an over-accentuated but under-resourced communal striving and a thwarted sense of purpose is employee stress or illness. In the university, as in any large corporation, ill health has a subtle but powerful symbolic place. The logic of incorporation enjoins white-collar workers not only to do their best, but always to be their best. The employee's body is simultaneously a signifier of the corporate body itself and a signifier of one's fitness to be a member of that body. Thus, its stress or illness cannot

---

two decades ago that despite complaints about work intensification and diminishing resources, overall European academics had a 'relatively high' level of satisfaction with their working life (2000: 27). He also noted, however, the plausibility of a future in which morale continued to decline as academics' disillusionment about their 'mission' grew (10).

be tolerated for too long, both because of the material drain it represents on the corporation's finances (a rupture of the principle of 'the profit imperative' [Mander 1992: 129]) and because it breaks the corporate principles of 'order', 'unity of direction', 'stability of staff' and 'esprit de corps' (Fayol, qtd. in Stoner et al. 1994: 38). And yet, in a big corporation such ruptures are not visible to the organization at large, but only to employees at the local level, who see its effects and may also have to put in compensatory practices, thus increasing their own workload. This places strain on colleagues and managers who may empathize on a human level but become impatient with making allowances for the stress or illness of others.

Occasional illness is permissible; indeed, it is one of the few valid excuses for the non-performance of certain duties (non-attendance at meetings, failure to meet a deadline, missing a lecture). Illness is, after all, believed to be somewhat beyond one's control. But only certain kinds of bodily dysfunction count as legitimate, hence the anxiety surrounding the question of the relationship between stress and illness, and the moral and legal question of responsibility for stress. Bureaucratic/corporate culture is happier with illness as uncontrollable event rather than chronic condition. Getting the flu, an infection, or food poisoning, slipping a disk or breaking a leg – all these are legitimate illnesses, since the body figures as powerless matter that has fallen prey to an unaccountable mechanical or biological mishap. The chronically weak or stressed ('unproductive') body is, however, another thing. It is the recalcitrant feminized matter that is out of control, unable to be 'mastered'. Chronic stress, mental illness, recurring illness are the bodily signs that one has not 'coped'.

As part of this subtle symbolics of stress and illness, a tacit and insidious equation between stress or weariness and professionalism has crept into academic life. I have heard 'jokes' in which looking well, fit or happy is interpreted as a sign of under-work. This is an ultimately logical, if perverted, response to professional overload. Such jocular observations are underpinned by mutual, and internalized, surveillance. In a very tight employment market, stress (or the visible markers thereof) functions increasingly and paradoxically as a signifier of both professionalism and weakness. The right amount of stress shows that you are working hard enough; too much stress signifies the body/person that 'can't cope', and therefore has no place in the strangled employment market of academia. The tired body may signify professionalism, but the less-than-well body signifies corporate deficiency. Having tipped one over some finely drawn and invisible line, the sick body signifies unproductivity, inability to cope, moral, intellectual and professional 'weakness'. Thus, by mutual surveillance and an increasingly internalized self-surveillance, we come to know who 'is' or 'isn't' up to the rigours of an increasingly demanding profession. To some extent, while-ever the academic marketplace is so strained, employed academics are condemned to an almost daily performance of their right to a job, and the same principle, working differently, applies to unemployed or casual academics seeking to gain a job.

Anxiety and fear about not working hard enough are in that sense systemic rather than incidental. Indeed, they are actually useful to the system:

> The individual's sense of agency and freedom ... are overlaid and in tension with an almost subliminal anxiety and fear of surveillance ... The fear and anxiety are useful, from a systems point of view, as they work to fuel a constantly renewed (though largely futile) resolution to remake a self who is appropriate to, and regarded as good enough within, the new system. (Davies 2003: 93)

In such a system, it is up to the individual to self-manage, often at private expense (Redden 2008, Fisher 2011, Gregg 2011).

The gendered dimensions of these struggles are significant. Not only is there the deep historical feminization of the body as weak vessel to contend with, but also the social dilemmas of reproductive life. Participants in Acker and Armenti's study of women academics in some Canadian universities reported that female academics of an earlier generation (those who were balancing childcare and academic work some 30 years ago) used to try to time babies for the long break (2004: 10). Still others missed the opportunity altogether. Today, when the interests of family and work compete, it is still usually women who resolve the dilemma by leaving work or working part-time (Horin 1995: 1). In the 1990s, full-time female academics were more likely than their male counterparts

> to be single and childless, not living with a partner, to have been a tutor (often within the university where they once were a student and now work) before becoming a lecturer, to have interrupted their own career by following their partner to another city or country, to have engaged in part-time employment or have spent a period outside the workforce through being a parent, and to have combined a full-time career as an academic with extensive household and childcare responsibilities. (Romanin and Over 1993: 425)

Despite this, there were no reported differences between women and men in academic performance. The authors of the study noted that

> Even when they had the added pressures of caring for young children and of combining this role and other family responsibilities with their work as academics, the women ... remained indistinguishable from their male colleagues on multiple indicators of academic performance. (Romanin and Over 1993: 425)

But at what cost?

Metrical systems have little to say about personal costs like tolls on health, wellbeing and relationships. But they do presuppose the measurability of all things and encourage the drawing of equivalences. It is, therefore, dismayingly reasonable that the question 'how many [research] papers is a baby worth?' has already been addressed. Answer? In the UK: one (Klocker and Drozdewski 2012: 1275).

Beyond Pessimism: Fumbling Towards a New Art of Academic Living

So far, I have painted a very gloomy picture, despite the hope promised in the title of this book. Perhaps things are worse in Australia than elsewhere; a 2007 international survey indicated that Australian academics are among the least satisfied in the world (Coates et al. 2009: 47). Now is a good time to grab hold of Romain Rolland's 'pessimism of the intellect, optimism of the will'.[22] As a generation of scholars prepares for retirement, we might hope for a useful crisis, in which some of the assumptions of recent decades about productivism and accountability have to be revised. Or perhaps we might find solace in the thought that we are on the verge of replacing and renewing the current generation of scholars with one not hidebound by the past – born into a new bodily and social regime and hence more prepared, and more able, to thrive in the one to come.

For me, the question that matters most in pondering their future is less what they will think or believe about universities, than what their bodies be will able to sustain, and what impact the demands of the new university life will have on their fuller social, family and economic lives. The scholars to come may be less subject to demoralization and despair about university life than the retiring generation, but how well – and for how long – can anyone thrive, physically and socially, in a regime hell-bent on productivism? Is it sustainable for an entire career? What does it mean for 'other' aspects of life: child-rearing, mortgages, even hobbies?

The early version of this essay, written some fifteen years ago, was impressionistic, emanating from intense experience and full of its rawness. Since the time it was written a substantial body of literature reporting, expressing and analysing academic distress has arisen. In reading academics' accounts of their new workplace life, I have become aware of the frequency with which they make use of narrative genres of varying types, including anecdotes, interviews, autoethnography or collective biography (for examples, see Pelias 2004, Davies

---

22 This maxim was made famous by Antonio Gramsci, who used it repeatedly in his letters from prison. It was on the masthead of the newspaper *L'Ordine Nuovo*, of which Gramsci was a co-founder (Morgan 1987: 306).

and Bansel 2005, Sparkes 2007, Watson 2009). Part of the academic response to the new university, then, has simply been to bear witness. The proliferation of first-person accounts might indicate that academics have collectively grasped the intimate yet shared impact of these changes and have sought new forms and genres in which to express this. Perhaps we have realized that in the face of seemingly unstoppable forces like neoliberalism and marketization the best, or maybe the only, response we have is to appeal to the minutiae of the everyday as it connects us together.

So it is with the aim of connecting the personal to the collective, the everyday to the sweeping, that I offer some concluding reflections. I offer them merely as springboards – faltering steps towards a new art and politics of academic living.

Setting limits   Melissa Gregg perceptively notes that today there is 'a diminished terminology to speak of work limits' (2009: 212, original emphasis). So perhaps a good place for new academics to start is to realize that no one in academia – no one – will ever tell you that you have done enough. They may tell you that you have done well; they will congratulate you on your successes; they may thank you for your hard work – but they will never tell you that you have done enough. Realizing this can be liberating. We ourselves have to cry enough, to take up the positive potential in the double-edged sword of the neoliberal insistence on agency and self-regulation. Rejoice in the realization that no one will ever tell you you have done enough, and stop waiting for it to happen. We are all unevenly placed to do this; it is not a particularly viable strategy for casual academics seeking permanent work. So senior academics have to take the lead here. Expectations about output can mount only if people keep setting the bar higher.

Embracing the game   Setting limits is made easier when you embrace the fact that productivity is a game – one you probably can't win. If you want to, you can choose to watch over-achievers with a bemused ethnographic regard, so long as you don't make the mistake of regarding the truths produced by auditing mechanisms as a brute indicator of worth. Reject the new-fashioned 'numerology' – the 'belief that somehow numerical information is always superior to qualitative, structural, and topological information' (Boulding 1996 [1978]: 416). Remain alert to the tiny ways in which auditing mechanisms begin to look like revealers of truth.

Embracing inefficiency   It helps to remember that all the fundamentals of our job – teaching, learning, understanding and creating ideas – have little to do with efficiency. They are messy and unpredictable, like life itself: 'Some of the redundancies and inefficiencies of universities are part of that ultimate product of human activity which is the reason for living at all' (Boulding 1996 [1978]:

416). They are the intellectual equivalent of the Amazon, harbouring seeds whose import cannot be known in advance:

> These redundancies are also an extremely important reserve of high-quality ability in times of crisis. To make universities narrowly efficient might well be the greatest disservice we offer society. (416)

Reclaiming the pause Perhaps we should try to do nothing, even if only for a few minutes each day. We can encourage each other in trying to refuse the machinic mentality of productivism whereby one output must follow another, with no time to breathe or digest. But it is probably wiser to talk publically of optimizing health rather than embracing laziness. When Barthes urged us to dare to be lazy, his job probably wasn't on the line.

Embracing multiplicity This chapter has argued that academics expend much physical, mental and emotional energy trying to be the human glue that binds the university's different institutional forms together – striving to preserve or salvage what they believe to be valuable in the university as an institution. This is an exhausting way to live and work. If trying to be multiple isn't your thing, try to spread the idea that there are many legitimate ways of being an academic. Fight for workloads formulae and auditing mechanisms that recognize this.

Harnessing contagion It is worth believing in the power of one body to affect another, and the surprising interpersonal impact of social networks (Christakis and Fowler 2010). Since we apparently influence others more than we realize, it is worth becoming rather more consciously contagious. We might, for example, find ways of refusing the tacit moral equation between being stressed and being a good employee. Senior academics in particular have an ethical obligation to lead in this, to be aware of the power of what they embody. They need to recognize that their mode of professional being in the world is itself a tacit pedagogy and they are therefore obliged to use it reflexively and ethically. Ethical leadership needs to reverberate right down to the minutiae of professional life – remembering that every time you send an email to colleagues at 3am, or cheerily announce that Saturday is your most productive working day, you are making a choice to participate in the normalization of overwork. Controlling this requires the kind of moral leadership that recognizes and repudiates the current system's aim of producing 'different classes of knowledge workers' (Redden 2008: 15).

These are, it might be retorted, individualized, or at least localized, suggestions – calls for people to better regulate themselves and manage their responses rather than to attack the fundamental ideologies or systems that produce the problem in the first place. They are – and in that they are complicit with the self-managing habitus (Redden 2008: 11) produced by neoliberalism and the privatization of solutions that results from it (Fisher 2011, Gregg 2011: 5). A traditional labour politics repudiates these. The Australian Council of Trade Unions, for example, notes that 'stress management, lifestyle changes, personality-change methods, relaxation techniques and the like are not acceptable as a first focus prevention' (qtd. in McKenna 1994: 2).

Perhaps then we might look to a more shared political strategy, such as;

Discourse jockeying What discourses can we harness and ride as well as the traditional discourses of labour politics?

One suggestion is that we might find political leverage in the call for social accountability – a call that we in the Humanities once repudiated so fiercely. We might argue to managers and governments that there are different ways that academics can be held accountable and that it is time to rethink the blunt and blinkered equation between accountability and an escalation in publication. We might point out that rewarding the rapid publication of many articles doesn't foster an innovation culture; it fosters a repetition culture. It discourages reflection, the maturation of ideas, and risk taking. It might goad a few recalcitrants into doing more, but in so doing kill off something more precious. 'Should we not', asks Kenneth Boulding, 'judge a system by its peak rather than by its average?' (1996 [1978]: 417). Perhaps if governments want to encourage social engagement, relevance and accountability, they should look at rewarding multiple types of academic work. To take just one example, outreach or community activities – such as running in-services, talking at schools or community groups, giving public lectures, reviewing for newspapers – could be taken out of the realm of sacrificial labour and rewarded in the same way that research is.

While it may be true that in the current climate research evaluation frameworks are 'inevitable' (Redden 2008: 8), the populist impatience with abstruse scholasticism might make this a call that could garner widespread public support. Why could there not be auditing systems that recognize that there is more than one way to be a good academic and which query the assumption that publishing yet another academic paper is always and for everyone the best way to be accountable, useful and socially relevant?

The obstacle to this more open understanding of accountability is the market model whereby universities are rewarded (by governments, but also by consumer mechanisms like league tables) for the amount of intellectual 'product' they shift. Arguing for a broader notion of accountability means seeing whether there remains any political traction in the idea of the social good. Since governments in the UK and Australia are still the major funders of higher education, asking this involves confronting the question of how much stake governments themselves still have in the idea of the nation state rather than the market state (Rutherford 2005: 299). Is there enough political life left in the idea of the university as a nation-builder in the face of the emerging reality of the university as a player in a global marketplace?

Playing the accountability and relevance game is, however, dangerous terrain, for it risks surrendering too much scholarly ground, such as the liberal humanist idea of knowledge for knowledge's sake or the scientific valuation of curiosity-led research, in favour of brute utilitarianism. But there is some scope for bridging the two, by arguing that we can never know in advance which intellectual pathways will end up being fruitful.

In any case, it is likely that no arguments, liberal humanist or utilitarian, will convince those members of the public who are staunchly convinced that academics are indulged dilettantes:

> Come off it. All academics do is read, think, tap on a keyboard, blow hot air and sit on their butts. How difficult is that? Do you actually believe that qualifies as hard work? Hard work is done in the mines, in the hospital wards, on construction sites etc (OFistFullOfDollars 2011)

Why waste one's time considering such vitriol? What could it possibly have to teach us?

First, it recalls, albeit in a populist and contemptuous idiom, the assertion that has rippled underneath this entire chapter, as both a perturbation and a productive spur to thought, that academics have actually had it easy when compared to other industries and for that reason should abandon the idea that there is something special or different about academic work and think themselves lucky that they have been protected for so long from the changes that have rocked other sectors. We might also note the irony that critical intellectuals, including those in Cultural Studies, have no doubt played an inadvertent role in undermining their own social authority, in their insistence on the historical contingency of knowledge and the power relations involved in its dissemination. The second thing such disparagement might teach us is that we can expect few favours from the general populace unless we make our case most strenuously about the value of our work.

Responding to this challenge involves bringing to the fore the consciousness of kind so important to traditional vocationalism and to political action. The tradition and social reality of the collegiate remains one of the strongest cores of academic life and one of its strongest sources of satisfaction and pleasure, so we should seek both to preserve it and to harness its political potential. And this is where our similarity to others can actually be made to work for us rather than being thrown in our face as an accusation.

First, our experiences of the dilemmas of vocationalism – the tension between creativity and coercion – can be shared and debated with other workers. As Andrew Ross (2004) has argued, the rise of sacrificial labour – or, to put it another way, the hijacking of vocationalism – means that academia has come to function less and less as the privileged exception to the alienated labour of mass capitalism than as the model for a new, postmodern, form of self-directed work, in which labour cannot so easily be separated from life: 'the extraordinary ability of academics to excavate working hours from a range of times in the day … has provided a model for the flexible work arrangements now formalised across many sectors' (Gregg 2009: 211).

Second, our concerns about the politicization and corporatization of knowledge should find us allies in the public sector, where debates about the dangers of both political interference and the new managerialism are widespread (Parker 1989, Weller 1989, MacDermott 2008).

Third, academics are not alone among white-collar workers in suffering a loss of professional morale alongside a decline in public support and respect. Doctors, for example, experience similar problems. They too have lost public authority, and are burdened by heavy workloads and the demands of a saturated information environment. They also share some not dissimilar paradigmatic difficulties, striving to uphold an ethic of the social good while burdened by a popular cynicism, which may accuse them of being self-interested, or mere puppets of big pharma, or mere technicians. They too are watching their clientele turn from being patients into consumers with rights.

Another profession with whom we share many predicaments is, ironically enough, politicians themselves. Like academics, they are subject to new, intense and inflammatory forms of public scrutiny; are relatively underpaid; and still bound by a belief in the public good while nonetheless being widely ridiculed as self-serving elites. The irony that politicians might be in the same boat as academics – watching their vocationalism ridiculed by popular cynicism and being subjected to unprecedented scrutiny – may give rise to some Schadenfreude. But a more useful response would be to open up a serious public conversation about the fate of the professions.

I cautioned earlier that the desire to be 'just one thing' might be regressive. But this chapter has not been driven by a nostalgic desire for a return to the simplicity of the scholarly model – a model that was based on privilege and social exclusion and which, in any case, certainly has to evolve as societies change. Rather, it has sought to outline the personal costs of a model where multiplicity means the requirement to be everything, at once.

What would a happier model of multiplicity involve? One answer is that multiplicity is empowering when it is recognized that we cannot do all things equally and that it is reasonable for there to be different seasons in academic life – some stages of your career when you write like fury; others when you read and reflect – as well as different types and styles of academics – some who intervene in international research; others who intervene in local communities; others who are exceptional teachers. The second, related, condition of happy multiplicity is eliminating the possibility that any particular idea of the academic can be wielded, randomly and punitively. Rather than striving to be the one who embodies it all, we should rather celebrate the fact that between us, as a collegiate, we have the bases covered.

CHAPTER 3

Pluralism and its Discontents: Teaching Critical Theory and the Politics of Hope

'We can no longer afford the luxury of pessimism'

David Brower, foreword to Shutkin (2000)

At this point, I turn, with some relief, away from the predicaments of academics toward those of the students we teach, and already I feel my spirits rise. For the classroom is at the heart of what most academics do and its capacity to generate dilemmas is not a sign of some contemporary decline, but a perennial feature of teaching. It is, moreover, a space where we can still unequivocally try to be a force for good.

The particular pedagogical problem out of which this chapter springs is the teaching of contemporary critical theory to undergraduates. While this is a case quite specific to the Arts and Humanities, it is a useful vehicle for exploring how the intellectual and institutional changes of the late twentieth century provide us with new challenges in the structuring of curriculum and in classroom practice. Exploring some predicaments in the teaching of critical theory shines a light on the problems of pluralism brought about by massification and by the rise of interdisciplinarity.

My starting point and core assumption is the inseparability of our intellectual and affective lives, and so this chapter on the difficulties of teaching critical theory discusses the impact of our teaching strategies and curriculum structure not only on intellectual rigour but also on quite fundamental emotional states and capacities, like hope and joy. Once upon a time I considered hope and joy to be something of a potential an embarrassment to Cultural Studies, which for so long concentrated on power and critique. Even its tectonic shift from the late 1980s towards celebrations of pleasure struck me as rather different from hope or joy. Over recent years,[1] hope has begun to make an occasional appearance

---

1 There seems to have been a little flurry of writing on hope in the late 1990s – David Hicks was writing on hope and environmental education in the mid-1990s; a special issue of the journal *Social Research* came out in 1999; Mary Zournazi's collection of interviews on hope was published in 2002. My own first foray into the area was in a conference presentation in 2001.

(for example in a collection of interviews by Mary Zournazi [2002]) but it is still more at home in the philosophy of education, or in psychology, religious studies or the self-help shelves. But a series of major global events – 9/11, the election of Barack Obama, the GFC, the Eurozone crisis, the threat of climate change – have thrust the matter of hope well and truly into public discourse. Moreover, the current climate of uncertainty and despondency within universities has likewise put hope on the agenda, both as an intellectual matter and as a matter of workplace survival. The unhappy state of universities is, indeed, the insistent backdrop to these ruminations – for it is this context that structures the kinds of teaching we can do and that obliges us to continually reconsider our teaching strategies.

My focus, as throughout this book, is on my own field of Gender and Cultural Studies. But the politics and ethics of hopeful teaching are pressing concerns in other disciplines. Most obviously, hope is a theme in the environmental disciplines, where the question of how to educate without producing despair is an urgent one. David Hicks, for example, has written extensively about the crucial need for a pedagogy of hope in environmental studies (Hicks and Holden 1995, Hicks 1996, Hicks 1998). And of course hope matters in other disciplines, including Peace and Conflict Studies, International Relations, Terrorism Studies and critical race studies. But for me, the question arose in the context of teaching Gender and Cultural Studies to undergraduates.

Hope, Despair and Leftist Politics

Hope is a core religious value, intimately linked to faith. In the Christian tradition, hope is a virtue. The sinfulness or otherwise of its opposite, despair, has been a recurring theme in Christian theology, with many Christian writers drawing explicitly on their own personal experiences of despair and doubt. Saint Augustine, for example, recounts in his *Confessions* his own battles between hopeful faith and despondency (1944 [399]: Bk 6). For Augustine, both hope and despair are gifts of God, since they keep each other in check: despair counteracts 'presumption', and hope leads us towards God (Snyder 1965: 35): 'For Augustine, the ideal spiritual state for a Christian is a fruitful tension between positive hope and negative fear' (35). In the sixth century, Saint Benedict warned that the devil uses despair as a subtle trap for those of whose sinfulness he is not assured (22). In the thirteenth century, the ambiguities and complexities of despair are evident in the writings of Saint Thomas Aquinas, who presents the arguments for and against the sinfulness of despair. In his *Summa Theologica*, he reiterates Augustine's contention that despair is a sin, since it indicates a lack of faith in God, even though it might seem not to lead to any gain on the part of the sinner (2007 [1911]: Q20, 1253).

Protestantism foregrounded even more the paradoxical nature of despair. Luther centralized it, 'plac[ing] despair of self at the very core of Christian experience' (Snyder 1965: 24). It was not merely some unavoidable human frailty, but rather one of the utmost tests – a necessary component of faithfulness. Man's salvation can come only once he recognizes his utter sinfulness; in that way, salvation is dependent on despair, which acts 'to terrify [man's] mind and cast out all complacency' (Luther, qtd. in Snyder 1965: 24). Luther repeated Benedict's vision of despair as the devil's most subtle weapon, aimed especially at the holiest of men, the saints (Snyder 1965: 25–6). The question of the sinfulness or otherwise of despair continues as a theme of Christian discussion today, as evidenced by numerous online forum discussions on the topic. This discussion is especially charged in the light of the contemporary medicalization of despair as depression.

It is a commonplace to point out the structural parallels between Christianity and Marxism (i.e. their shared narrative of a utopian past, a Fall, a contemporary struggle and hope for/belief in a utopian future). Marxism, with its promise of revolution, has 'represented the immanent version of hope available outside the Christian eschatology' (Deneen 1999: 578). Patricia White argues that something she calls 'social hopes', in contradistinction to 'private hopes', is intrinsic to both the Marxist and the Christian worldview, and that in both cases lack of hope is envisaged as a flaw or a cause for guilt, since it signals lack of political commitment or lack of faith in God respectively (1996: 10).

Hope is, it would seem, central to left-wing politics. Indeed, the philosopher Richard Rorty claims that 'The Left, by definition, is the party of hope' (1998: 14). And yet, the versions of leftist theory I encountered when I first began studying Cultural Studies didn't feel like they had much to do with hope. On the contrary, I experienced both sides of the coin of French critical theory – its trenchant critique and its romantic utopianism – as subtly demoralizing, in different ways.

By the time I was a university teacher, confronting the issue of hope in the Cultural Studies classroom, I still hadn't come across any Marxist writings on hope. I later discovered that there is in fact a Marxist discussion of hope, Raymond Williams's *Modern Tragedy* (1979) and Ernst Bloch's *The Principle of Hope* (1986) being two examples. Hope is also, of course, a major theme in the left-wing project of critical pedagogy. In this tradition, political projects cannot help but be affective projects: critique and resistance find their affective counterparts in rage and hope, which are needed in equal measure. As is clear from the epigraph to this book, hope was a central animator of the work of Paulo Freire, who saw education as a tool for liberating the oppressed. Freire himself made hope more visible over the years, reworking the ideas he had made famous in *Pedagogy of the Oppressed* (1970) under the title *Pedagogy of Hope* (1994 [1992]), which he presented as a 'reliving' of his life-long belief in the personally and socially transformative power of education. As Freire put it, *Pedagogy of Hope* 'is written in rage and love, without which there is no hope' (1994 [1992]: 10). Hope continues as a theme in those influenced by Freire, such as the critical pedagogue Henry Giroux, whose work has been influential in one vein of Cultural Studies.

Some academic bodies of thought, especially in the US, are driven not so much (or not only) by a discourse of hope as by one of optimism. For example, optimism is both the object of study and the core virtue of the subdiscipline of positive psychology, a field emerging out of the work of Martin Seligman. This new field has gained considerable momentum since Seligman first called in 1998 for a major reorientation of psychology away from a focus on the negative (Baumgardner and Crothers 2009: 3). It attempts to shrug off some of the influence of Freudian thought, with its systematic 'unveiling' of the self-serving roots of most behaviour (2009: 2), and to move away from contemporary psychology's disease-focused model (3). It notes the importance of a positive disposition and/or a self-imposed retraining ('learned optimism' [Seligman 1992]) on health, wellbeing and happiness. Optimism, insists Seligman, can be learned as a set of techniques, even if one is not, dispositionally speaking, an optimist (2002: 24).

Unsurprisingly, this work flourishes in the US, where optimism is a national virtue. It connects with and seems to provide scientific legitimation for currents in contemporary American popular culture, such as the self-help movement, which has long championed the psychological benefits of positive thinking (Norman Vincent Peale's bestseller *The Power of Positive Thinking* was first published in 1952).[2] The New Age uptake of this popular psychology goes so far as to claim the material and spiritual as well as psychological benefits of positive thinking, contending that it has the power to alter all aspects of material reality, including health, wealth and relationships (Hay 1987).

Some, however, are critical of the role optimism has played in American popular and political culture. Drawing on the work of the American social critic Christopher Lasch, Jean Elshtain (1999) castigates a certain strand of (particularly American) political philosophy that is driven by optimism rather than hope. She reprises Lasch's claim that much American political philosophy has bought into 'the dominant story America likes to tell about herself — a story of optimism and unboundedness' that can easily tip into arrogant 'triumphalism' (Elshtain 1999: 532). Elshtain makes the contrast between 'unwarranted optimism' and hopefulness (531). The latter recognizes and respects the limits of human

---

2 Though very popular, the book was not uncontroversial. Peale was a Christian minister, who was criticized for the fact that his training was theological rather than psychological or psychiatric. The largely anecdotal nature of the book made it a target for criticism from trained psychologists.

projects and does not seek, unrealistically, to 'insulate' a polity – let alone every individual in it – from 'experiences of loss and defeat' (531). In Lasch, this emphasis on limits was a secular humanist 'equivalent' to the Christian formulation of humanity and human lives as inherently and inexorably frail, fallible and vulnerable. 'The texture of daily life', wrote Lasch, is made up of 'an experience of loss and defeat' (qtd. in Elshtain 1999: 531), a view that would seem to have derived from his early Marxism but which lacks its insistence on a redemptive political project to rectify this alienation. Like Lasch, Elshtain sees much of the Western philosophical tradition, especially political philosophy, and most especially American political philosophy, as complicit with an idealistic denial of limits. In this it is, paradoxically, not hopeful enough – not because it is gloomy but on the contrary because it is unjustifiably optimistic. As an intellectual and political project, it is, she states, an 'anti-tragedy' (1999: 531).

Barbara Ehrenreich (2009) is likewise highly critical of the American cult of optimism, which has, she argues, 'dark roots' (74), for it emerged out of an attempt to overturn the 'Calvinist gloom' (78) of the pilgrims but retained, she says, 'some of Calvinism's more toxic features – a harsh judgmentalism ... and an insistence on the constant interior labor of self-examination' (89). She analyses its workings in a number of contexts, including in cancer care and positive psychology. Like Lasch, she considers it a driver of American military triumphalism, and notes its connection to the 'absurdity' (8) of ideologies of unfettered growth. She considers that its insistence on the centrality of personal responsibility makes it complicit with 'the cruder aspects of the market economy' (8). Indeed, she sees it as having entered 'a kind of symbiotic relationship with American capitalism' (7).

Such critiques are useful as prompts to consider the differences between optimism and hope. But I do not want to insist on a watertight distinction between the two. Both are conceptual formulations rather than simple empirical realities, and taxonomic games are therefore of only limited use. Instead, I'd like to focus on a number of properties that recur across many discussions of hope, which are useful in an exploratory rather than definitional way.

For example, hope is usually understood as not 'calculative' (White 1996: 9), having little to do with a rational assessment of how well things may or may not turn out in the future. Hope is, in Schudson's words, 'undaunted by statistics' (1999: 628). Though it is normally seen to be future directed (Zournazi 2002: 18), it is not predictive, nor even necessarily precise about its objects. Nor is it the same as expectation (Lingis, in Zournazi 2002: 23). Indeed, the phenomenologist Alphonso Lingis claims that it is actually the logical opposite of expectation: 'hope is [by definition] always hope against the evidence' (in Zournazi 2002: 23, original emphasis).

A turning point in my own thinking on hope and its opposite came, in fact, when I went to hear the High Priest of Theory. Hearing Jacques Derrida speak in Sydney in 1999, it became clear to me that rather than despair being as it were, a failing, a lack or a cause for guilt, it can be, in fact, productive. When Derrida spoke about the negative term as logically producing its positive opposite, it dawned on me that despair was, in fact, the logical precondition for hope.[3] While I found this philosophically encouraging, it still wasn't enough, in that this extended only to hope and despair as abstract terms. The actual embodied state of despair need not always bring about hope, as we all know. And nor do critical, utopian or subversive ideas always feel positive or hopeful. Clearly, I was searching for something more than an ideology, theology or even a psychology of hope, but something more fully embodied, more like a phenomenology of hope.

Something like this can be found in a number of writers who have seen hope as an innate feature of human embodiment. Lingis, for example, sees a certain type of hope as a kind of energy or 'animal courage' (in Zournazi 2002: 23). Patricia White likewise sees it as something rather like a life-principle. Citing Mary Warnock, she notes its fundamental place in human life: 'To lose hope is to lose the capacity to want or desire anything; to lose, in fact, the wish to live' (qtd. in White 1996: 8). The anthropologist Lionel Tiger, viewing hope through the rather different lens of evolutionary sociobiology, sees this life-seeking principle as operating at a species level. He considers hope to be 'a real [vital] force located in the body and hence in human nature' (1999: 613). For Tiger, hope is a biological necessity: 'Hope is a central functional component of human action' (617). Indeed, he elevates it to a kind of evolutionary mechanism: 'Nothing ventured nothing gained' is, in his view, something like an evolutionary principle (617).

In this view, not only is hope not rational, it enables change precisely by overriding reason: 'in the see-saw ... conflict between reason and emotion, the function of this emotion, hope, is to sufficiently disable the constraining prudence of reason as to permit action to occur' (Tiger 1999: 618). For Lingis, despite his passing suggestion that certain types of hope function as vital forces, this is an existential rather than a biological matter. He believes that each of us as has to make 'a very fundamental kind of existential decision' (in Zournazi 2002: 25): 'do we believe our joy or do we believe our neutral states' (25). The latter is, of course, 'pruden[t]' (25) but, in Lingis's view, life-denying.

I will return later on to the question of whether this existential orientation can really rightfully be construed as a 'choice', raising the objection that some people are better positioned socially than others to have this level of self-reflection and self-entitlement. Who (if anyone) actually does get to choose to believe in their emotional states, and what might 'choice' mean in this context? For this fundamental existential decision of which Lingis speaks is often not a decision at all, in a literal sense. Rather, it is often already given to and for us,

---

3 Had I been reading Luther, I might have learnt something similar a lot earlier!

through our family and social circumstances and through accreted experience. In that sense, hope, unlike optimism, which is essentially cognitive, can be pre- or non-ideational.[4]

Despite these reservations, I am attracted to the possibility that phenomenology might give us one way of conceiving of hope as an active force, rather than a series of negations (i.e. claims that it is not calculative, not predictive and not expectation). A phenomenological characterization of hope as an active principle is less interested in how hope might be yoked to particular individual or political projects than in hope as a precondition for any form of action, and indeed, as generative of action (Gabriel Marcel, qtd. in White 1996: 9). This, indeed, was Freire's view. For Freire, hope actively demands action:

> As an ontological need, hope needs practice in order to become historical concreteness. That is why there is no hope in sheer hopefulness. The hoped- for is not attainted by dint of raw hoping. Just to hope is to hope in vain. (1994 [1992]: 9)

Perhaps, more modestly than either Lingis or Tiger, we could think of hope less as a force than as a potentiality – an embodied openness to possibility. For hopelessness, as Freire noted, 'paralyzes us, immobilizes us' (1994 [1992]: 8).

A number of writers see hope as having collective or social dimensions and/or operating as an engine of sociality itself. Patricia White (1996) lists hope among the 'civic virtues' necessary for a vibrant democracy. From Tiger's evolutionary biological perspective, hope is not only a necessity for individuals, but 'an essential vitamin for social process' (1999: 622), in that it is impossible to imagine a society continuing to function, let alone develop, in its absence. In a rather different vein, the conception of hope as the collective potential for action allows Mary Zournazi (2002) to imagine certain forms of social processes themselves as hopeful. Zournazi sees hope at work when we act on the desire for change – especially through engagement, dialogue and the attempt to imagine things differently (2002: 19). For Zournazi, there is an element of hope in the collective nature of the critical enterprise whenever it transcends individualism or conventional politics in order to 'engag[e] with wider senses of belonging which relate to our life experience and how we "fit" into a "cosmos" of global concerns' (2002: 19). Zournazi believes that this is best undertaken not as the enactment of some ideological 'vision' but rather in 'a spirit of dialogue, where

---

4 Ehrenreich considers hope to be an 'emotion', and optimism a 'cognitive stance' (2009: 4). Centuries earlier, Aquinas argued that 'the type of hope that is an *emotion* is not a virtue, only the hope that is a feature of the *mind*' (2012 [1269–72]: 218, original emphasis). The phenomenological approach bridges this dualism, allowing us to conceive of hope as a (contextual) embodied orientation to the world.

generosity and laughter break open a space to keep spontaneity and freedom alive – the joyful engagements possible with others' (12). In this view of things, hope is about openness, possibility and generosity rather than the elaboration and execution of a precise ideological project.

This leads us to a conception of critical theory – which is, after all, supposed to be about imagining things differently – not as pessimistic but, on the contrary, as intrinsically hopeful, even when it is not cheerful, and as necessarily entailing some connection between social hope and private hope. This is, perhaps, what a Cultural Studies colleague meant when, after I told her I was writing about hope, she spontaneously said: 'That's what we teach! Hope'. When I asked her what she meant, she said that the structuring assumption of disciplines like Gender and Cultural Studies is that change is possible, and that we can think interestingly and differently about the world. 'We offer students curiosity and interest, and that is why they come to us', she said.

So my question is, why doesn't it always feel like that? Why do some students and many social commentators experience cultural theory as joyless – an instrument of demoralization and alienation? Obviously, political views are one important reason, but they do not explain it all. After all, I teach under the rubric of Gender and Cultural Studies and yet for years I found some of it quite demoralizing – and I don't mean just the social problems it identified, but also its proposed 'solutions' and its favoured stances and approaches. I don't think we can assume an easy overlay of intellectual positions, political views, and emotional responses. We can see this by remembering that the 'arrival' of theory proved a problem for traditionalists of all kinds, including those of the left.

The 'Problem' of Theory/The Joy of Theory

The introductory essay to a collection called *Post-Theory* (McQuillan et al. 1999) is titled, perhaps somewhat optimistically, 'The Joy of Theory'. The trope is unusual, in that the advent of theory in universities in the 1960s was so often heralded not as something joyous, but as a challenge, a threat or a sign of decline. It was frequently described in terms of metaphors of death and disease. Wallace Martin, for example, described the rhetoric of 'growth and decay, health and disease, crisis, death, and birth' (1996: 15) with which theories are announced and decried. He himself used the metaphor, but knowingly: 'In pathology, a crisis results from a disease. In criticism, it is a sign of health' (16). 'In America, the source of the plague is said to be Europe', he continued (Martin 1996: 16–17). With similar irony, Terry Eagleton called the arrival of theory 'a really virulent outbreak of theory, on an epidemic scale' (1990: 25–6). Perhaps it's just a metaphor, but if metaphors are truly something 'we live by', as the title of Lakoff and Johnson's (1980) famous study puts it, then they are part of our psychology and our embodiment.

As both an intellectual and a professional event, the coming of theory was at the same time productively tumultuous and deeply divisive. It threatened careers, and produced polemical rhetoric from both the 'pro'- and 'anti'-'Theory' camps.[5] The coming of Theory placed particular strains on established academics. In 1992, Ken Ruthven pithily expressed the alternatives open to older academics 'faced by mounting evidence of [their] own intellectual obsolescence': 'either to retire gracefully or to become a student again' (ix). By now, most academics have in fact, faced and dealt with Ruthven's Choice. Moreover, a new generation of younger, theoretically literate academics has now taken its place in the academy. For younger academics, 'theory' is unlikely to be a turning point so much as the very stuff of their undergraduate, and indeed school, education.[6]

My own first encounter with critical theory was not, on the whole, joyful. I encountered theory fairly late in the piece, having had a rather astonishingly apolitical New Critical undergraduate education, and thus fell into Ruthven's Category B – one who needed to become a student again. When I did belatedly encounter Theory, there was, for the middle-class school teacher that I then was, something of loss as well as gain in the undoing of my intellectual formation. While some on the left claim that the rise of theory operates in counterpoint to the decline of politics (see McQuillan et al. 1999: xi), this is not necessarily so. For me, theory operated not as the suspect opposite to politics, but as the very mode of my politicization. For those whose first politicization is deconstructive in nature, theory poses a particular set of problems, and they differ from those it poses to the political activist – who may see theory as a sign of the decline of politics, the spinning off of political energy into an abstruse and self-indulgent world of intellectual speculation. For the apolitical subject who is politicized via theory (as many of today's students are) theory is paradoxical: it is both too political and not political enough. Too political, in that it gives one an acute and nuanced sense of the problems of the world, and not political enough, in that it doesn't

---

5 I'm aware that I'm using this term monolithically, perhaps rather too flippantly following those writers who avoid the question of the different kinds of theory by recourse to irony. McQuillan et al. (1999), for example, write it with a capital 'T'. I'm sure there are many different kinds of theorist, from Freud to Derrida, who might point to the importance of this avoidance, but my preoccupations lie elsewhere.

6 'Theory' per se is not taught in Australian schools, nor is Philosophy. But a critical ethos has filtered through the curriculum such that feminist perspectives, for example, are commonly encountered in English or in upper high-school subjects like 'Society and Culture'.

seem to offer much by way of solution. Rather, it teaches one to analyse and deconstruct the solutions as well as the problems. Theory, in that sense, becomes its own answer, and a constantly shifting one at that.

For some, that makes theory an exercise in cynicism. Raymond Tallis (1999), for example, objects to the 'industry' of cultural criticism, applying this not only to anti-humanist theory but also to humanist laments. He decries what he calls the 'intellectual sport of diagnosing the ills of society', claiming that this sport is itself 'one of the chief of our social ills' (1999: 89), with an alarming potential to generate despair or defensive cynicism. Some on the left agree. Henry Giroux, for example, has concerns not only about the intransigency of traditional Marxist politics, which leaves, he argues, little space for faith in cultural interventions (2000: 6), but also in the more self-serving forms of Cultural Studies. He notes with alarm the 'growing academicization' (13) of Cultural Studies, in particular its complicity with careerism and its potential to be obscurantist and insular (14). Against these twin poles of dogmatic political culture and self-serving academic culture, he champions the project of critical pedagogy, within which he includes 'the best work in cultural studies and cultural politics' (14). This approach, he argues, offers the best pathway through this dilemma, since it remains utopian without being 'messianic' (129), thus offering, in his view, the best chance of promoting what he calls 'educated hope' (129). The philosopher Richard Rorty, however, considered left-wing critical pedagogies themselves to be incompatible with hope, claiming that you cannot 'find inspirational value in a text at the same time as you are viewing it as a … mechanism of cultural production' (qtd. in Giroux 2000: 22).

I have never thought of Cultural Studies as 'cynical' but my early encounters with left-wing theory left me believing that it was the inheritor of something of an intellectual bias towards pessimism. On the whole, I thought, joy has played only a bit part in the grand drama of leftist theory. Terry Eagleton, indeed, considers that Marxism has traditionally seen the revolutionary and the comic as incompatible:

> There has been, so far as I know, no Marxist theory of comedy to date; tragedy has been a considerably more successful contender for the attention of materialist criticism. And there are good enough reasons why Marxism has suspected the comic: for what after all could more securely rivet us in our ideological places, having provisionally jolted us out of them? (1981: 159–60)

There are of course exceptions to the dominance of tragic theory; Mikhail Bakhtin's (1984) theory of carnival, which is widely used in Cultural Studies, is an obvious example.[7] On the whole, though, I have experienced critical theory as a practice marked by its suspicion of hope or joy, perhaps because they are seen as religious values. Rather than experiencing hope as a Marxist virtue (White 1996: 9), I felt on the contrary a tacit equation between optimism, intellectual inferiority and political betrayal. If you are optimistic or joyful about the world, it's because you're not bright enough to realize how corrupt it is, or not politically committed enough to jolt yourself out of your bourgeois comforts. If you seem too cheerful you are obviously not thinking hard enough. (Interestingly, this equation is also made in mainstream psychology. Seligman calls it 'depressive realism', or, more colloquially, the 'happy-but-dumb' thesis [2002: 37]).

Critiques of pessimism have often come from anti-theory camps, who see many forms of contemporary theory as programmatically pessimistic (see Tallis 1999). But pessimism isn't restricted to the left side of politics; there is no shortage of gloomy conservatives. In fact, many forms of intellectual positioning and posture rely on it (from the irony of an Oscar Wilde to the ironic detachment that characterizes a certain style of contemporary intellectual hipness). As Bertolt Brecht put it: 'The man who laughs hasn't been told the bad news yet'. This is usually cited with cynical approval. It is quite startling, then, to discover that in its full context it is, in fact, a lament for lost innocence, a critique of the assumption that to be hopeful is to be politically naïve.[8] This foreshortening of Brecht's fuller meaning is an ironic reinforcement of his poetic claim that for those disappointed in the world, be they intellectuals, artists, or the chronically cool, pessimism can serve as both a moral and an intellectual virtue. (This is, perhaps, an intellectual equivalent to the workplace principle described in Chapter 2 that makes a virtue of overwork. If you arrive at work looking too cheerful, it's a professionally incriminating sign of underwork.)

---

7 Indeed, Eagleton's comment is made in the context of a discussion of Bakhtin, in which he considers the political limits to Bakhtin's 'vivaciou[s]' utopianism (1981: 148).

8 Precise translations of this line differ. The one cited in here is perhaps the most common version. The line comes from Brecht's poem 'To Those Born Later', which opens as follows:

Truly, I live in dark times!
The guileless word is folly. A smooth forehead
Suggests insensitivity. The man who laughs
Has simply not yet had
The terrible news.
What kind of times are they, when
A talk about trees is almost a crime
Because it implies silence about so many horrors? (1976: 318, lines 1–8)

But is it right to see theory as gloomy? After all, in our reading and teaching we constantly see how theories can serve as an invitation, a platform from which to spring. Here is Lucy Lippard, for example, describing the way the social theorist Dean MacCannell uses theory: '[H]e deploys the speculative nature of theory in the service not of nitpicking cynicism but of freedom to dive in, to question everything about everything – especially those concrete phenomena that he has seen, experienced, and pondered firsthand' (1999: x). The poetic style of feminists like Hélène Cixous or Luce Irigaray, the in-your-face brashness of some queer theory, the playfulness of deconstruction, can all be read as energetic and utopian responses to social inequality. Moreover, a sense of community and common purpose can animate even the most critical of critical theories. Finding a framework, a language, and an audience for one's personal and political discontents can be intensely liberating. Annette Kolodny, for example, speaks of the pleasure given her by her early encounters with feminism, which enabled her and her peers to 'make public our otherwise private discontents' and to find that others shared them (1980: 1). Doreen Massey likewise writes of the belated sense of affirmation she felt once she discovered a feminist theory that could confirm and give voice to things that she already knew to be true about the world (1994: 185–7). Clearly, despite the intellectual allure of pessimism, there is, in fact, nothing intrinsically or inevitably pessimistic about critical theory at all. Derrida has always said as much about deconstruction. He understood it 'not as a violent demolition but as a positive undertaking that stakes out and foregrounds the unarticulated, forgotten, subordinated, or repressed possibilities of the philosophical tradition' (Cox 1996: 122). For many people, including myself, theory has changed the way we see the world, as well as providing a language and a conceptual framework for articulating things we already felt or knew. It has reinvigorated our disciplines, produced new disciplines, created communities and provided political purpose and focus, as well as division and difference.

In any case, Cultural Studies has to a substantial degree defined itself against the dourness or the puritanism of, to take a classic example, the Frankfurt School. Indeed, this is one of the things for which it is commonly condemned – for not being serious enough, for having capitulated to populism and become, in the words of one detractor, 'a cultural court jester' (Stuhr 1995: 9).[9] But do any of the postmodern celebrations of desire, resistance, diversity, mess, plurality or uncontainability amount to joy or hope? Despite the resistance and the jouissance, the pleasure and the desire, I am left with the lingering

---

9 Cf. a comment from a different author within the same collection: '[M]any of the followers of Barthes and Derrida seem more interested in the jouissance and erotic frissons of post-structuralist linguistics than they do in exerting practical influence on the media and on governments' (Myers 1995: 34).

suspicion that optimism, joy, and hope might still be a little suspect – as either politically soft, intellectually weak or religiously inspired (and hence Bad), even though I know that optimism, hope, or joy, are not inimical to the left and are, moreover, emotional states whose availability can be thought of at least in part in social terms. This returns me to the question I hinted at earlier: to whom, and in which contexts, are hopeful encounters with critical theory most readily available? We can begin to explore that question by thinking about people who don't find theory uplifting, so I turn now to some of my classroom experiences of student resistance to theory.

Student Resistance

The contradictoriness of my own theoretical conversion left me alert to the dilemmas of those among my students who might be experiencing something similar. From my own experience I can remember that while there are many pleasures to be had from learning to see the world anew, there are also potentially some painful losses to be negotiated. This sense of loss can result from a perceived assault on religious belief (all the more powerful for being almost always tacit), or on ideals (like truth or authenticity or consensus), or on identity itself (especially the notion of an essential self). In my early days as a university teacher I actually heard a student waiting for a lecture turn to the current week's topic and say, 'Oh, don't tell me they're going to take that away from us too'. I am not suggesting that all student encounters with theory are of this kind – by no means, for many students have embraced theory joyfully – merely that this is *one* of the effects that becoming aware of a critical theory and politics can have, and that it's something I have rarely heard addressed in relation either to the curriculum structure or to an ethics and a strategy of teaching. Rather, I have seen either an ignorance of the potentially life-changing impact of such teaching, a simplistic celebration of it, or a tendency to see it as some form of necessary initiation. I have heard tutors who taught in a particularly comprehensively deconstructive first year course at one Australian university speak of it with a machismo of the 'Well, I had to go through that and it didn't do *me* any harm' variety. Resistance, it would seem, is futile.

But some students do resist, and being the formalist I am, I've constructed a little taxonomy of modes of resisting theory. This by definition omits the more heartening student types such as the Enthusiastic Convert, the Diligent Scholar, the Open-Minded Agnostic, the Passionate Specialist and so on. In making this list of 'Resistors', I intend the term ironically, for the trope of resistance is too often an easy professional option that protects us from having to think about and develop strategies around the impact of theory on the lives of those whom we teach.

153

I will return to this below, but before embarking on a quick list of the 'Why-Bothers?' Humanities academics might encounter in the course of duty, I'd like to note that resistance is not the only problem – programmatic uptake is another, when we see theory degenerate into something that I would consider to be both bad intellect and false morals. At its best, theory provides nuanced and insightful ways of understanding the world. At its worst, however, theory is taught (or learnt) as a catechism, a set of repeated and repeatable moral precepts that add up to a corpus of predictable banalities (binaries are bad; subversion is good; singularity is bad; diversity is good; rationality is bad; radicality is good; everything is (sigh) a 'cultural construction'). This is theory – the provoker of questions, the opener of minds – turned into its opposite – a mode of preventing thought. My focus here is not on this impoverished version of theory, however, but on the question of student resistance.

Why Bothers I have Met

The Ideologue's Why-Bother   I met this in a course I taught on Consumer Culture, with a Christian student who repeatedly met any of the theoretical discussions with 'But we don't live in an ideologically perfect world'. The ideologue's why-bother can come from *within* theory as well as from outside it, since it can be the tactic of anyone who deals with fluidity and multiplicity by finding their truth and hanging on to it – the hard-core Deleuzian, the person who can understand the world *only* through Foucault, or Dworkin, or whoever.

The Existential Why-Bother   All this is untrue, so why bother with it? It's all just opinions.

The Complacent or Threatened Why-Bother   If I go along with this, I'll have to change myself and my world.

The Despairing Why-Bother   Why bother? It won't change the world. This 'you're-pissing-into-the-wind' why-bother can come from despairing greenies, Marxists, feminists, postcolonialists...

The Overloaded Why-Bother   Stop it. I don't want to know anything more. Possibly a Lazy Why-Bother, but the subject is equally likely to be suffering from Issues Fatigue (see below), in which case it may be a subcategory of the Despairing Why-Bother.

The Pragmatic Why-Bother   Why bother? It's not in the exam.

The Utilitarian Why Bother Why bother? It won't get you a job. If you successfully diagnose this as a Lazy Why-Bother, perhaps they simply need to work harder. Geoffrey Bennington's definition of theory as thinking hard comes to mind here (1999: 105).

The Dilettantish Why-Bother Don't worry, if you miss this theorist there'll be another one along in a minute. Possibly a product of transdisciplinary overload and/or curriculum design flaws.

A colleague also suggested a genre of resistance that he called 'generic anti-extremism', which he defines as when students say things like 'Feminism is OK, but I think it has gone too far'.

All in all, though, I think the trope of student resistance all too often masks our own resistance to thinking more about why some students don't want to hear what we have to say. Like many accusations of false consciousness, it itself proceeds from weariness or despair. Perhaps we could ask, rather, whether student resistance to theory is:

1. Resistance to (or lack of familiarity with) abstract thought per se, that is, lack of familiarity with the *kinds* of thinking that will be required of them. Many Australian students, studying no philosophy at high school, reach university unused to critical or analytical thinking itself, which they may experience as a baffling or unwelcome intrusion into their everyday pleasures. There is probably no Humanities teacher reading this who hasn't come across a student who is unwilling to analyse some text, whether it be a Jane Austen novel or an episode of *The Simpsons*, because they experience analysis as a form of robbery of unselfconscious pleasure.
2. Resistance to working hard. Note, too, that we usually teach theory as a mode of *reading*. (The teaching of theory can of course be enhanced using visual aids, but can theory itself be visual?)
3. Fear of falling: Lippard's definition of theory as 'questioning everything about everything' (1999: x) may not be, for everyone, an inviting prospect.
4. Resistance to the ideologies structured in to particular theories. We may think the ideological content of our courses is obvious and that students choose accordingly, but it need not be, as my colleagues and I discovered each year when reading the student evaluations of first-year Gender Studies subjects and repeatedly finding the recriminatory comment 'Contained too much feminism'.
5. Resistance to being overwhelmed. Some students may suffer from what a colleague of mine calls 'issues fatigue'. Our undergraduates are among the first who've grown up with issues-based, social problem-based, thematic teaching from the primary school curriculum onwards, as well as having had the dubious benefit of knowing more about world problems than most of the people who have ever inhabited the globe. Perhaps resistance is the best available

psychological strategy in the face of an all-pervasive incitement to care.

6. Resistance to having their ideas undone. As teachers, we rarely discuss the ethics of undoing religious and cultural belief systems, perhaps because of a lack of time and energy, a suspicion of pastoral discourses, or an impatience with political positions other than our own. I myself have taken great care to warn students when we were doing, say, a visualization or relaxation exercise in my course on the body – seeking permission from the class to do something a little 'dangerous', giving students the option to opt out – but I have never warned them that the same subject might give their ideas and beliefs an overhaul. Why is the body something that has to be regarded as dangerous territory, and the mind not?

So far, my discussion of resistance has tended to imply that it comes down to a matter of disposition or personality. I need to correct this by giving a sense of the social and educational context out of which these reflections arose, as it is instructive.

I first devised this rather flippant list of resistive strategies when I was working in a highly transdisciplinary Humanities department, which came to being in the 1990s. This department was a positive product of the intellectual tumult that followed the advent of theory, the birth of Cultural Studies, and the expansion of the Australian tertiary sector. Because of its newness it enjoyed[10] the rare privilege of escaping deep ideological division, having been formed entirely on the premise of the joys of both theory and transdisciplinarity. Eclectic and quirky in nature, it encouraged a theoretical hybridity that went beyond the interdisciplinarity even of Cultural Studies and that was, for me, a delight. It was located in a university in which the greatest proportion of the students came from non-English speaking backgrounds. They came from a range of cultural backgrounds, and from across the social spectrum. A large proportion appeared to hold religious or spiritual beliefs, including significant cohorts both of Muslims and of fundamentalist Christians. Many were the first in their family to go to university. Most were engaged in substantial amounts of part-time work (figures of 20 to 30 hours per week from supposedly full-time students were not uncommon), and, given this and the distance of the campus from many of their homes, most students used to stack up their classes onto two to three long days a week and never visit the campus outside of those times. As a consequence, there was not a great deal of campus life, except for the few Humanities students who chose to live in the residential college.

10 I am using the past tense here not only because I no longer work there but also because the department as such no longer exists, having been swallowed up and re-formed several times in a wave of institutional restructure that typified Australian universities in the late twentieth century.

These days, as I noted at the start of this book, I teach at a 'gargoyled' university – a prestigious, well-resourced university whose students come overwhelmingly from privileged backgrounds. The university is taking action to redress the social imbalance, but in the meantime, the demographic is still predominantly a privileged one. In this new context, I still encounter student resistance to critical theory, but far less.

The discrepancy between my fairly frequent experience of student resistance at a newer university with a diverse student base and my less frequent encounters with it at my current university signals more than just the march of time – the normalization of theory through its influence over the last decade on the national schooling curriculum – though that is one factor. It also has the potential to teach us a lot about social class, knowledge mastery and social and cultural capital – in particular, the differential social impact of the way we teach critical theory.

At first glance it is a seeming paradox that it should be the privileged students (whose social power, one might imagine, Cultural Studies is interested in unmasking) who are happy enough to see hegemonic values called into question while those with less social and cultural capital were more resistant. This paradox draws our attention to the role that socio-economic factors (social class, economic wellbeing, career prospects and so on) play in intellectual life. Someone with a secure economic base and social position may have a greater buffer against intellectual and existential upheaval than someone in a socially more precarious position. Some people, to recall Lingis's claim about 'deciding' to believe one's joy, are better placed to do so than others.

Second, the disparity in student reaction points to certain contradictions and dilemmas about the transition from a Humanities education based on the mastery of a canon of knowledge to one centralizing the acquisition of skills, especially critical thinking skills – what Karl Maton calls a shift from 'knowledge codes' to 'knower codes' (2009: 46). While on the one hand this newer mode affords the possibility of experiences of recognition, community and hope to those from disadvantaged or minority backgrounds, it also potentially robs them of the ability to acquire a body of knowledge that might accord them greater social, cultural and even economic capital than they currently have. Barry Kanpol (1998) identifies this as one of the core dilemmas for teachers within the critical pedagogy mode: how can they simultaneously teach students to be 'critical citizens' while nonetheless opening up concrete economic and career options for them? The Marxist feminist Judith Williamson (1986) made a not dissimilar argument some decades ago, at the point when Cultural Studies was consolidating its position in the academy and a celebratory approach to popular culture was beginning to displace not only the liberal humanist canon but also a traditional Marxist feminist ideological critique of popular culture. She was concerned about the effects that an over-emphasis on the delights of popular culture might have on working-class and minority students' access to the cultural capital associated with familiarity with the literary canon. This was, for her, more than just a political matter (robbing working-class students of hegemonic knowledge at precisely the moment when they were entering the academy in greater numbers), but also a question of intellectual and personal impoverishment – the loss of access to cultural products that have the potential to be life-changing and life-enriching: 'I can't say this too strongly, people's lives are transformed by the discovery of radical ideas, and it is a terrible abdication on the part of the left if we cannot continue to develop these (14). These radical ideas can, she claimed, come equally well from 'high' culture and from critical theory, but not from the vacuous forms of theory that characterized the high point of Cultural Studies' celebration of the popular in the latter decades of the twentieth century. Depending on how truly critical it is, 'theory', then, might offer community, but it might also invite too much upheaval and proffer insufficient psychological, cultural or social compensation in return.

I remember with some pain an incident where the personally confronting nature of theory for those with little social capital was made all too obvious to me. I was called on at very short notice to take the first class of a further education course for mature women hoping to re-enter the workforce after a period of absence. The notice was so short that all I thought to do was arrive with my standard feminist kit-bag (the magazines plus images-of-women approach). One woman who had had a hard life and knew more about gender issues lived on the pulse than I ever will found the discussion, which I thought was the simplest introduction to feminism, deeply upsetting and she never returned. She didn't want critique; she wanted something that would take her somewhere different.

This was a devastating example of the emotional potency of 'Theory' and of the ill-effects of wielding it naïvely or inexpertly. For this woman was exactly the kind of person feminist theory and politics traditionally aims to engage and indeed help. Yet one poorly framed encounter with it was enough to stop this already disenfranchised woman in her tracks – or at least, that particular track.

It is precisely this disruptive potential that, I believe, means we must think carefully about what it means to change the inner worlds of those we see in our classrooms each week. I hope it's obvious that I'm not saying we shouldn't challenge students or make them uncomfortable – that's surely what universities are for. Rather, I'm saying that for ethical, intellectual and indeed political reasons it's worth putting some thought into what our current intellectual and institutional contexts might mean for the ways in which this can be done. This means thinking about critical theory not only as a set of ideas and propositions, but also as a set of encounters, including in the classroom.

Hope in the Classroom: From Ethos to Pedagogy

'Rage and hope' is the title of one critical pedagogy website (Williams 2004). But what does this mean *in the classroom*? How do we think and 'do' rage and hope together, and how do we bridge the gap between hope as a general ethos and hopeful (or hope-producing) teaching as a set of classroom strategies and practices? It starts, before we even enter the classroom, with curriculum structure and design.

Curriculum Design in the Pluralist Context

Although some forms of social theory might seem to give greater scope for hope than others, the possibility for hope nonetheless depends in part on the context of the encounter. Ideas do not occur in a vacuum, and how we as teachers shape, pattern and organize them has a big impact on how students process them. As teachers, we need to consider the psychological and intellectual impact of the ways we *structure* students' encounters with theory. This is especially pressing in those universities in which academics' right to determine the sequencing and structuring of ideas has been diminished by degree rules that encourage a more and more random, unsequenced and uncontextualized encounter with life-changing ideas.

The big-picture changes discussed in Chapter 1 have given rise to a variety of fragmented structures and processes, including (and here I reduce vast changes to a representative list): the multiplication of modes of teaching (e.g. off-campus, intensives, summer school, web-based teaching; individual study contracts; video conferencing); the rise of cross-servicing within and between universities; the large-scale abandonment of pre-requisites (in Australia); the opening up of subject choice and a consequent inability to regulate student pathways through a degree; and the contraction of face to face hours (e.g. via the shortening of semesters, the rise in flexible delivery modes and the cutting of tutorial times). All of this results in a fragmentation of the student community, a diversification of student pathways, and a reduction in control over the combination and sequencing of subjects. Moreover, the student base itself is changing as it grows, diversifies and internationalizes. Expansion (of institutions, of courses, student numbers) meets contraction (of time, hours, staff and money). Such are the material and psychological conditions in which we and our students 'do theory'.

This institutional fragmentation coincides with, responds to, and exacerbates the pluralism that dominates the intellectual landscape today. Pluralism is a value within much contemporary critical theory in the Humanities, and it is also an oft-touted solution to the problem of the multiplicity of theories and of possible ways of teaching them. To the question of why we should teach theory and which theories we should teach, we all too often find ourselves responding that we want to offer diversity, to give our students a range of ways of seeing the world, to offer choice. 'Create your own degree' was the marketing slogan of one transdisciplinary Australian Humanities department some years ago. But there is something of the knee-jerk about this (to say nothing of the para-consumerism of celebrating 'choice'). In any case, pluralism itself is not singular – it takes different shapes in different contexts – and its intellectual, structural, and affective dimensions need to be considered.

So too, the ideological effects of pluralism are not simple. Crucially, it is pluralism itself that is the problem for many of our students. According to Raymond Williams (1988), the dominant modern understanding of the term 'theory' is as the opposite of something proven; in other words, the idea of theory encompasses the possibility of its own untruth. If a theory is, according to this definition, neither true nor provable, and if there any many competing theories, then some students find themselves wondering who will tell them the 'truth', or why they should study so many 'untruths'. For some students, the problem with Theory is that it alerts them to problems without solutions.

Plurality, diversity and multiplicity are not ideologically neutral precepts and we shouldn't offer them up as such, as can happen in quite subtle ways when they are structured in as core metaphors or base assumptions of a given theory. To take one example, Terry Eagleton has critiqued 'diversity' as the unquestioned moral good at the base of postmodern and postcolonial theory:

> Historically speaking, there has been a rich diversity of cultures of torture, but even devout pluralists would be loath to affirm this as one more instance of the colourful tapestry of human experience. Those who regard plurality as a value in itself are pure formalists, and have obviously not noticed the astonishingly imaginative variety of forms which, say, racism can assume. (2000: 15)

Seumas Miller has argued something similar, writing from a position hostile to post-structuralism. He is vehemently critical of what he believes to be 'postmodernists" uncritical assumption that 'cultural relativism implies tolerance of others cultures' (1995: 57). 'Nothing could be further from the truth', he asserts. I would want to say, more moderately, that relativism sometimes can promote tolerance, but that it can also produce the opposite, for example in right-wing historical revisionism.

Even if pluralism weren't a value in itself of many of the theories that we in Gender and Cultural Studies teach, it is in any case structured into the curriculum via the kinds of fragmentation, multiplication and contraction described above. Given the current institutional imperatives towards 'openness', 'diversity' and 'flexibility', our students are likely to encounter a pluralism that is casual or accidental as well as programmatic or ideological. It is not only a matter of the diversity of assumptions and approaches likely to be found in any one department (essentialists teaching alongside post-structuralists; humanists alongside postmodernists). Nor of course is there anything wrong with a student encountering dissension, difference and diversity. Rather, my concern is that there is often structurally no forum in which such differences can be even recognized and articulated, let alone considered and debated. In Australia at least, our teaching arrangements all too often mean that subjects are almost inevitably separated from each other, and insufficiently sequenced; it is no accident that they're now often called 'units' rather than subjects. In many programme structures there is less and less of a core to hold things together and in any case, the student cohort itself is likely to be fragmented – wandering tourist-like from discipline to discipline. In the Australian context this is often actively encouraged. In many Australian universities, pre-requisites have been drastically reduced and occasionally eradicated, and students can do much of their study outside their home department.[11] This latter innovation has much to recommend it, but what will hold the increasingly disparate little blocks of knowledge together, or, rather, what will be the forum that will allow students to see, name and debate these differences? What will give ideas shape and pattern? For I think the shape, pattern and structure in which we encounter ideas can have as much impact as 'content' itself.

Consider two contrasting hypotheticals. A student might encounter depressing material in a systematic, coherent and focused way and leave with a positive feeling (e.g. of familiarity, control or mastery over a body of knowledge). On the other hand, a student might encounter a whole raft of cheerful matter in a more random and unfocused way and may leave a course with an uneasy sense that something is missing; they may lack a sense of history, or of discipline, to hold wheeling ideas together. Whether or not this is unsettling depends, of course, on an individual student's desire for systematicity and order, and the extent to which they even recognize the disjunctions. These hypothetical examples illustrate a dual point about the infamous opposition between form and content: firstly, that the two can't neatly be separated, and that form may act as a kind of content in itself; and secondly, that form and content can sometimes be in tension with each other.

A real-life example suggests just how painful the consequences of this structural fragmentation can be. Many years ago, a young man came up to me at the end of a first-year lecture on postmodern approaches to selfhood and said, with some distress, 'But I don't understand. Everyone has a self, don't they?'

---

11 At one university at which I taught there was a time when *all* pre-requisites in the Humanities were to be disallowed, since they hindered student 'freedom of choice'. The only exceptions allowed were, bizarrely, ones where an Occupational Health and Safety case could be made for them and, grudgingly, in the learning of languages.

Perhaps I had given a particularly confused lecture. But I think too that he himself was in confusion, and the last thing he needed was the kind of intervention I was offering him. Subsequent weeks proved that he was indeed struggling to hold his own in turbulent psychological waters. When he dropped out of the course later that semester, I hoped he would find something that worked for him – that he would go away and forget the half-truths he had taken from us.

Ideas, I soon realized, are dangerous and need to be handled with care. This young man might perhaps have been helped to a clearer view on what it means to be a self had he come across that same lecture within the context of a more carefully structured sequence of ideas, or within a smaller tutorial group, where his concerns could have been discussed better. Subversive ideas are like antibiotics – you need to take the entire course, otherwise you might breed something even worse than what you started off with.

Gerald Graff recognized the problem when he wrote of the laissez-faire nature of the pluralism that characterizes North American Humanities departments. He questioned the effectiveness of what he calls the 'privatized classroom' in an era of great heterogeneity within Humanities departments (1994: 27). That is, he wondered whether 'an accessible picture of the humanities can emerge for students' (27) when universities are characterized by theoretical dissent. Graff celebrates the radical plurality of contemporary Humanities, but he's concerned about the pedagogical and political effects of a laissez-faire pluralism that can result from a compartmentalized approach to such differences. He argues that we should try to structure 'the latent connections between courses and discourses' (27).

In those universities governed by the 'free-range' ethos, however, this is very difficult. Even so, we can think about the different ways we might organize the teaching of contemporary critical theory within any given subject.

A Taxonomy of Possible Ways of Teaching 'Theory'

Within this institutional context of diversity, fragmentation and abundant choice, students of critical theory encounter a relativistic and pluralist intellectual universe. How do we guide them through it? The following taxonomy is intended as a fairly ad hoc sampling of some of the ways in which Gender and Cultural Studies academics can 'do theory' with our students. I offer this brief and informal list because it is one way to make visible the fact that the choices we make in designing curricula have political, affective and ethical effects as well as intellectual ones.

1. Theory or theorists as an object of study: In this mode a theorist or a body of theory is studied in a systematic, detailed, and contextualized way e.g. a

study of Freud, Lacan, Derrida, feminist psychoanalysis, postcolonial theory. This is theory conceived of as a body of knowledge in which one can gain a specialization.

2. Theory as a form of intellectual history: Again, this sees theory as a body of knowledge worthy of study in its own right. A subcategory of this is an argument about cultural literacy. That is, if one wants to be a conceptually literate member of our current society, then you *should* know, say, Foucault, Derrida or Butler. The difficulty here is not so much the underlying claim (it's hard to argue that a Humanities graduate *shouldn't* be familiar with such thinkers) as a pragmatic difficulty. How does one structure a curriculum around such key figures? This includes not only the banal but important question of who gets taught and who gets left out, but also, more deeply of how and why they get taught. This mode need not, by the way, constitute a return to the Great Men version of history; it could be organized around themes, discourses, problematics or the historical development of conceptual categories. The argument for theory as a form of history may take the form of a debate around a theoretical canon, oddly similar to the one about a cultural canon made by Allan Bloom in *The Closing of the American Mind* (1987), in which he laments the decline of a shared knowledge base.[12]

3. The next mode of doing theory is one I call the toolbox mode, in which theories are valued for what they allow you to *do*. Or, to switch metaphors, theories are like different pairs of glasses that you can pick up and put down and that allow you to see the world differently each time.

4. Theory can also be taught and practised in a methodological vein – as something to be 'applied' as a method, a technique or perhaps even a 'style'. Some might object that this is like theming a restaurant or picking a colour scheme for a house ('Will I go for the Deleuzian look this summer, or something lighter?'. 'Surely not Baudrillard, he's *so* twentieth century'.) Applied theory can easily become either faddish or programmatic. McQuillan et al., editors of the *Post-Theory* collection, are critical of what they call 'Theory as sausage machine, pouring texts in at one end, producing 'new' readings at the other' (1999: x). The

---

12 I think Bloom is actually a little less conservative than he is given credit for. While it's undoubtedly the case that he values the canonical Western tradition for its own sake, his argument is nonetheless couched in rather more relativistic terms. He is making an argument not (only) about the intrinsic merits of the canon, but also about the social importance of sharing a language and a body of knowledge per se. If we want to understand each other and communicate, he argues, then we need a common currency. Of course, he's fighting a losing battle against the diversifying and fragmenting forces of globalization and postmodernity, but there is still an argument to be made about coherence and internal consistency within the circumscribed context of a given university curriculum.

fact that theory can challenge dominant traditions, they say, does not mean that Theory should be applied universally and mechanistically as a set of techniques, procedures and operators to every book ever written, exposing them one by one as vile inscriptions of reactionary western logomachy. (1999: x)

5. Theory can also, of course, be something we believe in as true (a possibility I am canvassing alarmingly late in my taxonomy). Everyone's list of True Theorists will of course be different (mine includes bits of Michel Foucault, Norbert Elias, Maurice Merleau-Ponty...). These Correct Thinkers should not be confused with the writers of incredibly useful fictions, like Freud.

6. Theory can be taught in explicit and overt alignment with a particular politics, such as indigenous studies, post-colonialism or queer.

7. Theory as thematics: theory can be used as a means to open up discussion of social problems or concepts. Accurate understanding of the theorist in question is, in this mode, a bonus, since theory is a means to an end.

8. As an intellectual exercise – 'skills' training. Theory can be used to help students learn consistency, internal logic, exemplification, close reading, abstract thought or rhetorical skills.

We can group these approaches. At one end of the scale, theory is a specialist enterprise – an end in itself, where accuracy and subtlety matter. Around the middle, theory is a means to various ends – the development of the student as, for example, a political subject, or an autonomous questioning individual. Its aim is to open up dialogue about society, and if it does this effectively, it doesn't matter too much if the students' understanding of any given theory is less than accurate or lacks sophistication. Finally, there is the 'skills' approach, which may be related to the goals of subject formation, but can also be rather more formalistic in nature. Across these approaches, we might see ourselves as training students for the academy, for politics, for democracy, for literacy, or for employment. We thus implicitly offer our students a potential subject position to occupy.

As I noted earlier, though, teaching academics often have little control over the rules and regulations that govern student progression at their university. Those with continuing contracts do, however, have considerable power to adjust the curriculum within a department or a subject, though casual staff may find themselves teaching curricula in whose design they have had very little say. But for all teachers the classroom remains an important scene for the staging of encounters with radical or disruptive ideas.

Classroom Practice

The way we stage encounters with challenging ideas will differ between disciplines. One starting point in the Gender and Cultural Studies classroom is to think carefully about being programmatic – willfully or accidentally implying that particular theories give a correct view of the world, that particular politics or approaches provide the best solutions to social problems, or that all students share the same political views. This might seem a redundant or even strange suggestion when Gender and Cultural Studies is, after all, so overt about its politics, and when one of its key approaches is to reveal and critique the hidden politics of *other* discourses. Yet, in an overtly politicized discipline it is easy to slip into the assumption that your students share your politics (or *should* share them). It is easy to teach Gender and Cultural Studies as though certain assumptions, values and goals are self-evident. Not only is this unlikely to be sufficient to the full range of students' views and expectations, it is also a reduction of the critical pedagogy aim of promoting a vibrant democracy where difference is respected and debate robust. Put simply, students hate being preached to.

Similarly, teachers in Gender and Cultural Studies shouldn't assume a secular society nor a student cohort made up of agnostics or atheists (this is no doubt self-evident in the US, which has a greater comfort with public displays of religiosity than is the case in Australia). Of course, this ought to go without saying in any multicultural society, but all too often in the Australian Gender and Cultural Studies classroom the secular is assumed as either a social reality or a social goal. This risks alienating whole cohorts of students, including those of minority backgrounds for whom religion might be a crucial part of individual and cultural identity.

We can go further than simply acknowledging differences in students' values and beliefs, and overtly discuss with them the transformative nature of the pedagogy in which we are engaged, including the process of values questioning and reconstitution this almost inevitably entails. It is more honest and more ethical to thematize the process of values breakdown and reconstitution than to assume it as a necessary but unspoken trial of university life. Discussions about why people believe certain things – what comforts, privileges, solace or power they gain from their beliefs – not only give students places of refuge, they also help them understand the affective, ethical and political dimensions of knowledge production.

Such conversations prevent us from consigning contradictions, differences, ambiguities and ambivalences in beliefs and values to the realm of the tacit. Such tacit pedagogies risk producing an invisible division between 'insider' students who can happily agree and identify with the theories being taught and a group of people who are pulled emotionally or intellectually in other directions but who may well feel themselves to be isolated in their uncertainty or resistance, since it is never available for public conversation. This, to me, is an alienating pedagogy that tacitly assumes a 'correct' way of seeing the world and hence an implied ideal student. It is inadequate to the diversity of actual student belief and, in its reliance on an unspoken fiction of shared belief, fundamentally unethical.

It is all very well to say that differences must be acknowledged and respected, but this is not easy to combine with critical theory which is, after all, driven by ideologies and political goals. How to be at once critical and compassionate without descending into a vacuous pluralism that stands for nothing either morally or intellectually is a real problem. Christopher Lasch, for one, abhorred the 'quasi-therapeutic subjectivism of the "I'm okay, you're okay", variety', seeing it as a 'cop-out' (Elshtain 1999: 541). How can we teach critical theory openly and generously without copping out this way?

In schools, the approach known as 'values clarification' was one attempt to develop a classroom practice out of the emerging problem of moral, ethical and cultural pluralism. This approach, which emerged in the 1970s, was still popular in Australia when I was doing my teacher training in the mid-1980s. The idea was that rather than inculcating a particular moral code, or teaching a particular ethical framework, the teacher's role was to help the student 'clarify' his or her own values. This was a recognition of diversity but it sidestepped the question of the social dimensions of morality – be that society's need to arrive at some shared moral code on certain questions or the very real social impacts of particular moral and ethical choices. It was, essentially, an egalitarian and individual 'solution' to the problem of diversity – a formalist one, in that it replaced moral content (particular precepts, claims or presumptions) with the goal of developing a set of reasoning skills and logical attributes, such as analytical capacity, self-consistency and self-knowledge. But, as any good dictator knows, self-understanding and self-consistency do not a virtuous person make; most dictators know pretty much what they are doing, and are pretty consistent about it.

Values clarification was limited, intellectually, by the tensions in the philosophical schema on which it was, in part, based – Lawrence Kohlberg's (1973) scale of moral reasoning. As many readers will no doubt remember, the psychologist Kohlberg drew on the developmental models of Jean Piaget to create a scale that aimed to evaluate not the moral content of any decision or attitude but the level of moral reasoning that goes into producing it. Kohlberg's schema was itself, inevitably, value-laden: it was, after all, a scale. At the bottom was moral reasoning aimed at the avoidance of punishment, and at the top a set of consciously chosen universal ethical principles. This highest level of 'Postconventional, autonomous, or principled' moral reasoning (632) attempted to bridge a number of tensions – for example between ethics and morals; moral choice and moral imperatives; and individual rights and human rights – through an appeal to transcendent values which, though they were not 'concrete moral rules like the Ten Commandments' (623), were understood as 'universal principles':

At heart, these are universal principles of justice, of the *reciprocity* and *equality* of human *rights*, and of respect for the dignity of human beings as *individual persons*. (1973: 632, original emphases)

Kohlberg, then, was explicit about the value-ladenness of his scale, and of its potential as a tool not only to analyse but to *evaluate* and *judge* moral reasoning.

In the uptake of his schema into values clarification programmes, however, the tension between promoting individual moral choice and encouraging responsible choices was evident. The strain between individualism and collectivism in the Kohlberg model was reflected in the dual role of the state education system as the instrument charged both with the development of autonomous individuals and the construction of functional citizens. Students were to be encouraged to 'make their choices freely' (Howe and Howe 1975: 29), but such choices were to be made '*after carefully weighing the consequences of each alternative*' (1975: 29, original emphasis). The assumption seemed to be that greater self-awareness brings greater moral responsibility.

The limitations of the values clarification approach in the classroom were made evident to me during my second-ever block of practice teaching, where its failings emerged as a concrete pedagogical problem. I was to take over a class of junior high school students for a four week period, teaching them English. When their class teacher briefed me, she drew my attention to a male student who was, she said, bright but troubled. At the very end of my practice teaching block, the students had to write something about their leisure activities. I forget the details now, but I have not forgotten sitting at the dining table of my suburban family home, a white, middle-class woman in her twenties, marking their final assignment, and encountering the piece of work this young man handed in. In it, he recounted in some detail his favoured regular weekend activity – going out and finding someone to bash. Of course, this confession may not have been true. It was – just possibly – a cry for help, but as he had a warm, perceptive and experienced classroom teacher I think this unlikely, as he was not without sources of help. Rather, he was, I believed, jibing and testing me, aiming, I assume, to jolt me out of my middle-class complacency and idealism with a dose of realism, if not reality.

I didn't know how to respond. Had I been his permanent teacher no doubt I would have been prompted to take some action, but as a soon-to-be-departing novice teacher my job was, simply, to give this piece of work a mark. After pondering the problem, in the end, with a sigh, I assessed it technically – grading it on its internal consistency of argumentation, written expression and grammar, my matter-of-fact comments making no reference to the heart of the matter. I had refused to take the bait, but nor had I done anything useful. This was a cop-out of the kind abhorred by Lasch, an example of a 'strange suspension of specific moments of judgment' (Elshtain 1999: 541).

I describe this piece of ancient history because it is the counterpoint to the alienating pedagogy described above. The refusal to pass judgement and the pretence that there are no different judgements are two sides of the same coin.

Some lessons take a lifetime. Some decades after these events, two principles now emerge for me from the painful moments of non-connection mentioned throughout this chapter. The first is a reminder that pedagogy is, ultimately, a set of relationships. In the case of the school student, I suspended judgement and marked technically not because I had no idea how to do it more meaningfully, but because I had no *context* in which to do it more meaningfully. I was a practice teacher, there for a few weeks only, and as such had no enduring pedagogical relationship with the student through which I could have opened up these difficult questions. Thinking about these events all this time later leads me to connect it with my current concern about the impacts of fragmented curriculum structures and massification on the quality of pedagogical relationships in the Humanities in universities today. Large student cohorts and fragmented attendance and curriculum structures have the potential to undermine the element of relationship in the classroom, both between teacher and students and between students themselves, who often do not even know each other's name by the end of the semester. As I noted in Chapter 1, the tutorials I experienced as an undergraduate – eight people in the lecturer's office for a whole year – have been replaced by 12 lessons spent in a formal classroom with up to 25 others. Clearly, classroom pedagogy in the age of massification and fragmentation has to work hard to develop the kinds of relationships that might encourage sensitive discussion of psychological, emotional and ethical issues.

The second reflection that emerges for me out of the inadequacy of pluralism and relativism is that in the critical Humanities we have to explicitly address the impacts of the theories we teach. We are good at doing this when it comes to the philosophical, social or political impacts of particular bodies of thought. But we are, I think, less good at integrating this examination of impact with discussion about the individual emotional and psychological ramifications of different bodies of thought.

I don't think I've learnt how to do this systematically. My experiment in teaching Gender and Cultural Studies without either preaching it or diluting it into vapidity remains a work in progress. But I have spent a decade or more blundering around these issues, led by the heart rather than by a systematically elaborated pedagogical formula. Or, to put it less romantically, I have been led by worry and concern – sometimes triggered by particular incidents, at other times by a more pervasive sense that something was not right.

To give an example: in teaching a course on embodiment, I might at one time have focused on the intellectual dimensions of, say, deconstructive accounts of the relationship between mind and body. Now I tend to accompany these intellectual manouevres with a consideration not just of their philosophical or even political ramifications, but also their potential personal ones. For example, when opening a course about the body with a critique of Cartesianism, I cannot teach the problem of mind-body dualism simply as some philosophical history, let alone outlining some true and correct way of conceiving mind-body relations, nor even push one particular formulation as being the obviously politically progressive way forward. Instead, I open it out as a problem not only of epistemology but also of ontology. When my students and I pick apart received ideas about the body (e.g. 'it's not who you are on the outside that counts, it's who you are on the inside'), we do so not only for what they might reveal about traditional conceptions of interiority and exteriority, nor only for the different political pulls and pushes of theories of embodiment. We also try to address the affective dimensions of these philosophical and political questions – why some of us might be strongly pulled by an idea of the body as the home of our identity and others not. In so doing, I hope to offer a version of pluralism that isn't reducible to a banal idea of 'choice', but that tries to intertwine the political, the emotional and the philosophical and to exemplify the complexity of belief.

What has all this got to do with hope? Well, I return to Zournazi's (2002) conception of hopeful exchanges as those that are conducted in a spirit of openness and generosity but which permit disagreement. This is, to my mind, what one approach to a hopeful pedagogy of critical theory might mean – not that everyone agrees, nor that we as teachers think we know the answer, but that difficulties are allowed to be spoken. More than this – if we want to avoid the moral and intellectual vacuousness of simplistic pluralism, difficulties sometimes have to be spoken. How to unsettle programmatic disciplinary assumptions while still allowing a sense of disciplinary belonging and mastery is, of course, a tricky question. We can't, in the name of psychological and emotional security, fail to give students a body of knowledge through a disciplinary orientation; otherwise we deny them a sense of secure and relatively bounded accomplishment.

Patricia White's (1996) discussion of hope proceeds from the assumption that hope itself is not unitary. I thought of ending on this typically theoretically playful note, by concluding that it is pluralism itself that needs pluralizing, that to solve the pluralists' malaise we need to pluralize hope. But really, I mean something rather more simple. I imagine hopeful teaching as a practice that helps students experience hope not as a set of beliefs, nor even necessarily as an optimistic frame of mind, but as an embodied intertwining of private and social hopes. This happens not by diluting our discussions of social problems or by seeking a cheery theory, but when our curricula are structured in such a way as to allow students to adequately name not only the social problems discussed within theory but also the private problems posed by theory itself (i.e. to articulate their despair, the sense of loss, or the ideals that they feel are being threatened by a given theory, or to discuss the contradictions that arise between their different subjects). This kind of hopeful teaching can occur only when we as teachers become aware of the tacit pedagogies we embody in our conversations, our silences, our ideas and our relations with others.

We know that critical theory isn't the opposite of practice but a form of practice (Martin 1996: 16). That's why it matters how we do it. It's the fact that theory matters, that theory does have effects on our students, that makes it worth the effort to find the curricular structures and pedagogical strategies that will do justice both to it and to them. If hope is, as Paulo Freire claims, 'an ontological need' (1994 [1992]: 8), then there can be no valid pedagogy without it.

CHAPTER 4

The Idleness of Academics: Hopeful Reflections on the Usefulness of Cultural Studies

Introduction

This hopeful chapter on the usefulness of Cultural Studies opens, perversely, with three rather discouraging stories, in the form of an evasion, an accusation and an insult.

The Evasion: As all academics know, at least two rituals can accompany the successful completion of a PhD, and the newly qualified must choose whether or not to participate in them: in some countries, the graduation ceremony, and in most countries, the changing of the name on one's credit card to 'Dr'. When my time came I participated in both rituals, and as a result of the latter I used to occasionally have shopkeepers ask me, rhetorically I presume, whether I was a doctor. 'Yes, but not the useful kind', was my stock reply for some time until I belatedly realized how unhelpful to the broader cause this escape route was.

The Accusation: was made on the occasion of my very first foray into ethnographic fieldwork. Armed with a kit bag of tape recorder, question sheet and university ethics approval number, I visited a beach as part of a study of nudism in Australia. Aware of the sensitivities of nudists with regard to privacy, I left this kit bag behind and approached a nearby group for a preliminary sounding out, to see if they might be willing to participate. An informal conversation began. One man was particularly forthcoming. He began a lengthy digression about a seagull he'd seen walking on the beach with an arrow stuck through its neck. My expression of wincing sympathy obviously sent the wrong signal; he stopped his story, and asked me abruptly whether I listened to the popular radio broadcaster John Laws. Forced to confess that I didn't, I was immediately denounced as a useless do-gooder. 'I mean, if you were coming up with a new formula for this', he said, holding up a bottle of sunscreen, 'then it might be some good to me'. A series of other angry accusations followed, and I beat a polite if shaken retreat back to lick my wounds and re-read my ethics application. I was comforted by my middle-class friends, who shared my understanding of the utility of intellectual work, and by the thought that this incident could be recuperated as a 'Useful Learning Experience'. That this accusation of uselessness should have been thrown at me and my kind on the occasion of my very first step away from the (evidently useless) textualism of my earlier Cultural Studies work towards the (patently useful) method of ethnography did add insult to injury. This, however, isn't the insult I promised, for I've been saving the best for last.

The Insult: The crowning insult came in 2000 from the then Prime Minister, John Howard, on the occasion of the re-launch of the conservative literary and cultural journal *Quadrant*:

> Perhaps the intellectual divide ... in our community now is not so much between so-called elite opinion and popular opinion, but between political correctness and common sense. Now, some may regard that as an unduly provocative remark; but I think one of the great roles of *Quadrant* has been its questioning of political correctness. And when I reflect, as probably many in this audience will do, on the idleness of so many in academia and, despite some notable and well-known exceptions, on the shameful assault on the reputation of [the conservative historian] Geoffrey Blainey that occurred during the 1980s and the early 1990s, you will have in mind the sorts of things that I think are relevant to the role of *Quadrant*. (Howard, Hayden and Shaw 2000: 2)

There is something very Australian about these three stories: the self-deprecating humour of my own response; the ferocity of the popular condemnation of 'elites'; and the condemnation of academics' role in battles over national identity. Each story touches on a set of tropes that are a recognizable part of Australian public life, as Benjamin Glasson's (2012) essay on anti-intellectualism in Australian newspapers makes clear. Glasson identifies four principal themes (and four corresponding ideas of the intellectual) in Australian newspapers in the late twentieth and early twenty-first centuries. The first theme is elitism and privilege (with a corresponding figure of the 'elite intellectual' [103]). The second is the idea that by dint of being an intellectual, someone has, in effect, 'relinquish[ed] their citizenship' (104). They no longer belong to the nation, a nation imagined as comprised of 'ordinary' people who speak the language of 'common sense' that Prime Minister Howard extolled. Glasson calls this intellectual 'denaturalized' (104). The third recurring theme – that expert knowledge cannot be trusted – continues this lauding of common sense: 'Expert opinion is no better, and is often worse, than that of the person in the street' (106). The corresponding figure is that of the 'suspect intellectual' (106). The fourth theme identified by Glasson is that of an intrusive intelligentsia trying to restrict free speech and/or impose its 'nanny state' ideologies on the public: the 'prescriptive intellectual' (107).

In the Australian context, then, a traditional hostility to intellectuals is interwoven into debates about national identity. The term 'elites' is one half of a binary of 'empty signifier[s]' (Glasson 2012: 104) used to create two imaginary polarized groups: elites and 'ordinary Australians'. Left-wing academics are frequently accused of undermining Australian national identity, and even putting Australian national security at risk in the age of terrorism (105). Glasson sees this 'antagonistic discourse of an "enemy within"' as arising from 'the ontological lack at the heart of the discourse of [Australian] national identity' (105).

Whatever the specificities of the Australian context, where the condemnation of elites[1] is not a recent phenomenon but rather a longstanding theme in the establishment of a post-colonial national identity, shifts in the nature of the university and the publics it serves mean that there are now some commonalities with the standing of academics in other nations. Jonathan Rutherford, for example, considers that in the UK, neoliberal and neo-conservative theorists and politicians have expressed 'implacable hostility toward left liberal intellectuals and public sector professionals' (2005: 308). It is probably safe to assume that the compliment is returned.

The intelligentsia are of course buffered better in some nations than in others, but an overall arc is clear: academic standing, along with that of many professions, is in decline. Jürgen Enders notes numerous comparative studies from the late twentieth century all reporting on the 'de-professionalization' of academia (2000: 8–9). This is, as we have seen, part and parcel of the marketization of universities, which requires and entails shifts in both the idea and the social standing of academics. The trust and respect associated with the vocational model give way to the 'coercive' forms of accountability associated with audit culture (Shore and Wright 2004): 'lack of trust in experts or professionals is replaced by trust in systems of accounting and accountability' (Cummins 2002: 109). Intellectual authority has, as Frank Furedi (2003) tersely puts it, been 'downsized'. The attacks on the credibility of climate science are one notable example. Of course, as I noted in Chapter 2, there is a certain irony in the fact that academics themselves have been major players in the larger cultural shifts that have encouraged this critical attitude to authority and a consequent erosion of trust.

As the twentieth century drew to a close, governments enlisted universities as 'partners' in the business of transforming old economies into new, knowledge-driven, economies, which needed 'workers who were autonomous entrepreneurs

---

1 An anti-authoritarian attitude is not new in Australia, but different discourses emerge through which to articulate and shape it. For example, Guy Rundle (in Glasson 2012: 103) notes that the term 'elites' came to Australian political discourse from the US, where it was first used against 'so-called Nixon Democrats' (103).

rather than dependent employees' (Rutherford 2005: 301). In the process, universities were required to transform *themselves* as well – from 'unproductive consumers of public money, into hubs of economic competitiveness and regional development' (301). In the current regime, all levels of the system are required to prove their utility to each other and, ultimately, the nation and its economy: universities must justify their usefulness and efficiency to the nation, staff must justify themselves to their universities, courses of study to the university, particular subjects to their departments, the student union to students and so on.

A call for accountability is a species of veiled accusation. Enders notes the body of research reporting on the increase in public blaming of academics (2000: 9). The European studies he cites describe critiques of the quality of academic work, the training of graduates and the ability of academic work to address the pressing problems of our time (9). In Australia, meanwhile, a nasty little cluster of rather more moralized accusations are able to hide behind the seemingly incontestable call for 'utility'. The first of them is the accusation of laziness. We have already heard what a Prime Minister had to say about 'idleness'; here is an 'ordinary person', contributing to an online debate about the job losses at an Australian university:

> I loved Uni, the lifestyle was just so lazy. The academics were no exception.
> If I had a high paying job, and almost no KPI's, then I would resist any being
> introduced. (Neil 2011)

As we saw in Chapter 2, such clichés bear no relation to the actual working conditions of contemporary academics, where overwork is in fact the more serious danger (Winefield et al. 2003, Jensen and Morgan 2009).

Neil's assertion that academics are answerable to no one voices a second common accusation – that of a lack of accountability. It is true that the intellectual autonomy traditionally enjoyed by academics could mask, or serve as justification for, an unwillingness to submit to the types of tedious protocols or surveillance that typify many workplaces. The transformation of the university into a bureaucratic corporation has largely put paid to that, and there can hardly be any contemporary academics slipping through the audit culture net.[2]

The third accusation is that of privilege. As Glasson notes, the term 'elites' is used by Australian politicians and the media to denounce, often venomously, the luxurious distance academics are perceived to have from the real world, and their consequent lack of empathy with the citizenry (of which the failure

---

2 Burrows notes that it would be 'quite easy to generate a list of over 100 different (nested) measures to which each individual academic in the UK is now (potentially) subject' (2012: 359).

THE IDLENESS OF ACADEMICS

to appreciate John Laws is metonymic).[3] It is of course true that academics have always enjoyed particular types of social, if not financial, privilege. Indeed, Jean Dunbabin sees the development of a sense of insiders and outsiders as characterizing the universities right from their very inception (1999: 41). Although the medieval masters were often very poor, it seems likely that they, and their students, would have been seen by outsiders as 'one privileged community among many' (40) – just another 'confraternity like those of craftsmen, merchants or devotees of a particular saint' (40). Medieval universities enjoyed freedoms, including exemption from local taxation and some degree of legal independence (41). They regarded these privileges as necessary but they were no doubt resented by the local community as unfair and financially burdensome (41). So accusations of parasitism and elitism are not recent, though of course the shape they take today is different. Dunbabin is careful to note, for example, that although 'those who lived cheek-by-jowl with the masters often detested them, they rarely dared to scorn their scholastic pursuits' (46). This is no longer the case.

This brings us to the fourth accusation, that of irrelevance, or uselessness. As we saw in Chapter 1, the powerful discourse of the university and a university education as contributors to the social good was refashioned in the late twentieth century into one of social utility more narrowly conceived, translating into strident calls by politicians for universities and academics to be more 'relevant'. Universities responded to these calls in a myriad of ways – cutting courses, changing pedagogies, strengthening links with industry, and branding themselves according to the new value set, as the slogans of these Australian universities attest: 'A University for the Real World' (Queensland University of Technology); 'Bringing Knowledge to Life' (University of Western Sydney); 'Bringing Ambition to Life' (Bond University).

Despite such changes, popular and political accusations of irrelevance continue apace. 'Irrelevance' or 'uselessness' can refer both to process (how we spend our time) and product (what our 'outcomes' are). It can refer to inefficiency and ineffectuality, lack of effort or outcome, or misdirected effort (i.e. irrelevant, inappropriate or valueless outcomes). It is increasingly likely to refer to a lack of an obviously pragmatic application, to teaching that doesn't train students for the workplace, or to research that has no immediately evident commercial application.

But it's clear that uselessness may also refer to work that has a politically unacceptable output, as indicated by the logic of the ampersand underlying John Howard's denunciation of idleness 'and' a shameful assault on the reputation

---

3 Glasson describes how John Laws's retirement was used in sections of the Australian media as an occasion to denounce academics' distance from 'ordinary Australians' (2012: 103).

of Geoffrey Blainey. The idleness Howard condemned was not *lack* of work; it was *misdirected* work – time-wasting and destructive assaults on common sense and national pride.

What all the accusations canvassed so far (including my own self-deprecating ones) have in common is the characterization of left-wing Humanities academics as idle, politically correct do-gooders, and our work as a valueless attack on common sense. Now, any number of French philosophers would encourage us to see these criticisms as signs of our success: Roland Barthes (1985 [1979]), who, as we saw in Chapter 2, dared modern people to be lazy; Michel Foucault and Jacques Derrida, whose methods are based on the deconstruction and disruption of common sense; Georges Bataille (1988), who warned about the dangers of cultures that tried to rationalize away all forms of waste – these and others might encourage us simply to reject the discourse of utility. But contemporary academics don't have the luxury of laughing in their detractors' face, especially when some of those detractors hold the purse strings.

In any case, since uselessness is a serious accusation – dangerous, powerful, and, in some nations more than others, commonsensical – academics are actually obliged to consider what our own investment in the discourse of utility might be, how we might fare within its parameters, and whether we can sometimes put it to work in our favour. This chapter, then, proceeds less from a rejection of the discourse of utility than from an ambivalence towards it, in the hope that we can engage with it not just as a political rationality but also in relation to our deeper interest in the purpose and meaningfulness of our work. After all, the idea of usefulness is a core component of the vocationalism that still characterizes much academic work. Most academics *do* feel a sense of responsibility to make the best of their knowledge and their privilege, whatever discourse they might feel comfortable using to think about this (whether it be a discourse of social utility, of professionalism, of radicalism, or of the public intellectual, to take a few likely examples).

In this chapter, I explore the question of usefulness by reporting on a series of surveys and focus groups I conducted with undergraduate Cultural Studies students at one Australian university. This project turned out to be an experience in disjunction. I conducted it at a time when public and political disdain for academics was high, and professional morale plummeting. What I discovered, though, was a very encouraging set of student responses, in which students affirmed the interest and the value of studying the Humanities, and Cultural Studies in particular.

This is an especially important message for the public and politicians (as well as academics themselves) to hear, especially since calls for utility and relevance hit the Arts and Humanities particularly hard. For the idea that the Arts and Humanities do not serve as a viable professional preparation has been a persistent popular trope for decades. In Chapter 1 I noted this cliché's elevation to formal government policy in the Thatcher government's 1985 Joseph Report, which worked actively to undermine the standing and viability of the Humanities, defending them only in ritualistic terms (Secretary of State for Science and Education 1985: 9).[4] The report was explicit in its agenda of trying to promote science and technology subjects in schools and universities, warning unambiguously that unless employers changed their thinking, too many bright students would be led into the economically and socially useless wastelands of the Arts and Humanities:

> Employers, understandably, often choose recruits for careers in management by reference to general ability and leadership qualities, but they must also provide clear signals of the importance they attach to competence in science and technology. If they do not, then it is probably that more able youngsters than would otherwise be the case will opt for subjects that will not contribute to the technological competence of our economy and our society. (Secretary of State for Science and Education 1985: 7)

Indeed, the report explicitly instructed employers to correct the misapprehension that the Arts might be useful in promoting the qualities needed by business:

> One of the potentially surer routes to a successful business career ... for those with an enterprising and innovative attitude of mind ought to lie through competences in science, engineering, technology or mathematics. It is important that employers should recognise this themselves and through their actions convince able youngsters and their parents. (7)

By the start of this century, this tepid endorsement of the Arts had sunk even further, in some popular discourse at least. We saw in Chapter 2 that the 2011 funding cuts to UK universities brought to the surface a growing belief that the Arts should be practised as a private hobby. Debates in Australia around the same time unearthed the same view:

> Centre for Peace and Conflict Studies, Digital Cultures, Philosophy, Classics ... are these people for real? Why the hell am I paying taxes to support this tripe? You want to spend your days doing this, you pay for it yourself then we

---

4 This defence came in a single sentence: 'For many occupations a rigorous arts course provides an excellent preparation for jobs which carry responsibility and are personally and intellectually demanding' (Secretary of State for Science and Education 1985: 9). This statement was followed a few sentences later by a warning that Arts places were about to be cut.

can concentrate on areas of national importance such as science, engineering, health, and education... (Tory Boy 2012, original ellipses)[5]

When forced to justify their personal and social utility, the Arts and Humanities are normally forced to rely on general statements about the cultural heritage and national enrichment, on arguments about personal development (which receive short shrift in the era of user-pays ideologies), and on difficult-to-substantiate claims that employers value the skills acquired in an Arts degree, such as critical thinking skills, confidence, communication skills, a tolerance for difference and the ability to work independently. When making these claims at university Open Days, I always feel slightly unconvinced myself. So, clearly, do others (see Fig. 4.1). But if sonnets, irony and the ability to conjugate fail to convince, perhaps semiotics, discourse analysis and deconstruction might do the job? Perhaps, in other words, it is slightly different for Cultural Studies?

Cultural Studies and Utility

Cultural Studies is, again, particularly interestingly placed in these dilemmas. On the one hand, it can be read as a success story: popular with students, cutting-edge theoretically, relevant, connecting abstract theories to real life. Perhaps Cultural Studies academics are champions of the new order. Jonathan Rutherford, for one, notes despairingly that though Cultural Studies was not bred for the corporate university, it has proved able to adapt to it: 'in its flight from its roots in romantic humanism Cultural Studies has found itself dispersed but quite at home in the valueless world of the corporate university' (2005: 313). In the allegedly post-ideological university – the one in which the university does not so much embody a set of values as extract surplus value 'as a result of speculation on differentials in information' (Readings 1996: 40) – perhaps it doesn't matter what we profess, so long as we profess profusely. Bill Readings notes, with typical irony, that this

---

5 At the time of writing (late 2012), this belief has been taken to its logical conclusion in the domain of the visual arts with the NSW state government's decision to withdraw all funding for the Visual and Fine Arts from the Technical and Further Education (TAFE) system. Arts courses have been given the summer break to become fully commercial operations. The rationale was two-fold: first, the contestable claim that Fine Arts are not an especially viable contributor to the economy, and second, the moralized argument that these measures were needed to prevent dilettantes and hobbyists from repeatedly doing courses at the taxpayers' expense. As women, often older women, make up a substantial proportion of students in these courses, there are also gendered assumptions and impacts at play, as was explicitly the case with Thatcher's cuts to the Arts.

Figure 4.1   Cartoon by Bradford Veley. Reproduced with permission

is perhaps a less heroic role than we are accustomed to claim for the university, although it does resolve the question of parasitism. The University is now no more of a parasitical drain on resources than the stock exchange or the insurance companies are a drain on industrial production. (40)

Readings argued that content had become irrelevant – or rather, relevant only in relation to how well it performs as a commodity. Readings believed that Cultural Studies was the discipline for this new moment. As we saw in the Introduction, he argued that, whatever the ideas and values presented in particular Cultural Studies *work*, as a discipline, Cultural Studies is animated by a conception of culture that is empty enough to thrive in the environment in which content has been replaced with 'excellence' (1996: 13), which 'has no content to call its own'

(24). The 'general applicability' of the concept of excellence, argued Readings, 'is in direct relation to its emptiness' (23). Cultural Studies work is 'fecund' and 'multiple' enough to suit 'the age of excellence' (17).

This, though, would be strange news to all those who condemn Cultural Studies precisely because it is too *full* of ideological content, as in the opening example from the former Australian Prime Minister John Howard. As that example attests, the new corporatism and the old conservatism are not one and the same thing. Even though the characteristic anti-humanism of Cultural Studies 'is no threat' to utilitarian values and marketized systems (Rutherford 2005: 313), it nonetheless still matters, to politicians, the media, and students and their parents, what types of values are being promulgated within the university. In that sense, Cultural Studies remains both ambiguous and contested.

The point is that everyone – traditionalists and radicals on the left and right – can find something to hate. As we saw in Chapter 3, familiar accusations are that Cultural Studies is too frivolous; or that it is characterized by a ludicrous imbalance between the arcane nature of its theories and the trivial nature of its objects; or that it lacks the credibility of media production courses, and so on. Cultural Studies is not useful enough (i.e. not vocational, practical, applicable, or income-generating). It is too heavy (i.e. too complex) and too light (too 'poppy', frivolous or fun). For some activists it is not political enough – a complicit sell-out to the forces of consumerism or intellectual faddism. Others on the left lament the fact that in the new marketized system Cultural Studies can no longer be political; Rutherford says that Media and Cultural Studies have been 'turned away from political engagement because academics fill all their time meeting the demands of the market in research' (2005: 309). For conservatives, by contrast, it is *too* political, reducing cultural practices to ideology.

In the face both of such variegated but sustained criticism and of the progressivist hopes that gave birth to the discipline, it is hardly surprising that discussions about the purpose, role and effectiveness of Cultural Studies have always been a core thread in Cultural Studies work itself, in a way that is no doubt quite bewildering to those in disciplines less preoccupied with debating their 'mission'. So when, towards the end of the twentieth century, political discourse started to turn to utility, the perennial debates interior to Cultural Studies about its purposes and use were doubly charged. In 1999, Martin Ryle, for example, wrote a thoughtful essay on 'the usefulness of Cultural Studies' in the context of British New Labour's understanding of higher education as the 'relevant provision' of a service to a clientele who already know what they need, and of Tony Blair's hope that Britain may have 'the best educated *workforce* in the world' (45, original emphasis). The familiar (and, to many, tedious) debates within Cultural Studies about the tension between politics and theory were also, in their own way, responses to this new climate.[6] I don't intend to take yet another stroll down the theory/practice cul-de-sac, nor its deconstructive resolution, having briefly surveyed this terrain in Chapter 3, but it is important to note that debates about utility have their place within Cultural Studies too.

Instead, this chapter reports on what some Cultural Studies *students* thought about the usefulness of the discipline. After all, it is in our interactions with students that many of us enjoy a sense of meaningful purpose. In any case, since calls on us to amend our ways are so often made in their name, the student body can also be thought of strategically as a site of intersection – between, on the one hand, the demands of government and managers to prove our worth, and on the other, our own desires to do a good job on our own terms. Getting a better sense of what students might think about the usefulness of Cultural Studies is a potentially quite freeing way of manouevring about in that space, and it may also well provide some rhetorical weaponry in the fight to defend what we (want to) do.

Student Interviews

During 2002 I carried out a number of surveys and interviews with current and past undergraduate students at the university at which I worked. The students were enrolled not in a named Cultural Studies degree or major but in a transdisciplinary Humanities programme centred on Cultural Studies but with a few quirkier edges. The first was a survey of around a hundred first-year students enrolled in a foundation unit called *Introduction to Cultural Studies*. Students were asked to respond in writing to a single question: 'Is Cultural Studies useful, and if so, what might its uses be?' They were given no background to this question; they were simply told that I was writing a research paper about Cultural Studies and wanted to canvass their opinions. The second form of survey was with 2nd/3rd year students in an elective called *Consumer Culture*. Students were given more context (i.e. a muted sense of the political context in which such questions were being asked) and were also given more

---

6 Variants of this opposition included the contrast between teaching and activism, or activism within the academy and outside it (Hall 2002: 9). As with all binaries, three predictable positions emerged: a defence of either term, or a deconstructive 'resolution' of the opposition itself. Gary Hall's book *Culture in Bits*, for example, is based entirely on a call to bring deconstruction to Cultural Studies, and on the claim that the questioning of politics is 'an inextricable part of what it actually means to *do cultural studies*' (6, original emphasis). For Hall, an ongoing commitment to theory is actually 'the most political thing for cultural studies to do' (6).

guidance (including questions that problematized the discourse of utility itself). Forty responses were received. The third forum was a series of small-group interviews with students who had finished their degree and were either doing Honours or were in the workforce.

It is important to characterize, as succinctly as possible, the nature of this particular student body. The study was conducted at the Blacktown campus of the University of Western Sydney, which drew students from quite a wide area. It drew from the Blue Mountains (a somewhat 'alternative' region), from predominantly working-class western Sydney suburbs such as Blacktown and Mt Druitt, and a few from the semi-rural western fringe of Sydney (Windsor and Richmond). Another major catchment area for this particular campus was the Hills area of Western Sydney, a district characterized by politicians as comprised of 'aspirational voters'. Broadly speaking, the students at that time were career-focused, low in cultural capital, but relatively affluent. Large numbers were from non-English speaking backgrounds. Many were the first in their family to go to university, but they did not appear to be as competitive as students at some of the other campuses.[7] While not necessarily overtly political, the students tended to be open to new ideas, and quite liberal, often in a *laissez-faire* way. At the campus in question they appeared to be pragmatic, and their motivations were often very evidently extrinsic (e.g. they went to lectures if they were made compulsory but otherwise would frequently absent themselves; they did the readings if there was an assignment based on them). Nonetheless, it's clear they were interested in the new things they were learning at university. They were very focused on future employment and most were concurrently engaged in large amounts of part-time work – up to 30 hours per week for full-time students. For this reason, they spent little time on the campus, which, partly as a result, offered very little by way of student life, especially in contrast to more established universities. Their absence from campus was also reflected in library usage, which was low compared to the other campuses of the university. I say all this not to lament the decline of an active intellectual and political life in this version of a contemporary university but to give as accurate a sense as possible of the demographic whose responses I am about to describe.

---

7 This is, of course, an assumption. I made it based on the observations of some of the Blacktown students after they began taking subjects on other UWS campuses following the university's major restructure. They commented on how competitive students at other campuses were. Tutors involved in cross-campus teaching for the first time also reported that students on other UWS campuses (which draw on different demographics) were, variously, more politicized, or more competitive, or had a stronger sense of themselves as a student body.

Findings

Broadly speaking, the values that students cited as 'useful' fell into four categories: intellectual/conceptual; personal development (with a very specific recurring theme of the link between self and society); skills development; and vocational. The relative proportion in each category differed across the cohorts I surveyed, but in the large first-year group, on whose responses I will focus, they fell roughly in that order (i.e. concepts; self/society; skills; jobs).

This was the cohort who were asked, 'Is Cultural Studies useful, and if so, what might its uses be?' The first thing to report by way of findings is how overwhelmingly positive the responses were. Of the 102 first-year surveys, all but five were entirely positive. One was totally negative, one was parodic, and three expressed reservations (mostly about the vocational usefulness of Cultural Studies) but even then nonetheless had positive things to add.[8] Pleasingly, they were clearly able to make the distinction between evaluating the *subject* (which they did a week later, and which produced the expected mix of gripes and compliments) and reflecting on the value of the field of study, which produced a far less equivocal range of comments. As we will see later on, students appear to have a good grasp of genre and context.

Now, one might argue that one would expect students with an investment in Cultural Studies to reply positively since it's bound up with their developing subject position as Humanities students – but it was their first year (and so they were not necessarily committed to it as a course of study) and in any case many were doing the subject because it was a compulsory Foundation for a wide range of different areas of study. Moreover, not all respondents were Humanities students; a fair proportion were doing a BA (Tourism). So what did the students find useful?

Overwhelmingly, the students found that Cultural Studies gave them a deeper, broader, more nuanced way of understanding society and culture. This was usually the first value cited, and it was among the most frequent. This was clearly considered a worthwhile end in itself, as evidenced in one response that said, simply and only: 'It's useful because it teaches us to study culture'. While it might sound an obvious thing that Cultural Studies is useful because it helps

---

8 The parodic answer was a lovely reading of the mating habits of the Spangled Drongo in relation to various theories of gender and of everyday interaction; the negative one was gloriously grumpy — accusing Cultural Studies academics of creating jobs for themselves (if only!) by intellectualizing the obvious. There was also one reply for the True Believers out there — a student who considered Cultural Studies to be 'limitless' in its usefulness, since any field of study that taught students to analyse the world *'from a Marxist perspective'* (original emphasis) was invaluable in helping people obtain in-depth insight into 'the workings of our tragic world'.

you understand culture, I was pleased to see an intellectual value repeatedly cited highest. Put simply, students valued having had their 'understanding' and 'insight' increased, and they particularly valued the sense that their understanding had been broadened, deepened, or rendered more subtle and acute. Some students valued the acquisition of specific new concepts, both for their own sake and for their usefulness in other subjects: 'Issues such as ethnography and relational readings have become very useful'. I must admit to being surprised at the high level of intrinsic intellectual value. This might sound unduly cynical, but it's not what I had expected from this particular student cohort.

There was a reasonable frequency of responses valuing the development of a *critical* understanding of society:

To question society and its structures

Prevents us from becoming too naïve in accepting certain aspects/elements of culture.

This may help us to identify elements of inequality within our system, and also reminds us to not take things on surface value – to critically analyse.

But this response, though reasonably common, was not as frequent as one characterizing the understanding gained through Cultural Studies as a form of new awareness, an opening up of one's eyes or mind: '[It] has opened my eyes and mind to the broader issues within society'; 'It has opened my eyes to the way people act, look and are'; 'You become more open and more aware of the issues around culture'. Having one's mind opened was widely considered of intrinsic value: 'Yes, I find studying the concept of "what is a culture" mind opening in itself'.

Students repeatedly valued Cultural Studies' ability to help them understand not only their own culture, but also that of others. They very frequently claimed that Cultural Studies had opened them up to a diversity of opinion, belief and ways of living. For quite a number, this was linked to a kind of social utility – the promotion of tolerance:

[It] enables me to see that each culture is different & to accept its differences

I think [it's] useful 'cause we learn about different religions and cultures…

It's useful 'cause it teaches us to be open-minded and it teaches us to see things on different levels and different perspectives.

This was intimately connected to understanding one's own social positioning:

Makes me remember that when judging or even just observing others that I inhabit a post-modern, pop culture environment and am a Westerner.

Relevance to the everyday was fairly frequently cited as a value in itself: Cultural Studies is useful because it 'comments on everyday activities'. Mostly, though, Cultural Studies' emphasis on contemporaneity was valued as a mode of connection. The connection between self and society was a major theme and a prize value, as one would expect from a generation schooled through the 'self and society' paradigm, much of whose education has valued 'knower codes' over 'knowledge codes' (Maton 2009: 46):

> Learning about Cultural Studies has helped me understand more the inner workings of society, the mind and the entire self.

> Cultural Studies are vital in providing ways and means by which to analyse ourselves and our place in society, and allows us to consider our own personal opinions of how societies are formed, and by whom.

For some students, there was clearly a connection between understanding the world and knowing how to live in it, hence the repeated finding (one that surprised me) that for many students, studying Cultural Studies was enhancing their actual way of living: 'Cultural Studies is useful to not only a BA Communications student but it's beneficial in life in general'. Or: 'It is a way to insightful experiences in our everyday life. A chance to rediscover what culture really is'. This answer seems to see conceptual understanding as contributing to an art of living. Some students used a vocabulary of enrichment; others one of applicability. Perhaps because this particular subject had a fairly strong focus on the routines and rituals of everyday interactions, Cultural Studies was repeatedly understood as promoting self-understanding:

> Yeh, it's useful for an individual to explore their place in society.

> Yeah. Personally it has opened my eyes on the way I view myself and others as individuals and the different styles of everyone.

> It helps us understand and make sense of the things we do and why we do them.

> Uses – I can observe my everyday life and systems I become a part of and analyse it.

> [It helps me to] broaden my own perception of identity.

Learning to understand their own behaviour connected up to other forms of self-understanding:

> Yes, it allows you to look at what isn't realised in one's self. It opens you up. Makes you see inner self. Teaches you about everyday life.

> Cultural Studies allows individuals to understand how their identity is created/formed in order to find meaning of the "self".

Indeed, many saw it as promoting self-transformation:

> It makes you think and question the way we live, and why we do what we do, so we can approach things differently and hopefully more positively.

> It is not merely a good subject, rather it is a critical element necessary for the individual to undertake in their journey to ultimately achieve the enlightenment of reason and rationality.

Even where self-transformation was not described as explicitly as this, it was still very widely implied, especially by the frequent use of phrases like 'you become'. For two students, Cultural Studies even enhanced self-*value*:

> It makes me proud to be individual. [complete response]

> The importance of being an individual in our mass consumer culture.

Meaning recurred as a common theme, sometimes slipping between semiotic and ontological registers. Students valued the way Cultural Studies taught them to see hidden meanings, and to get a sense of the multi-layering of meaning. This took familiar forms, such as 'making you think about the meaning behind the adverts', but it was also frequently connected up to larger questions of social and cultural meaning-making: 'Looking at everyday life, and looking for the deeper meanings'. Sometimes, the link between seeing cultural meanings and finding personal meaning was quite explicit:

> Individuals need to understand how and why life is structured and the meaning behind it.

> I do have a natural curiosity and fascination with the Why? question – why are we here, why do we behave the ways we do, why do we live this way etc. Cultural Studies has proven worthy of exploring such issues…

The subject's focus on the routines and rituals of everyday life appeared to have a similarly reassuring function for some. Despite the focus on diversity, the use of theorists like Erving Goffman (1959) and Harold Garfinkel (1967)[9] reassured some students that 'we are "all the same"'. Studying the shared nature of particular social predicaments evidently reminded some students of their own 'normality'. For one student, reassurance came from the critical tools learnt through Cultural Studies:

> It's useful because it shows how wrapped up in consumer culture society is and almost shows how not to be wrapped up in it, and how some aspects we worry about are normal and fit to make up our own culture! It uses these aspects to get people to become more aware and proud of their culture and what aspects of themselves make up culture and contribute to it.

In sum, a great number of responses connected an altered perception of the world, the development of critical faculties, self-knowledge and an enhanced ability to live. This matrix was unexpected to me, but it's clear that Cultural Studies' focus on the everyday, on subjectivity and on the social provided a vehicle for connecting up questions of cultural meaning-making in the broadest sense to many students' sense of the individual quest for meaning. Students also valued the integration and connection of knowledge itself – they valued Cultural Studies because it connected up with other subjects they were studying, something that was understood as both intrinsically and pragmatically valuable. It turned out, then, that this student body could be characterized as both extrinsically and intrinsically motivated.[10] They were pragmatic but they were also equally apt to put a high weight on intellectual values.

Some students in the upper levels had some reservations about how likely Cultural Studies was to help them get a job. But even there, there was a reasonable degree of sanguinity. First-year students imagined that Cultural Studies' stress on understanding difference would prepare them well for teaching and counselling, and some (though not all) Tourism students were quite confident that an enriched understanding of culture would help them engage in the business of packaging, promoting and selling culture to others. The graduates I interviewed

---

9 Goffman and Garfinkel, in slightly different ways, studied the hidden patterns, codes and rituals that help structure everyday life, such as the tacit rules of conversation, of queuing in public places, of pedestrian behaviour, and so on.

10 I am drawing loosely on a taxonomy of four categories of student motivation devised by John Biggs and Phillip Moore: intrinsic, extrinsic, social and achievement (1993: 259ff.). I haven't more rigorously applied it, because it applies to motivation (which I didn't ask students about) rather than perceived value, which was the object of my questioning.

were clear about what they had got from their studies that was useful in the workplace (both in getting a job and in understanding workplace culture), but they were also aware of how hard they had had to (or would have to) work to gain entry into the workforce. Once there, though, they were surprised at how much of their studies were of use (including both practical tools like writing and conceptual tools like an understanding of gender).

In the responses from first year students, the rhetoric of skills development was largely absent. I was surprised at this, because it had been a strong feature both of the 2nd/3rd year responses and of the interviews with graduates. These latter had been much more comfortable discussing the development of communication skills, analytical skills, research skills, critical thinking and so on. They spoke the language of curricula vitae comfortably. Some prodding on my part made it clear that they valued a whole lot more than this, but their first impulse had been to speak in terms of skills and outcomes. This may have been because it's a more comfortable discourse one-on-one than the discourse of personal development, or because, as recent graduates, they were more focused on the creation of a marketable, competent persona than first year students were, or perhaps, intriguingly, because I had given the interviewees more sense of the political context of my enquiries into the utility of Cultural Studies, and the skills and competency discourse is an obvious political strategy in defence of the Humanities.

Either way, these upper-level students certainly showed themselves to be proficient at moving between different discourses to describe what they valued in their study, and to be entirely reflexive about the role of context in determining which discourses to mobilize. They had clearly learnt a lot about discourse, genre, strategy and power! They were comfortable and pragmatic about the need to adopt different discourses in different situations, as became clear in a discussion we had about the gains and losses of a discourse of social utility. I told them a story about a student who had come to see me about handing work in late. He had always appeared pretty laid-back, if not lazy. In the course of our conversation, he told me how much the Humanities course, especially the Gender Studies component, had changed him. He described the masculinism of his upbringing, and his sense of shame at his own former homophobia. He was close to graduating, and he now wanted to work in the community sector as a heterosexual advocate for gay rights. I later passed this story on to a colleague, and we debated whether the change in this student should rightfully be considered a form of social utility. My colleague considered such a tag not so much false as a gross impoverishment of the story. The students, however, saw it much more pragmatically:

Kate: I think you're too ethical. [laughter]. You're too ethical. I don't think it robs it; you have to use that.

Interviewer: You have to use the discourse?

Kate: Absolutely. I don't see that as robbing it.

Interviewer: Why?

Kate: Because it's not going to get out there if you don't, and that's more important than, I'm not saying how you go about it, but I don't think it's devaluing to put things in terms that are, you know…

Miriam: It's just an example. It's just a little case study that you're showing.

Anthony: Yeah.

Miriam: It doesn't devalue it.

I still can't say whose side I come down on, but it was certainly clear that the students were entirely pragmatic and willing and able to adjust discourses to suit the context.

Graduate labour market studies hint that these students may not be atypical in their interweaving of intrinsic values and pragmatism. In 1990, Jim Taylor published results from a survey of UK graduates, in the context of the then Conservative government's policy of ensuring that 'the needs of the economy' rather than demand from applicants should be paramount in determining 'the right number and balance' of graduates in different subject areas (239). Predictably, graduates in Business, Law, Maths and Computing did very well on labour market indicators like job placement and salaries, in contrast to graduates in the pure sciences, the Arts and the Humanities (250), who were also not certain that their study had helped them to get an interesting job (251). While graduates across the board were not very likely to see a link between their degree and obtaining a good income, this belief was strongly marked by discipline: predictably, graduates in Arts and Humanities considered that they had become well educated but were less confident that their degree had paved the way for a lucrative career, compared to graduates in Law, Engineering, Maths or Computing. Interestingly, however, most graduates in all disciplines felt that they would do the same or a similar degree if given the choice again (251).

Conclusion

To a cynic, this exploration of what some students valued and considered useful in Cultural Studies might seem to confirm Cultural Studies' total incorporation into the institution and into the logic of customer satisfaction. Cultural Studies' favour with this particular cohort – aspirational, pragmatic and coming from a region that has moved from traditional Labor voting towards the Liberal-National Coalition – might seem to confirm Readings's (1996) and Rutherford's (2005) gloomy visions of Cultural Studies as a discipline suited for the consumerist times. Except that the things the students valued, again and again, were the *critical* perspectives opened up by Cultural Studies, the incitement to look at their world *afresh*. Even those who see Cultural Studies as having abandoned its critical edge in favour of overly celebratory populism need to acknowledge that these students were valuing not some comforting reaffirmation of their place in the world, but the ability to view their world differently.

Our students – who, unlike politicians and online commentators, actually engage with what we *do* – spoke of the *worth* of what we do and, again unlike many politicians and indeed university managers, had not abandoned a language of content and value. Their responses were, in that sense, almost anachronistic – perhaps some hint that what Readings (1996) called the 'university of culture' might still continue to exist in shadowy form within the university of excellence. But instead of seeing this student rhetoric only as a self-deluding and 'atavistic' desire to belong to something that no longer exists, as Readings does (11), we should see the student desire to be part of a university of culture as something to be celebrated and harnessed.

CHAPTER 5

Feeling Like a Fraud: Or, the Upside of Knowing You Can Never Be Good Enough

'What is viewed collectively as structural inconsistency is felt individually as personal insecurity, for it is in the experience of the social actor that the imperfections of society and contradictions of character meet and exacerbate one another'.

Clifford Geertz, 'Ideology as a Cultural System' (1973): 204

The Fraudulence Problem

A few years ago, at a conference on new pedagogies, I decided to accost a longstanding fascination of mine. In the lead-up to that conference, I started casually mentioning to colleagues 'my academic fraudulence paper'. I didn't have to say much more, as I was usually met with a laugh and a piece of comradely encouragement. Still, at that point in time, I was a little twitchy about too publically professing an interest, if not expertise, in fraudulence, lest collegial judgment tip away from a warm appreciation of my 'quirkiness' towards altogether less generous thoughts.

But my unexplained use of this phrase was also, in its own delicate way, a kind of experiment – a testing of the waters – to see what would happen if I pretended to a bland assumption that fellow academics would automatically know what I was talking about. In fact, I've been testing this assumption one way or another for the last 15 years, through conversation and reflection, gradually transforming fraudulence from my own private affect to a little leitmotiv in my thinking about the interplay of ethics, politics and pedagogy in the changing university climate. Over the last decade, my thinking about fraudulence has transformed from a private distress to an intellectual curiosity, a pedagogic challenge and an ethical imperative. So now I approach the subject quite straightforwardly, convinced of its political, ethical and human importance, especially, but not only, to postgraduates and early career academics, and also to the discipline of Cultural Studies itself, which prides itself on centralizing ethical matters in its scholarship and teaching.

My passing conversations on the theme of fraudulence over many years have convinced me that there are at least some academics for whom the idea has a certain instant recognition value, notwithstanding a moment of shock or surprise when it is actually articulated. Of course, as with so many things, once you start thinking about it, it seems it magically appears everywhere. Since becoming a fraud-watcher, I have stumbled across it in numerous feminist accounts of doctoral research (e.g. Reger 2001, Bondi 2005: 238), and in an essay by the Australian writer and critic Robert Dessaix, in which he describes academic writers as 'spend[ing] their lives examining and being examined, finding others wanting while on the edge of being found wanting themselves' (1998: 122). Up it pops too in Ann Game's and Andrew Metcalfe's description in *Passionate Sociology* of a bad writing day – a day when, as they so resonantly put it, 'the words are sullen, when the possibility of hope seems absurd, when examination processes creep into my study and pronounce me a failure, when I'm only surprised it has taken people so long to discover that I'm a fraud' (1996: 31). And it appears yet again, in Elspeth Probyn's matter of fact claim that 'feeling like a fraud is routine in the modern university' (2005: 131).

There's presumably nothing unique to academia about feeling like a professional fraud. Any profession that is subject to a constant barrage of new information and intense public scrutiny no doubt creates conditions in which it can flourish. The medical profession is an evident example. But it could well be the case that teaching is a profession particularly prone to it. (I vividly recall my father's advice to me before I launched myself into my first school teaching post – that when he had been a school teacher he used to console himself that at least he was keeping somebody *worse* out of the classroom!) Nor can one claim the fraudulence phenomenon as a purely recent phenomenon, though my argument is that recent decades have produced conditions that have greatly intensified it.

So, feelings of fraudulence may well be quite common in many professions. But what does it mean to think of the feeling of fraudulence, and the strategy of bluff that may well accompany it, as *routine* in the modern university? Perhaps it means that as well as thinking of it as a *symptom* – something private which we attempt to repress in professional life but which slips out every now and then – we should also think of it as shared, deeply entrenched, tacit, but easily recognizable – 'both self-evident and obscure' (Lusty 2009: 199). That is, we might consider it as a submerged feature of the academic professional everyday. Viewed this way, the feeling of being a fraud has much to teach us about the entwined intellectual, ethical, and pedagogic issues in the contemporary university, and the institutional conditions that produce and frame these issues.

The bigger context for this argument is the contemporary scholarly interest in affect, and in particular feminist methodological debates that refuse to see emotions or affect merely as some form of 'interference' (Bondi 2005: 234) in academic work, and which call for 'a wider appreciation of researchers' emotions in research practice' (231). While my focus in this chapter is not on this theoretical literature, it is nonetheless worth pointing to the important link between this theme in feminist methodological writing, the burgeoning literature on the marketization of higher education, and the ongoing debate, including within Cultural Studies, about the nature and role of academics in the contemporary critical disciplines (e.g. Wark 1993, Bennett 1998, Gregg 2006). And, insofar as feeling fraudulent is a paranoid mode of being, my argument also speaks to Eve Kosofsky Sedgwick's (2003) now well-celebrated call to rethink the nature and role of 'critique' away from what, following the psychoanalyst Melanie Klein, she terms 'paranoid' modes of enquiry and scholarship.

This chapter extends the reflections on emotional 'contagion' broached in Chapter 2 to explore the idea that academic affects have quite marked political, intellectual and ethical implications not only for those already in the profession but also, crucially, for those who may aspire to join us in the academy: Honours and postgraduate students and the ever-increasing pool of qualified scholars seeking permanent academic work. The chapter has three aims: to reframe fraudulence as an intellectual, political and pedagogic issue; to situate it within an analysis of the institutional and intellectual climate of the contemporary university, especially the Humanities; and to consider some pedagogical strategies we might employ to help turn the feeling of fraudulence from a personal and professional hindrance or interference into an opportunity for modes of Honours and postgraduate training that address students' potential futures.

Before embarking, here are some thumbnail sketches of the fraudulence phenomenon. Some of its typical public forms, acceptable because they are implicit critiques of institutional conditions, are: 'We never have enough time'; or 'We don't do anything properly anymore'; or even 'I wasn't trained in this'. But quiet conversations with colleagues and students over the years (and indeed, some of the published examples I cited a moment ago) have made it clear that there are more agonizing, usually private, versions of this professional affect: 'I don't know enough;' 'I really shouldn't be here'; 'one day they're going to find me out'. Liz Bondi, for example, describes the feeling that she got her PhD scholarship by a mistake rather than through her abilities and that she was at risk of being 'found out' (2005: 238). Such feelings may be exacerbated by the writer's social positioning (as in Bev Skeggs's description of being a working-class student researcher [1995: 195]). Viewed in this light, refusing to allow our students to feel that they are the only person in the room who doesn't know enough, or shouldn't be there, or doesn't understand, or isn't convinced, or doesn't have the right background for this, is not only an ethical imperative, but also a political pedagogical challenge.

People can also feel at risk of being found out for reasons germane to their discipline. A former colleague who taught quite unconventional material within a Sociology department some decades ago told me that she used to be afraid that someone was going to walk into her lectures and realize that she wasn't 'doing Sociology' and give her the sack. These questions of disciplinary orthodoxy are intertangled with the more personal forms of self-doubt to the extent that they reflect the historical institutionalization of hierarchies of classed and gendered knowledge and values.

Clearly, some forms of fraudulence are discipline-specific. If you work in a department of languages, having an accent as good as one's native-speaker colleague might be the issue. In Media departments 'theorists' may feel less authentic than 'practitioners' and vice versa. Technological comfort and proficiency can also be an issue, given the constant changes to teaching and learning technologies as well as research software.

In Cultural Studies, expertise takes a particularly personal turn since the business of subject formation is absolutely at the core of its disciplinary enterprise. As engaged critics of Cultural Studies such as Ian Hunter (1992) and Gary Wickham (2005) have argued, Cultural Studies is essentially a 'moral discourse' (Wickham 2005: 74) that has at its heart the cultivation of a particular form of ethical subjectivity. In that sense, Cultural Studies academics are invited to embody their discipline, and its politics, in quite intense and personal ways. To take just one example, the centrality of popular and youth culture to certain strains of Cultural Studies obliges its practitioners if not to remain youthful, then to remain in touch with, and – harder as one ages – *sympathetic to*, youth culture. Indeed, for some styles of Cultural Studies academics, this may manifest as an unspoken obligation to somehow continue to *embody* the area of youth culture in which they are experts. I myself have rarely been accused of being hip, so such pressures will not be particularly pointed for me, but I have nonetheless begun occasionally to feel old in relation to my students. I no longer have the heart to pretend to recognize every allusion to a currently fashionable nightclub or band. I can more or less happily trade-off this lack against some of the other kinds of things one can offer to students after spending a while in the field. But more fundamentally, I realize that there are now moments (happily, not all the time) when the questions that really excite them (for example, about resistance or transgression) and the utopian impulses that underpin their political engagements are not the same questions or impulses that excite me. Since I refuse to develop into a pathetic ageing wannabe hipster, my whimsical response is to imagine that I will need to retire early, develop an interest in some obscure but hip band, or to radically retrain myself in French, or Archaeology, or some altogether more *seemly* discipline in which I can age gracefully.

As these brief characterizations suggest, the feeling of fraudulence, though experienced as a sense of personal inadequacy, is often linked to the social positioning of the academic and/or to a critique of institutional organization, pedagogical frameworks, or disciplinary orthodoxy. But in the absence of widespread collegial discussion about such matters in any mode other than the confessional, it is very easy for such intellectual, pedagogic and systemic questions to be privatized, internalized and wrestled with as individual lack (and hence managed via a range of coping strategies, including evasion, bluff, secrecy and overwork) rather than considered as evidence of particular or changing intellectual and institutional conditions. The core argument of this chapter is that rather than considering the feeling of imposture to necessarily or always reflect personal failings – yet more evidence of our own unsuitability for the job – it might better be considered as an invitation to a richer debate about mastery, expertise and about the contemporary structuring of labour and knowledge in the academy. If it is true that the spectre of fraudulence silently haunts many academic communities, then we must make the case for the ethical and political importance of normalizing discussions about this experience, especially for postgraduates and early career researchers.

The first half of this chapter considers some of the structural features of the contemporary university that can contribute to the feeling of not being good enough. The aim of this is not to lament these features but to join the dots between them and the usually private feelings of incapacity experienced by many in the system. The second half of this chapter uses this analysis as a pedagogical prompt. I argue that in our current situation there is both an ethical and an intellectual imperative to discuss these matters with those whom we are ostensibly 'training' to be the academics of the future, and rather than bluffing them, to invite them to consider alongside us what 'expertise' might mean in the near academic future. This is pedagogy in a broad, holistic sense. It involves rendering more overt some of the tacit pedagogies already implied or embedded in our academic personae, our modes of writing and address, and our modes of negotiating the borders and the limits of what we know – in the corridor, the conference and the classroom. In fact, it's also about considering the corridor and the conference as themselves versions *of* the postgraduate classroom – venues for an ongoing, largely tacit, pedagogy about what it means to be an academic and what expertise can and should mean in the transdisciplinary, time-poor, outcomes-focused academy. As the subtitle to the chapter makes clear, in the face of such external circumstances, it is all the more imperative that we frame this as an invitation to a potentially quite enabling professional discussion. We must mine these often debilitating affects for their liberatory potential, without losing sight of the intellectual and political necessity of structural critique.

Structure, as always, is where I begin, via a brief survey of five institutional and intellectual contributors to the experience of fraudulence, before I consider its ties with social identities.

Structural Contributors: Hybridity, Post-Disciplinarity, Globalization, Productivism, Casualization

The Hybrid University

In Chapter 2 I made the argument in detail that the university is now a composite institution – part scholarly community, part grandiose bureaucracy and part corporation. In the face of the implicit requirement that universities be all things to all people (at once the custodians of tradition and the standard bearers of innovation; responsive to student demands yet mindful of standards; vocational without 'losing their soul', as a former Australian Education Minister put it [*Four Corners* 2005]), the pressures and contradictions are great. It is less that the university is in ruins, to recall the title of Readings's (1996) incisive book, than that it is a palimpsest – an institution trying to serve disparate values, visions and ideologies, with academics themselves all too often trying to bridge these gaps with their own bodies and labour. As I argued in Chapter 2, academics all too often serve as the glue that binds the disparate paradigms into something resembling a coherent whole, their bodies fighting to put the 'uni' into 'university'. In such a climate, it is easy to imagine that academics might sometimes feel that they can never get it right. We are *structurally* never good enough. My contention is that, in these circumstances, the only sensible and ethical strategy is to unleash the liberatory potential of this realization and to be quite open and sanguine about the fact that we can never be good enough.

Post-Disciplinarity

The large-scale institutional changes of the late twentieth century were accompanied by and interwoven with shifts in the structure of academic knowledge itself. The big-picture intellectual changes that Jean-François Lyotard (1984) shorthanded as the 'postmodern condition' include the challenging of disciplines by the rise of interdisciplinary and even transdisciplinary approaches; the emergence of new disciplines or fields of study; the rise of identity politics and critical theory and resultant tensions about how disciplinary knowledge should be conceived and passed on; the emergence and validation of new objects of study (e.g. popular culture); an increasingly overt politicization of knowledge in the wake of identity politics; and political and philosophical critiques of the ideal of objective knowledge.

As we saw in Chapter 2, the most obvious structural outcome of such a 'radically dissensual climate' (Graff 1994: 23) was a pluralistic curriculum, manifested on an institutional level in the reformation of organizational units (departments, centres, programmes), the breaking up of year-long subjects into single semester 'units', and the loosening of pre-requisites and sequencing, resulting in what literary scholar Gerald Graff calls 'a disjunctive curriculum', in which there is greater potential for students to encounter at least some of their subjects 'as an isolated unit' (23). Australian students, especially in the Arts and Humanities, are encouraged to select and combine a substantial portion of their degree according to their own interests, which usually means in practice a combination of cruising the 80-word blurbs in the undergraduate calendar and speaking to fellow students about their experiences. The undergraduate student cohort is thus fractured and diversified. Someone majoring in Cinema Studies, for example, may well be sitting next to a stray student from Mathematics who wants to fill up a spare spot in their curriculum with a fun film unit. While this broadening of the student experience has many intellectual benefits, from the teacher's point of view it makes questions of assumed knowledge and interests harder to manage, and all too often results in a kind of common denominator teaching that might leave some students with more specialist interests feeling cheated and some teachers experiencing fraudulent feelings of the 'we never cover anything properly any more' variety.

Meanwhile, staff themselves may have had equally disjunctive intellectual experiences, as they move from, for example, a disciplinary training to post-disciplinary teaching, or from the intellectual climate of one department to a potentially different one in another. Many academics have had to re-form themselves one way or another. This is especially so for those who spend a decade or so in the casual zone, moving between short-term contracts often in different departments, programmes or universities, before eventually securing the 'happy ending' of a tenured position. On the upside, this is a valuable intellectual training. On the downside, in a pluralist intellectual climate, and a marketized education system in which courses of study change frequently, moving even from one Cultural Studies department to another, even within the same country, can be a disorienting experience[1] – things that mattered in one place scarcely rate a mention in the next; one department's pet theorist is considered passé or problematic in another; even undergraduate students can seem to know more than you do, because they innocently reflect the intellectual interests of those who have taught them. All this can make one feel isolated, or

---

1 A senior figure in Australian Cultural Studies, Graeme Turner, claims that one of the features of contemporary Australian Cultural Studies programmes is that they are idiosyncratically organized around the teaching academic's interests, making them 'highly contingent' (2012: 77).

alienated, or stupid. This is another obvious source of the feeling that one does not know 'enough', or the right things.

Globalization

This experience of intellectual disjunction is even stronger for students and staff who take up study or academic work in a different country from the one in which they have trained. The increased global mobility of students and academics means that there is now significant movement between disparate systems, curricula, canons of knowledge, and indeed languages. This experience may well force a crisis in feeling about knowing enough, or the right things.

Concern about the wellbeing of international postgraduate students is well documented in the higher education and psychology literatures (for a sample survey, see Khawaja and Dempsey 2007). Indeed, as far back as 1967, Ward coined the expression 'foreign student syndrome' to describe the forms of anxiety, alienation and distress that all too often accompany the experience of studying overseas (qtd. in Khawaja and Dempsey 2007: 14). Adding to the welter of well-known contributory factors – language difficulties, financial strain, loneliness, homesickness, academic challenges – Khawaja and Dempsey also note the stressful effects of students' dual interpellation as both students and 'customers of a service organisation' and of the gap between 'expectations of service and experiences of service' (16). In other words, the palimpsestic effects described in Chapter 2 affect international students too.

Academic staff can themselves suffer from some of the disjunctive effects of a globalized system. When they take up a position away from their home country, they are often hired solo (though there are rare exceptions when a staff cohort is hired to set up a new programme). Like most students, they may also leave their partner or family behind, perhaps semi-permanently. These difficulties are compounded for those who take an overseas posting not as a career-advancing or career-capping move, as some senior scholars may, but as their only pathway to full-time employment. The isolated negotiation of differences between national systems, canons, styles and values gives mobile academics every reason to internalize these differences as individual lack.

The Rise of Productivism

One component of the marketization of the university has been the relentless rise of the productivist imperative. In Chapter 2 I described the way work and time itself have been refashioned, noting the myriad systemic changes to academic labour, including (to pick a random selection): increasingly instrumental relations to thought, to writing and to time itself; a reduction in the types of intellectual endeavour recognized as 'counting'; a concomitant disincentive to participate in unrecognized or undervalued university, community or scholarly activities, like writing book reviews or socializing with students; the slipping out of sight of non-instrumental or non-monetized 'outcomes'; and pressure to take low-risk teaching and research options.

It is not hard to see how this institutional climate, in which output is regularly and visibly measured against norms derived from budgetary and regulatory frameworks rather than scholarly ones, works to produce the academic subject as one who is always already inadequate. The ideal academic subject it implies and produces is, as in the classic account of capitalist alienation, disembodied – their output quantified on spreadsheets that have no connection with the conditions of actual living and working, let alone with the vagaries, contingencies and unpredictability of intellectual thought. This is the institutional substructure that makes it all too easy to feel insufficient because, after all, one can never, by definition, have done 'enough'. It is, in fact, the downside of the same academic freedom that allows us to navigate our own research trajectory, output and timelines, which makes us individually responsible for our own professional sufficiency. Academics are self-regulating professionals in a system without intrinsic limits and in which hyper-productivity is contagious. And when hyper-productivity is contagious, so too is the feeling of fraudulence.

The Casualization of Academic Labour

The expansion of postgraduate study in the latter decades of the twentieth century produced a new form of academic community. Where once postgraduate study was something that might have been carried out while occupying a full-time position (if at all), now most university departments have a distinct cohort of aspiring academics who are an important part of their social and intellectual life. The creation of this cohort went hand in hand with the casualization of academic labour itself, to the point where a large portion of university teaching is carried out by casual staff (statistics vary, but figures of around 40–50 per cent are not uncommon in Australia).

Postgraduate students and post-doctoral scholars are invited as participants and trainees into this alluring but nonetheless mixed, pressured, internally contradictory and evolving system. They are invited, however, only conditionally, since this is a workplace divided into what Megan Kimber (2003) calls a 'tenured core' and 'casual periphery'. In the Foreword to a 2008 report on casualization in the tertiary sector, the Deputy Vice-Chancellor of the University of Wollongong, Rob Castle, describes this hierarchical system even more drastically:

In many ways the lifestyle of the traditional teaching research academic is totally dependent on the contribution of sessional staff, in the way that Victorian middle class lifestyles were dependent on the domestic servant. They slept in the attic, ate in the kitchen and you grumbled constantly that what they did was actually not quite what you wanted. But nonetheless, they were absolutely essential to your being and to your lifestyle. I think this applies equally to many sessional staff today. (2008: n.p.)[2]

I do not want to deny or downplay this unpalatable image of a stratified system in which the privileges of tenured staff are bought at the expense of the un- or under-valued labour of the equivalent of the academic 'proletariat' (Castle 2008: n.p), but it can be rendered even more complex. We can paint an even more intricate picture of a typical medium-sized Humanities department, in which the centrality of the so-called 'casual periphery' to the teaching, social and intellectual life of a department is foregrounded, at the same time as tenured academics are not seen simply as an enfranchised superstructure but a group who *themselves* have to work to achieve and maintain a secure sense of academic subjectivity. The overworked permanent staff and the undervalued casual staff are two sides of the same coin.

A contemporary Humanities department is characterized by a diversity of modes of affiliation, belonging and access, and a distribution of academic functions beyond the core of tenured academics. Its paid academic workers may include a sometimes large cohort of postgraduates and an extended departmental community of casuals, research assistants, honorary associates and postdoctoral and other affiliated scholars. This makes for vibrant communities, but ones in which material privileges are unevenly distributed and in which scholars have different access to, relations with, and remuneration for their work and hence for time itself.

Questions of institutional access (to such tangibles as funding and offices and to intangibles like security and the ability to plan ahead) are thoroughly mixed in with the aspiration to and attainment of different forms of academic subjectivity. I'd like to consider three groups in particular: those in training; those in waiting; and those in permanent employment. Those in training include students enrolled in Honours or postgraduate degrees, who are typically interpellated as apprentices and scholars. This is a time when academic subjectivity is often vigorously aspired to, emulated and negotiated. A second group is those who

---

2 An interesting point of comparison and contrast is the two-tier system that emerged in the French higher education system post-World War Two. France met the challenge of post-War massification by creating a second tier of lecturers, who represented a challenging new guard, but one with less power, prestige and influence than the professors (Bourdieu 1988: 152–3).

have completed their PhD and are now symbolically[3] 'ready' for a market that is nonetheless unlikely to accommodate them in an immediate and secure future. They are, in a sense, liminal academics (though not liminal *scholars*, an important distinction) – academics-in-waiting as opposed to academics-in-training. They are often not remunerated for their research time but are nonetheless required to have an ever-expanding CV of research publications if they want to secure permanent employment. This means that research is taken on in an unpaid capacity and/or through movement into the increasing array of other liminal positions, such as postdoctoral scholars and honorary associates.[4] They are accorded some, but not all, of the privileges of full-time academic professional life (e.g. they typically have no permanent office) and many of their professional rights are provisional. For example, they may have to continually renew library borrowing rights and email addresses with each new contract (one of the rites of passage from PhD candidate to graduate being, at some institutions at least, the unceremonious dumping from email accounts and library privileges). On the one hand they are liberated from the burden of PhD study, but they are also subjected to a set of new anxieties – how long should I give it a go? Do I have to be prepared to move away from home, partner or family in search of a job? When should I give up? All too often I hear these questions individualized, transformed from engagements with a *system* to engagements with self-image in the form of the recurring self-doubt: 'Am I good enough?'

While entry to the third group, that of tenured academics, obviously represents the crossing of a significant industrial, financial, and symbolic threshold, it doesn't mean entry into a homogenous group. For although tenured academics share much in common, as a group they are also internally stratified in ways that result in big differences in security, working conditions and professional opportunities. There are hierarchies, for example, between contracted and tenured staff; research-only staff and those with large teaching loads; staff at relatively well-off universities and those at the battlefront of funding cuts; those who have been able to buy themselves time through grants and those working in snatches of time; and between those burdened by heavy administrative and managerial roles and those who have managed to escape such fates.

---

3 They may also be ready in a number of other ways, including intellectually and financially, but I use the term 'symbolically' in order to emphasize the symbolic function of the PhD as a marker of the end of the professional apprenticeship. I am not assuming that all Humanities PhD graduates aspire to a career in academia, but characterizing the situation of some of those who do.

4 As well as being personally unfair, this arrangement also means that the knowledge produced by younger scholars working autonomously will be skewed away from anything that requires substantial funding and/or long-term commitment to a single project. This is a serious issue from the point of view of the nation's investment in knowledge production.

Before turning to the question of what fraudulence may look and feel like to these different groups, I want to stress that the picture I paint is a disjunctive one, where the structural fact of a large group of people competing for a tiny number of precious jobs is as true as the very real practices of care, collegiality, support and encouragement that so often characterize these groups. For the existence of a large cohort of people in a variety of academic roles has greatly expanded academic communities and ensured a lively turnover of people and ideas. The creation and expansion of a cohort of Honours, postgraduate, and post-PhD academics has in many departments helped create large, complex and vibrant cultures of debate, intellectual co-operation and social engagement, where projects are discussed and co-created between scholars occupying a variety of academic roles – students, research assistants, casual teachers, full-time academics. Postgraduate cohorts themselves are typically characterized by mutual support and productive intellectual exchange in a variety of forms including readings groups, the exchanging of drafts, social occasions, shared teaching, and engagement in departmental online forums. So the phenomenon of casualization has perversely been an intellectual and social boon for academic departments. But it is a boon predicated on the uneven distribution of privileges, in which the seemingly democratic social and intellectual engagement is rippled in myriad subtle ways by the differing structural positioning of the community's members and their different personal and professional aspirations. Envy, admiration, emulation, competition, friendship and the pressure to perform run crossways, sideways, back and forth in many directions rather than up or down a simple hierarchy.

The complexity of such departmental communities means that feelings of fraudulence can work in both predictable and unlikely ways, and can apply throughout the academic life-course, not just at the beginning of one's career. It is not unexpected, of course, to find it early on, and for students who are turning to Honours or postgraduate study to feel deficient and fraudulent. These are, after all, self-evidently transitional years, where one is most explicitly moving from being a student to an apprentice, a scholar, and often an academic, whether in training, in waiting, or in permanent employment.

But crossing that magical threshold into permanent employment can in fact intensify rather than neutralize the sense of not being good enough. In a tight employment market, newly employed staff often very acutely feel their obligation to perform their right to a job, not only to new colleagues but also to all those hungry job-seekers in the casual periphery whose ranks they have just left. In such circumstances it is easy to feel that one has been given the job by mistake. Meanwhile, established staff may feel intellectually fraudulent in relation to their department's postgraduate cohort, sensing or fearing, perhaps, that the postgraduate cohort is where the intellectual action is – that postgrads are forming reading groups, are up with latest theory, and may even read a book from cover to cover rather than cherry-picking it for quotable quotes.

It may be hard for those on the other side of the forbidding fence between casual and permanent work to believe that tenured or senior staff have such feelings. In fact, such an assertion may well make some of those in the casual periphery *angry*. How dare anyone who actually *has* a prized job feel uncertain or unhappy, and even if they do, how dare they express it? And yet, while tenured staff are protected from the precarity experienced by casual staff, job losses and pension cuts at universities world-wide have made it evident that overworking is essential to job security. There can, it seems, be no more academic seasons: a time to prepare, a time to plant and a time to sow. Every year must be a bumper year.

Social Contributors: Mastery and Social Positioning

So far, I have surveyed a range of features of the contemporary system that may encourage the feeling that one is not up to scratch. But as the epigraph from Clifford Geertz points out, the 'imperfections of society' also buffet up against personal considerations – what he calls the 'contradictions of character' (1973: 204).

Discussions about fraudulence with postgraduate students over the years have prompted me to think further about how structural questions intersect with questions of personality or psychology. Some students have responded to my thoughts on fraudulence by asking how it differs from simple anxiety or feelings of inadequacy.[5] This has been a useful prompt to explore what one student called 'a fascinating, and subtle, distinction' (Murrie pers. comm. 2009).

Fraudulence implies some equivocality about the fundamental question of one's *right to be somewhere*. This feeling speaks not just to self-doubt but also to socially sanctioned roles and identities. As Greg Murrie put it, 'one is about role and the other about execution or performance' (pers. comm. 2009).

Performance seems, at least on the surface, to be about the successful acquisition of a set of intellectual and professional skills, while role evidently encompasses something more holistic, embodied, social ratified and conservative. It involves being seen as 'the right type of person'. The sociologist Pierre Bourdieu (1988) analysed how this worked in the context of the late-twentieth-century French academy, where, especially in the more prestigious and conservative disciplines like Medicine and Law, what was at stake in the credentialing activities of the university was not just knowledge but a type of embodiment, an art of living which is, as Bourdieu notes, 'inseparable from a *habitus*' – that is, a socially conditioned mode of being in the world (57). Role and performance are, of course, not distinct. Rather, judgements about how well one executes one's job (how skilful one is, how much capacity one has) are inevitably infiltrated by these broader judgements about 'fitness' (and 'fitting-in-ness'). And as new types of

---

5 Thanks to, among others, Sarah Cefai for conversations on this point.

individual break into established roles, the roles themselves and the institutions in which they are embedded slowly begin to change.

An obvious place to start thinking about the embodied performance of role is with the historical figure of the academic 'master'. The master-student relation was central to the medieval university; in the Oxbridge model, it was one of 'moral tutorship' (Dunbabin 1999: 43). Students bonded more with their college, hall or nation than with an idea of a 'university' as a defined entity. Indeed, according to Jean Dunbabin, this attitude continued to characterize students' experience in the Oxbridge model right up till the 1960s (31).[6] 'Mastery', then, involved both an intellectual capability and a social bond, and the identity of the master, drawing as it did on the clerical model in its fusion of the scholarly and the pastoral, was a masculine one. As Murrie so cogently put it about the difference between feeling fraudulent and feeling anxious:

> One might be a legacy of having to "sit in" on or borrow a subject position designated as masculine (the master); while the other is about the rigours of hierarchy – not *whether* one is allowed to occupy that space but whether one lives up to it. (Pers. comm. 2009)

One can, of course, never predict who can carry out this 'occupation' comfortably. All sorts of variables influence the extent to which social factors like class, gender and sexuality support or undermine one's sense of being in place. Some people can acquire a new *habitus*, or the semblance of one. Others can break through the structures regardless. John Higgins, in his biography of the Marxist literary scholar Raymond Williams, a foundational figure for Cultural Studies, comments on Williams's account of his experiences as a 'scholarship boy' at Trinity College, Cambridge, in the late 1930s and early 1940s. Higgins notes that although Williams was highly alert to the class differences, he was 'unwilling to be intimidated', and faced them 'with a sturdy self-confidence and political identity which were the products of a deeply supportive family environment' (1999: 7). So there can be inoculating factors. There are also, of course, strategies for rebuffing these internalized judgments about professional worth.

Before turning to what I see as some potentially useful ways of channelling the feeling of fraudulence, I want briefly to comment on one common professional strategy – that of bluffing.

Academic life has always involved the creation and maintenance of an academic persona – the public performance of oneself as authority or expert. Indeed, any professional has to learn the arts of what sociologist Erving Goffman (1959) called 'impression management'. Certainly, many academics would be familiar with the subtle strategies of managing – and/or being publically *seen* to

---

6 She notes that the sciences were different in this regard.

manage – both the question of difficult workloads and the tacit requirement to be master of all subject areas. Those emails sent at three in the morning to prove how overworked one is; the finely calibrated displays of stress (not so much as to demonstrate professional incapacity but not so little as to suggest under-work); the *de rigueur* dropping of the name of the theorist *du jour*, or references in departmental meetings to the 'current literature'; the in-jokes that assume and test the boundaries of scholarly knowledge, and so on. But my argument is that this form of professional impression management is particularly acute, and takes particular shapes, by the now routinely transdisciplinary contexts of much contemporary scholarship, and by the outcomes-focused, time-poor, bureaucratic contexts in which so many of us now work.

Impression management is an equally real issue for those hoping or trying to break *into* the world of tenured academia. The cultivation of an appropriate academic persona accompanies the labour of the PhD. This is a very self-reflexive process, and students are increasingly aware as they progress through their studies of the rigours of the profession they are seeking to enter. Take this example of a discussion from an online postgraduate forum about the necessity or otherwise of hiding 'deficiencies' from those permanent staff who may be in the position of offering work or otherwise furthering one's career. It tells a sad tale:

> I am a graduate student in humanities pursuing my terminal degree. As the semesters go by … I get more and more panicky in anticipation of the deadlines. This is getting worse. I have vomiting, uncontrollable shaking, harmful ideations and irrational fears that distract me from my work. It's a very serious problem…
>
> Should I confide my struggles in a friendly professor so she knows I'm not a garden-variety slacker, but struggling to control a disorder? Should I register with the disability office…? It is my natural inclination to be open and unashamed, but I've been cautioned against this … I tend to think of my department as a friendly place, at least as far as the faculty is concerned, and I can't imagine this professor in particular breaking a trust. But as I hope to become their colleague upon matriculation, I don't know what to do. (Anonymous 2010)[7]

The 27 replies to this post inevitably give differing advice, ranging from the suggestion to publicize, medicalize and normalize one's anxieties (by, for example, registering with Disabilities), to strategic advice about carefully micro-managing revelations of fallibility (only raise the issue when you're well; build up a bank of 'brownie points' in the good times so you can weather the bad times), through to advice to completely hide all vulnerability:

---

7 'Anonymous' was the original user name.

> I would not disclose this if it were my issue. It is so hard to get an academic job in the humanities these days that any potential drawbacks are going to be seized upon by the people sorting the field, just to winnow the hundreds of candidates down to a manageable number. (Sidhedevil 2010)

Clearly, there is already a tacit pedagogy about 'correct' academic behaviour at work. Can we develop a better one – one more open, more compassionate and more ethical? This would be a pedagogical project in the broadest sense.

Fraudulence as a Pedagogical Issue

In an essay about the impact of the turn to theory in the Humanities in the 1990s, Gerald Graff argued that the turmoil, contestation and uncertainty that characterized debates about theory, the canon and the teaching of literature were not in and of themselves a bad thing for students. 'What is really injurious to students' interests', he said, 'is not the conflict over culture but the fact that students are not more active participants in it' (1994: 19). In a pluralist and democratic university, what could be more practical, he asked, than a curriculum that 'treats cultural and ideological conflict as part of its object of study?' (19). I want to propose a similar approach to the question of feeling fraudulent – that we should aim to take it out of the realm of personal agony and into the realm of pedagogy, understood broadly as what we learn and teach not only in the classroom but in extended spaces like the conference, the corridor, the journal paper.

Breaking the polite silence around the conditions of contemporary academia – or, perhaps more accurately, removing questions of expertise out of the genre of the confessional, the whinge or the lament and putting them into the realm of the pedagogic – might be an important move both for established academics and for those who aspire to join us. In the section that follows, then, I consider five broad principles that could help us develop particular pedagogical strategies: 1) rethinking failure as a pedagogic resource; 2) rethinking expertise and mastery; 3) finding a place; 4) finding a voice; and 5) creating a persona.

Rethinking Fraudulence: Failure as a Pedagogic Resource in Training Researchers

A recurring preoccupation of feminist methodological reflection has been to explore the 'feeling rules' of academic research (Young and Lee, qtd. in Bondi 2005: 240), especially in relation to a theme of failure. It is not only that negative feelings like inadequacy, shame, guilt or self-doubt are paralyzing and interfere with the learning and writing process, but also that omitting to consider them represents a lost opportunity. As John Dewey put it, 'failure is not *mere* failure. It is instructive. The person who really thinks learns quite as much from his failures as from his successes' (1933: 114). Or, as Grandpa Potts in the children's film *Chitty Chitty Bang Bang* put it rather more exuberantly: 'There's magic in the wake of a fiasco'. In thinking as in living, much can be learnt from failures, 'bad' emotions, gaps, problems, experiments gone wrong. The researcher's emotions are, as Liz Bondi puts it, a 'potentially valuable resource' (2005: 242), whether or not they are explicitly discussed in the research. But the opportunities to change one's way of seeing or to understand a problem better are only available when one is able to reflect analytically on such emotions. This involves, according to Bondi, '*suspend[ing]* normative judgements about why one feels in order to reflect on emotions in their full richness and complexity' (241, original emphasis).

In a contemporary qualitative research framework, the researcher's emotions can be usefully thought of not as distortions but as 'a crucial aspect of the data' (Grossman, Kruger and Moore 1999: 124). This might involve thinking about objectivity itself as 'a form of emotion work taught in graduate school' (Reger 2001: 606), or it might involve the intellectual thematizing of other types of emotions and experiences. A supervisor or postgraduate teacher can fruitfully address aspects of the research or learning process like feelings of fraudulence, failure, or ignorance, perhaps using examples from their own career of things that didn't go well. But the sharing of experience in order to combat feelings of isolation and alienation is only a small part of what the thematizing of failure can do. Refusing to ignore or downplay emotions like feeling fraudulent is not necessarily about letting ourselves be more emotional; rather, it can be used as a way of becoming much better at *analysing*. Rethought thus, the ability to analyse emotions is an intellectual skill, a form of good thought rather than its classically feminized antithesis. For example, when teaching a fieldwork practicalities class in an Honours research skills unit, it turned out that there was far more to be learned from stories of interviews gone wrong than from the simple reaffirmation of correct interview procedures or protocols. It became clear to me and the class that even the most mundane practical matters, like confirming dates and times, can go awry because of the 'emotional intensity of ethnographic relationships' (Skeggs 1995: 198) and because practical arrangements are subtly embedded in the 'culture of indebtedness' (197) into which ethnographers, especially feminist ethnographers (197) are drawn. These were themes we were, after all, exploring by reading researchers like Bev Skeggs, Valerie Hey (2002) and Angela McRobbie (1982).

There are many ways of mining mistakes for their intellectual value. Assessment pieces that focus on the processual, shared and temporal nature of thought, for example, tacitly remind us that developing, altering and abandoning ideas is an important component of intellectual work. This is a latent feature of all those courses in which assessment is organized around the sequential development of an idea (e.g. the not infrequent assessment structure of making students work from proposal to draft to chapter). It could be augmented by assignments that specifically thematize supposed 'mistakes'. The essay form, despite the etymology of the word 'essay', tends very often to be used to argue a point, rather than to 'prove' it in the old sense. What about occasionally setting an assignment that focused on analysing the *abandonment* of an idea, project or concept, or detailing the *failure* of a project? Not only can one be analytical about why one no longer finds a concept viable or useful, but the underlying, deeper, pedagogy is one that reminds us that all thought is processual, and that there is no shame in things that don't work. (For an example of an assignment that focuses on challenges and difficulties see the Appendix). Such strategies are a way of conceiving of expertise not as the repudiation of failure but as made and continually remade through dialogue, revision and occasional error. Such a conception is a way of refusing, at least sometimes, the structure of argument that Sedgwick (2003), in her well-known call not to limit ourselves to only one tool in the intellectual toolbox – that of critique – calls 'paranoid'. In a refreshing refusal of the 'habitual practices' (124) of the critical disciplines, Sedgwick calls for greater diversity in what she calls the 'ecology of knowing' (145), so that we do not always have to be caught up in the game of attacking others while covering our backs (or, to repeat the quotation from Robert Dessaix, 'finding others wanting while on the edge of being found wanting [our]selves' (1998: 122)). The literary scholar Paul Ricoeur's famous 'hermeneutics of suspicion' is, Sedgwick argues, to be thought of less as a 'mandatory injunction' than as 'a possibility among other possibilities' (2003: 125). There are, she implies, different ways of being an expert.

Rethinking Expertise in a Pluralist intellectual Climate

Personal Strategies: Not Being a Know-All One way of publically performing a stance about mastery is to refuse to shy away from acknowledging the limits of one's knowledge or understanding. Such an acknowledgement can function not just as a personal commentary but also as an implicit statement of principle. Matter of fact statements of incomprehension, lack of knowledge or lack of interest and so on might thus be seen as a subtle part of an extended postgraduate pedagogy, in which we refuse to perform the illusion that one person can know all things or should be expected to try. Many years ago a senior colleague of mine unknowingly liberated me in this way. A junior academic tutoring in someone else's course, I was battling some dense theoretical text that another lecturer had set as a reading and I asked this colleague for some assistance. She bluntly told me that she had never understood the theorist in question and wasn't interested in trying. Now, perhaps you may consider this anti-intellectual, but as a junior academic, I didn't know you were allowed to *think*, let alone say this, and it came as a great relief. This, then, I consider a pedagogical act in the broad sense, since it was a blunt commentary about refusing pressures towards impression management via bluff. It was a very useful collegial performance.

Experts in Information Management   Of course, a serious look at the question of mastery involves not just the individual negotiating the limits of practicable knowledge, but a more sustained and public interrogation of the idea of expertise and the role of the academic. A more systematic example of an attempt to bring questions of expertise into public dialogue is the debate around the meaning of expertise in the information age. Some see that the only appropriate way forward in the digital age, especially for those who work in transdisciplinary contexts, is to modify our understanding of what it means to be an expert. In the age of the Internet, argue educationalists such as Marc Prensky (2008), who needs to remember facts?

In 2008, one private Sydney high school trialled the technique of allowing students to access the Internet, including social media, and to phone a friend during exams. The teacher coordinating the project said:

> In their working lives they will never need to carry enormous amounts of information around in their heads. What they will need to do is access information from all their sources quickly and they will need to check the reliability of their information. (Patty 2008: 1)

This may well be true, but it fails to address the question of uneven access to social capital. Not everyone has academically skilled friends. One of the girls who took part in the trial described how in a task requiring them to write a sonnet she texted her father – a former English teacher – for advice (Edwards 2008).

In academia, the argument about the importance of higher-order skills over factual content (or 'knower codes' versus 'knowledge codes' [Maton 2009: 46]) is quite commonly made in relation to postgraduate supervision, since supervisors need to be found for an ever-increasing number and array of projects. We are invited to see ourselves less as masters of specific content than of a particular skill set – information collection and management, critical thinking, conceptual development and specialist forms of analytical writing. This conception of the Humanities scholar is not new for, as Readings argues, the idea of critical thought as the intellectual skill that transcends and overarches particular disciplinary knowledge has been a characteristic feature of the modern university, at least in its Romantic formulation, where the university was understood as a 'site of critique' (1996: 6). But this idea nonetheless traditionally stood alongside the image of the professor as the accruer of specialist knowledge, the hero of 'the adventure of a liberal education' (Allan

Bloom, qtd. in Readings 1996: 7). But nowadays, says Readings, the fracturing of disciplinary knowledge and of the aims of the university mean that no such grand adventure narrative, and no such hero, exists (9). Perhaps, then, if we can no longer be heroes, nor even fellow journeymen, we might want to reconceive, or perhaps reduce ourselves, to being expert conduits and nodes in information flows, specialized collectors, arbiters and managers of information, experts in process rather than in content. Such a reconceptualization would accord with Readings's idea of the contemporary university as cultivating a highly translatable, reference-free, principle of excellence (24) over and above its role in inculcating particular knowledge. As we saw above, Readings saw Cultural Studies as having a particular place in this new regime, given the openness of its core concept, culture. Whether or not this is so, it is true that the conception of the academic as an expert in critical thinking and information management might be more attractive or plausible to some disciplines than others, or in some of our functions than in others.

I do have a measure of sympathy for this view, mostly when it comes to postgraduate supervision. Certainly, years of teaching a subject in which Honours and postgraduate students develop their thesis projects in relation to a body of literature has taught me that there is something technical about the ability to help students develop their projects. Asking the right questions can be far more important than knowing the answers, or even having read their theorists, and being an expert in structuring thought is an important skill, especially in transdisciplinary or problem-based environments.

As a strategy for teaching more obviously content-based units, though, this approach has its limits and it is unlikely that many academics will be content to become experts in pure form or process (professing an expertise in *how to* research, rather than in 'content') – certainly not in the bulk of our teaching, even at postgraduate level. Nonetheless, this triumph of knower codes over knowledge codes (of 'thought' over 'content') has become such an orthodoxy that it has made its way not only into accounts of postgraduate supervision but also into expectations of postgraduate *candidature*. Since intellectual content is so specific, and beyond the reach of the kinds of generic teaching and learning policies instituted at a university-wide level, university regulations focus instead on graduate attributes. Margaret Kiley notes the high level of consistency between Australian universities about what the PhD is meant to demonstrate, and that is, a set of *skills*, including, *inter alia*, working in teams, time management, project management, critical thinking, problem solving and so on (2009: 33). Such lists make it sound as though the aim of a PhD were, in fact, to test whether you can do a PhD.

'Mastery' and the PhD   The PhD is a particularly acute example through which to explore the borderlands of bluff and authority, since its very function is to

recognize mastery, to confer authority and to (pretend to) secure entry into full professional life. In his 1995 essay 'Monstrous Knowledge: Doing PhDs in the New Humanities', Bob Hodge ponders the authorizing functions of the PhD by, among other things, analysing the language of university PhD regulations. Hodge argues that although ideas like mastery and originality hang heavy over postgraduates and supervisors, they are actually much more equivocal requirements of the PhD than we tend to think. The 'idea' of the PhD is, according to Hodge, more powerful than the bureaucratic regulations that actually govern it; 'originality' and 'mastery' are requirements more mythic than literal. Hodge contrasts what he sees as the 'idealism and paranoiac excess' (36) of the idea of the PhD with the actual regulations governing the infamous 'original contribution to thought', which, he claim, tend more towards encouraging 'industrious conformity' (36) than grand disciplinary iconoclasm. If this is so, then to whom or what should the PhD student address his/her thesis – to the handbook regulations or to the idea of the PhD which, after all, is likely still to be a functioning myth in the eyes of the examiners, and thus needs to be taken into account regardless of the regulations? Clearly, a number of professional conversations need to be had, not just between supervisors and students but between academic colleagues since we are, whenever we examine a PhD, upholders (or not) of ideas about mastery and expertise.

Such questions have especial pertinence in transdisciplinary contexts, which challenge the relevance of traditional criteria for successful PhDs and the meaning of mastery itself. Willetts et al. argue that in the absence of the limits imposed by classic disciplinary frameworks, the student's *values* play an important role in guiding and shaping the boundaries of the project (2012: 129).[8] They note that transdisciplinary PhDs take place in the challenging, and sometime destabilizing, terrain of 'epistemological pluralism' (129).

For Hodge, similarly, the distinctiveness of what he calls a postmodern PhD would be its 'awareness of the problem of discourse' (1995: 38). For example, it necessitates:

- A heightened reflexivity of the shape of what one is doing, including its borders and a necessary awareness of what lies outside it.
- Demonstrating an awareness of the existence of other relevant theories, debates or approaches and their import without aspiring to a mastery of these. This involves understanding where your projects sits in relation to dominant lines of thought or endeavour.

---

8 They also note how the different expertise required in a transdisciplinary PhD requires a renegotiation of the supervisor's role and the supervisor-student relationship (2012: 137).

- Demonstrating not just a non-specific 'sufficient literacy', but a literacy that also demonstrates, perhaps implicitly, an awareness that negotiating disciplinarity involves negotiating genres and textual strategies.

To me, this represents not a weakening of PhD requirements as the doomsayers might have it, but in fact a more stringent approach, since it involves not only the mastery of certain skills and content areas, but also understanding where one's knowledge and approach fit within in a wider intellectual schema. In short it involves finding a place and a voice.

Finding a Place: Developing a Sense of Intellectual Project   The project of finding one's intellectual place involves developing a heightened awareness and reflexivity about the particularity of one's intellectual skills and training, aims and focus. This involves understanding one's own animating intellectual themes – one's developing intellectual biography – and how they fit into a bigger scheme. Getting the necessary distance and overview is not always easy; we normally can't see the intellectual wood for the trees, and we may, in any case, be prone to read our own distinctive intellectual shapes as a lack of something that others have – which is why developing this skill is of necessity a collegial undertaking. Colleagues may see themes, continuities and distinctiveness in our work that remain opaque to us. Mirroring back the contours and the distinctiveness of the student's intellectual project is certainly an important component of the supervisory role. It is in fact a very particular intellectual skill, which can be sharpened and developed.

Finding a Voice: Teaching Thesis Writing Strategies   In the 'Monstrous Knowledge' essay mentioned above, Bob Hodge (1995) makes an enthusiastic case for the transdisciplinary PhD. He urges PhD students in the New Humanities to 'be open to the monstrous'; to be transdisciplinary; to 'detect the shadow' (37). 'Work with the old prohibitions as well as the new knowledges', he insists; take seriously problems that are 'annulled' by being designated 'quaint', 'naive', 'outrageous' or 'unthinkable'; mix disciplines 'promiscuously', monstrously (37). For Hodge, shameful ideas, intellectual mistakes or conceptual misfits are not awkward problems to be hidden by strategies of evasion or bluff but signs that should be celebrated as pointers to the conditions of disciplinary discourses (37). But of course, well aware that to write such a thesis is to invite risk, and to encourage students in this manner irresponsible, he urges students *sous rature*, offering up his suggestions as 'practical advice (along with the further advice not to take it)' (37). His essay is at once utopian – imagining a revolution in disciplinary knowledge – and cautious, if a little disingenuously. He is, of course, aware that the ultimate requirement of a PhD is that it be passable. Indeed, he describes its definitive function as being 'simply the next stage in a career of study, a further qualification that allows the person to take up a position in academia' (36), a promise whose seeming modesty is now somewhat ironic, 15 years on, since the PhD as a guarantor of a job is now more a utopia than a mundane come-down. So, if we are all agreed that we do not want our students to offer up an unpassable PhD as a sacrifice on the altar of disciplinary politics – to produce knowledge so monstrous that the PhD cannot fulfil its authorizing functions (35) – then what kind of voice can we responsibly encourage our PhD students to develop?

I return here to Robert Dessaix, who makes the distinction between what he calls including and excluding texts and voices. The including voice is, he says, 'more openly emotional and personal (emphasising vulnerability)' (1998: 124). Whereas the excluding voice says, 'I'm now going to eat my dinner. Watch me', the including voice says 'Let's go shopping, shall we? Let's go and buy something together, then come home, cook it and eat it. What do you say to that?' (124–5). Dessaix explicitly genders these two voices; the personal, vulnerable, more openly emotional voice is a feminine one (125). This use of the phrase 'more openly emotional' and not 'more emotional' subtly makes the same point made by feminist methodological reflection that argues that objectivity is not the absence of emotions, but the *hiding* of emotion, in other words, a form of institutionally sanctioned bluff. The excluding voice, licensed to bluff, uses, Dessaix claims, jargon, habitual phrases, Latinate constructions, passive verbs and so on to render itself impregnable. This vision of a text armoured in orthodoxy is reminiscent of Dewey's account of the dangers of over-abstraction:

> Genuine ignorance is more profitable [than partial or confused understanding] because it is likely to be accompanied by humility, curiosity, and open-mindedness; whereas ability to repeat catch-phrases, cant terms, familiar propositions, gives the conceit of learning and coats the mind with a varnish waterproof to new ideas. (1933: 237)

Dessaix considers the excluding voice to be patronizing, since ultimately it refuses to share power with or confer authority on the reader. Game and Metcalfe say something similar, when they associate honest writing not only with lack of bluff but also with a lack of condescension (1996: 33). They consider bluff to be a paralyzing defence strategy, and they recommend that as writers we should try to liberate ourselves from the fear of our own inadequacy (36) by 'imagining a sympathetic readership, made up of people somewhat like [us]' (30):

> Writing for an imagined readership that you trust and respect is the source of the deepest writing pleasures, because it allows the fullest testing of your writing capacities, the freshest and most honest arguments, the least bluff, defence and ventriloquism, the most play, the least condescension. (33)

Both Dessaix (1998) and Game and Metcalfe (1996) celebrate gaps, holes and openings. Dessaix values texts that 'create an aperture in ourselves that others can enter' (1998: 131); while Game and Metcalfe celebrate both the incompleteness of the self and 'the incompleteness of knowledge' (1996: 35), seeing it as the condition of creativity: 'To write is to open up and be open to possibilities for creation and self-creation in the world' (35). Like Dessaix, they see the most pleasurable writing as that which invites, rather than declares: it is 'not a statement from the dock but an invitation to a dance' (35).

This celebration of openness and incompleteness is almost the contrary of what we are normally taught about making an argument: to make sure your back is covered, that every possible objection has been countered in advance, that you have left no visible gaps or holes. The gendering of these metaphors in these writers is also quite manifest: gaps, holes, apertures, openness, dancing, shopping all make it clear that these are feminized texts and strategies. But does writing a vulnerable text involve obligatory recourse to feminized genres of writing, such as the first-person narrative or the confessional mode (Bondi 2005: 243)? Should we perhaps be teaching students how to *avoid* feminizing their texts so they are not left open to attack? After all, the function of the invulnerable text is, Dessaix observes, not so much to demonstrate that one is right (although it may do that) as to demonstrate to one's peers that one is 'in the club' (1998: 122). Since gaining a PhD is, in a nutshell, about entry into a club, do we want to encourage our postgrads to write open, vulnerable texts or to cover their tracks, producing a hard, polished surface around their thesis – making it safe, invulnerable – less of an invitation to go shopping or dancing than a masterful performance?

For Game and Metcalfe, writing honestly appears more like a *writing strategy* than a recipe for a finished text – a strategy for liberating one's writing from the burdens of institutional rules (1996: 34) and the twin evils of boredom and the blasé attitude (29). So it comes down to a question of particular instances – when is it OK to admit you do not know and when should you bluff? Sometimes honesty is not the best policy, and bluffing is an important professional skill, which students should learn. But is the PhD thesis one of those times?

Creating a Persona   The question of strategy leads me to my final consideration, which is pedagogic only in the broadest sense of the term. I want to suggest that many of the ethical and intellectual precepts I am discussing can best be summed up as the development of a particular professional persona. The palimpsestic nature of the contemporary university now means that the ideal of the hero-professor is quite a composite figure indeed: an efficient administrator, an able manipulator of many types of technologies, a rigorous scholar and a caring teacher. Few of us can meet all these demands. Since it is, I think, no longer sufficient to act as if 'expertise' were simple to conceive but hard to achieve – it is now hard both to conceive *and* achieve – as my final strategy I want to propose the reflective and ethical creation of a professional persona as a self-conscious pedagogic strategy. In these days of ostensibly student-centred learning it is easy to forget the power of role models.

The importance of role models was reinforced to me during a small-scale study I conducted in 2012 in which I interviewed postgraduate students about their professional aspirations (Barcan 2014, forthcoming). I asked them, among other things, how they were learning to be an academic. The most common response was by conscious but selective emulation, observing permanent staff and by consciously trying out potential techniques and trying on elements of professional style. This confirmed my already developing sense that as academics we can wield ourselves as ethical instruments – not just in our overt actions but also in the way we craft our modes of being in the world. This is, I guess, a version of the academic impression management I described earlier. But it is a self-reflexive, politically aware version – one striving towards an ethics of embodiment.

Ironically, the development of an open, non-defensive, vulnerable academic self itself constitutes a self-conscious academic performance – as much a strategy as the protective and defensive strategies like bluff and evasion. It is a matter less of simply sharing the real vulnerable you with your students as of performing a particular version of authenticity – a persona organized not just around easing one's own anxieties but around that old feminist project of a rigorous examination of the seemingly personal, made in a spirit of critique and solidarity. This would be a self-conscious crafting of an academic persona, in text, speech and flesh – a persona that is not based on the creation of a polished surface, but, rather, on making the self into an interested participant who is sometimes bemused, sometimes lost, sometimes passionate, and – just occasionally – a master of something.

Conclusion

A few years ago, this paper belonged to a genre I now whimsically call 'Print 'n' Sprint' – referring to those drafts where I press 'Ctrl P' then sprint madly up the corridor to the printer before anyone could possibly pick it up and see what I am up to. For underneath the feeling of fraudulence is a form of professional shame, and writing about shame is, as Elspeth Probyn (2005) points out, inherently shaming. Shame itself 'is seen as deeply shameful' (Probyn 2005: xiii), and it acts as a hindrance to clear analysis (Bondi 2005: 241). But Probyn's work on shame also reminds us of two things – that shame reflects the fact that we actually care (that we are animated by what she, using the language of Silvan Tomkins's affect theory, terms 'interest') and that it can therefore be instructive and productive. In any case, these days I confront these feelings far more matter-of-factly as a realistic facet of contemporary university life and something which we are morally obliged to discuss, if not with colleagues, then certainly with postgraduate students, so many of whom face an uncertain future of moving between a series of short-term contracts, institution to institution, and hence having to move across multiple teaching areas, methodological approaches and collegiates, not only as tutors but increasingly as contracted convenors – with relatively little by way of infrastructural support and with less access, perhaps, to the sense of professional stability that comes with full membership of an academic community. If it is true, as Melissa Gregg argues, that cultural studies has 'made the scholarly vocation a more attractive and likely prospect for different kinds of people' (2006: 2), then perhaps a rousing and realistic discussion about what it really means to inhabit that vocation – and how we can make it easier on ourselves – would have much to offer both those who already live out that vocation and those who aspire to join us.

Conclusion

As I neared completion of this book, anyone asking me what I was working on was likely to be met with the reply that I was 'finishing a depressing book about universities with hope in the title'. And certainly, for a book advocating hope, these essays may appear rather too indebted to despair. But hope is like that: it is not an antithesis to worry, doubt or melancholy but, rather, emerges from them. Hope is a *discipline*. It must be practised, sometimes against the odds.

Contradiction, then, is part of the work of hope. And out of the mess of contradictory feelings that gave rise to these essays, I have teased out a number of threads:

The first is that I have realized that it is important to make the distinction between lamenting changes to the university as an institution and being worried about academic wellbeing. The serious questions raised by academics about how healthy, viable and prosperous a life a prospective academic might have within a university are not arguments against, for example, massification. They are, rather, grave interrogations of the intellectual and personal sustainability of a mass system organized around exploitative labour, whether that be the precarious labour of the ever-increasing casual staff or the overwork of the diminishing tenured staff. Such questions concern us doubly – as they bear on both the individual welfare of thousands of workers and the higher education system's capacity to systematically, impartially and carefully generate knowledge into the future.

The predicament of casual workers is particularly urgent. In response to critiques of casualization, we all too often hear the riposte that *all* contemporary industries need to be flexible, mobile and productive. We in turn must continue to make a double response: first, by continuing to insist that the production of knowledge must be understood to differ in certain crucial ways from other forms of industrial production; and second, and concurrently, by using our privilege to denounce the flaws in and violence wrought by disembodied models of flexibility on behalf of *all* workers.

In terms of our own ways of inhabiting the system, a second, similar, distinction may be of help in an everyday sense: that between the big picture – what is happening to the sector (over which I believe we have very little control) – and closer to hand, in the contexts in which we still have influence, such as the corridors and the classrooms. I am not trying to idealize the space of the classroom as outside or beyond politics. On the contrary, the types of students in our classrooms, the number of them, the nature of the equipment in the classroom, and the security, reimbursement and stress levels of the teacher – all these and more flow from that all too real politics. Still and all, teaching academics can draw some comfort from that fact that from the moment that classroom door closes, we are trusted, by students, colleagues and the general public to do our job – a job, moreover, that no one else can do. We must never lose sight of the classroom as a space of possibility.

Third, I continue to believe in the importance of contesting the discourse of efficiency. Efficiency, as Kenneth Boulding noted presciently in 1978, 'can be dangerous' (1996 [1978]: 415). Creativity and innovation rely on experimentation, and hence on the potential for failure and waste; drain away inefficiency and you risk losing the stuff you need most. Drawing on an ecological metaphor – the diversity necessary to ensure future survival – Boulding noted that narrowness (over-adaptation, if you like) is dangerous, and that inefficiency is the way societies keep doors open for a range of possible futures:

> [A]n inefficient species has reserves in redundancy and irrelevance, which are the sort of things that universities have, and can draw on these reserves for survival. This is a fairly comforting thought, that universities are repositories of redundancy in society, so that in a crisis they constitute an important reserve on which society may draw. (415)

Just as Barthes taught me to reflect that there are different types of inactivity, so Boulding has taught me to see that there are different types of inefficiency. Waste, for example, is 'inefficiency beyond the optimum' (1996 [1978]: 416). And then there are different temporalities to consider: 'there is a great deal of difference between short-run, narrowly measured efficiency and the long-run efficiency which leads to ultimate survival' (416). We may, he argues, have to have a bit of both, but we must never let the former become the enemy of the latter (416).

So, for reasons that concern innovation as much as human wellbeing, we have to continue to contest the ideal of ceaseless productivity and the strange fantastical cosmologies on which it reposes. What kind of cosmology – what theory of creativity, economics, let alone embodiment – could be supported by an ideal of ceaseless productivity? There are no bodies that can do output without sufficient input; no outbreath without the pause after inspiration. I don't want to live in a work world in which people become prompts for jobs – a world in which you bump into a colleague and they don't say 'Hello', they say, 'Oh sorry, I haven't replied to your email'.

Finally, writing this book has made me realize the importance of fighting for a quite simple principle – the principle that it is reasonable, fair and necessary for there to be different types of academics, and different ways of being an academic. Without our stylistic, philosophical and procedural differences there can be no deep intellectual diversity, no investment in unpredictable futures, no workplace justice, no possibility of responsiveness to local contexts – only a dangerously singular investment in one model of professional identity and intellectual production. Our professional variegation – sometimes exhilarating, sometimes deeply irritating – is something we can and must fight for.

Bibliography

[Augustine]. 1944 [399]. *The Confessions of St. Augustine*. London: Sheed & Ward.

Abdulghani, H.M. et al. 2012. Sleep disorder among medical students: relationship to their academic performance. *Medical Teacher*, 34(s1), S37–S41.

Abouserie, R. 1996. Stress, coping strategies and job satisfaction in university academic staff. *Educational Psychology*, 16(1), 49–56.

Acker, S. and Armenti, C. 2004. Sleepless in academia. *Gender and Education*, 16(1), 3–24.

Adams, D. 1998. Examining the fabric of academic life: an analysis of three decades of research on the perceptions of Australian academics about their roles. *Higher Education*, 36(4), 421–35.

Adams, D. 2000. Views of academic work. *Teacher Development: An International Journal of Teachers' Professional Development*, 4(1), 65–78.

Albury, K. and Crawford, K. 2012. Sexting, consent and young people's ethics: beyond *Megan's Story*. *Continuum: Journal of Media and Cultural Studies*, 26(3), 463–73.

Aldrich, R. 1996. *Education for the Nation*. London: Cassell.

Alfino, M. et al., (eds). 1998. *McDonaldization Revisited: Critical Essays on Consumer Culture*. Westport, CT: Greenwood Publishing Group.

Alley, S. and Smith, M. 2004. Timeline: tuition fees. *The Guardian* [Online, 27 January] Available at: http://www.guardian.co.uk/education/2004/jan/27/tuitionfees.students [accessed: 14 October 2011].

Althusser, L. 1971. Ideology and ideological state apparatuses (notes towards an investigation), in *Lenin and Philosophy and Other Essays*. London: NLB, 121–73.

Amis, K. 1960. Lone voices: views of the 'fifties. *Encounter*, 15(1), 6–11.

Anderson, D. 1990. Access to university education in Australia 1852–1990: changes in the undergraduate social mix, in *Ideas for Histories of Universities in Australia*, edited by F.B. Smith and P. Crichton. Canberra: Division of Historical Studies, Research School of Social Sciences, Australian National University, 116–47.

Ang, I. 2006. From cultural studies to cultural research: engaged scholarship in the twenty-first century. *Cultural Studies Review*, 12(2), 183–97.

Anonymous. 2010. Is outing panic disorder academic suicide? Metafilter, December 12. Available at: http://ask.metafilter.com/172936/ 'Is-outing-panic-disorder-academic-suicide [accessed: 16 May 2011].

Aquinas, St Thomas. 2007 [1911]. *Summa Theologica: Volume III – Part II, Second Section*. New York: Cosimo, Inc.

Aquinas, T. 2012 [1269–72] On hope. In *Thomas Aquinas: Disputed Questions on the Virtues*, edited by E.M. Atkins and T. Williams. Cambridge University Press. Available at: Cambridge Books Online http://ebooks.cambridge.org/ [accessed: 12 October 2012].

Arnold, M. 1869. *Culture and Anarchy: An Essay in Political and Social Criticism*. London: Smith, Elder and Co.

Arvidsson, A. 2005. Brands: a critical perspective. *Journal of Consumer Culture*, 5(2), 235–58.

Auchmuty, J.J. and Jeffares, A.N. 1959. Australian universities: the historical background, in *The Humanities in Australia: A Survey with Special Reference to the Universities*, edited by G.A. Price. Sydney: Angus & Robertson for the Australian Humanities Research Council, 14–33.

Australian Research Council. 2011. *Australian Laureate Fellowships Funding Rules for Funding Commencing in 2012*. Available at: http://www.arc.gov.au/pdf/FL12/FL12_funding_rules.pdf [accessed: 16 March 2012].

Bakhtin, M. 1984. *Rabelais and His World*. Cambridge, MA: MIT Press.

Ball, C.S. 1990. *More Means Different: Widening Access to Higher Education*. London: RSA [Royal Society for the Encouragement of Arts, Manufactures & Commerce].

Barcan, A. 1980. *A History of Australian Education*. Melbourne: Oxford University Press.

Barcan, A. 2011. *From New Left to Factional Left: Fifty Years of Student Activism at Sydney University*. North Melbourne, Vic: Australian Scholarly Publishing.

Barcan, R. 2014, forthcoming. Learning to be an academic: tacit and explicit pedagogies. in *Cultural Pedagogies and Human Contact*. Abingdon: Routledge.

Barthes, R. 1985 [1979]. Dare to be lazy, in *The Grain of the Voice: Interviews 1962–1980*. Berkeley: University of California Press, 338–45.

Bataille, G. 1988. *The Accursed Share: An Essay on General Economy*. New York: Zone Books.

Baumgardner, S.R. and Crothers, M.K. 2009. *Positive Psychology*. Upper Saddle River, N.J.: Prentice Hall.

BBC News 2010. Spending review 2010: key points at-a-glance. [Online, 21 October] Available at: http://www.bbc.co.uk/news/uk-politics-11569160 [accessed: 25 January 2012].

Bellah, R.N. et al. 2008 [1985]. *Habits of the Heart: Individualism and Commitment in American Life*. Berkeley: University of California Press.

Bellotti, V. et al. 2005. Quality versus quantity: e-mail-centric task management and its relation with overload. *Human–Computer Interaction*, 20(1–2), 89–138.

Belsky, S. 2010. *Making Ideas Happen: Overcoming the Obstacles Between Vision and Reality*. New York: Penguin.

Bennett, T. 1998. *Culture: A Reformer's Science*. St Leonards: Allen & Unwin.

Bennington, G. 1999. Inter, in *Post-Theory: New Directions in Criticism*, edited by M. McQuillan et al. Edinburgh: Edinburgh University Press, 103–19.

Berdahl, R.O. 1977 [1959]. *British Universities and the State*. New York: Arno Press.

Biggs, J.B and Moore, P.J. 1993. *The Process of Learning*, 3rd Edition. New York: Prentice Hall.

Blake, H. 2010. Grants, loans and tuition fees: a timeline of how university funding has evolved. *The Telegraph* [Online, 10 November] Available at: http://www.telegraph.co.uk/education/educationnews/8057871/Grants-loans-and-tuition-fees-a-timeline-of-how-university-funding-has-evolved. html [accessed: 14 October 2011].

Bloch, E. 1986. *The Principle of Hope*. Oxford: Blackwell.

Bloom, A. 1987. *The Closing of the American Mind: How Higher Education Has Failed Democracy and Impoverished the Souls of Today's Students*. New York: Simon and Schuster.

Bogart, G. 1994. Finding a life's calling. *Journal of Humanistic Psychology*, 34(4), 6–37.

Bond University n.d. *Important Information for International Students* [Online] Available at: http://www.bond.edu.au/prod_ext/groups/public/@pub-sa-gen/documents/guideline/bd3_013773.pdf [accessed: 13 April 2012].

Bondi, L. 2005. The place of emotions in research: from partitioning emotion and reason to the emotional dynamics of research relationships, in *Emotional Geographies*, edited by J. Davidson, L. Bondi and M. Smith. Aldershot, Hampshire: Ashgate, 231–46.

Booth, C. 1999. The rise of the new universities in Britain, in *The Idea of a University*, edited by D. Smith and A.K. Langslow. London: Jessica Kingsley Publishers, 106–23.

Boulding, K. 1996 [1978]. In praise of inefficiency, in *ASHE Reader on Finance in Higher Education*, edited by D.W. Breneman, L.L. Leslie and R.E. Anderson. Needham Heights, MA: Simon and Schuster Custom Publishing, 415–18.

Bourdieu, P. 1988. *Homo Academicus*. Stanford: Stanford University Press.

Bradley, D. 2011. *Academia: An Exciting Life*. Keynote address, *Academia: A Scholarly Life* conference, University of Western Sydney, 21 July.

Braidotti, R. 2011. *Nomadic Subjects: Embodiment and Sexual Difference in Contemporary Feminist Theory*. New York: Columbia University Press.

Brecht, B. 1976. To those born later, in *Bertolt Brecht Poems: Part Two 1929–1938*, edited by J. Willett and R. Manheim. London: Eyre Methuen.

Brett, J. 1991. The bureaucratization of writing: why so few academics are public intellectuals. *Meanjin*, 50(4), 513–22.

Brigg, B. 2010. [Untitled comment]. The stay at home students: university fees rise will force middle classes to live with their parents, by J. Groves and L. Clark. *The Daily Mail* [Online, 13 October] Available at: http://www.dailymail.

co.uk/news/article-1320027/Vince-Cable-Tuition-fees-force-middle-class-students-live-parents.html# [accessed: 7 July 2011].

Brookfield, S. 1995. *Becoming a Critically Reflective Teacher.* San-Francisco: Jossey-Bass.

Brown, R. 2010. Multitasking gets you there later. [Online, 29 June] Available at: http://www.infoq.com/articles/multitasking-problems [accessed: 19 April 2012].

Brown, T., Goodman, J., and Yasukawa K. 2010. Academic casualization in Australia: class divisions in the university. *Journal of Industrial Relations,* 52(2), 169–82.

Bryson, C. and Barnes, N. 2000. The casualisation of employment in higher education in the United Kingdom, in *Academic Work and Life: What it is to be an Academic, and How This is Changing,* edited by M. Tight. Amsterdam: JAI/Elsevier Science, 187–241.

Bunderson, J.S. and Thompson, J.A. 2009. The call of the wild: zookeepers, callings, and the double-edged sword of deeply meaningful work. *Administrative Science Quarterly,* 54(1), 32–57.

Burgess, P.W. 2000. Real-world multitasking from a cognitive neuroscience perspective, in *Control of Cognitive Processes: Attention and Performance XVIII,* edited by S. Monsell and J. Driver. [Cambridge, MA]: The International Association for the Study of Attention and Performance/The MIT Press, 465–72.

Burrows, R. 2012. Living with the h-index? Metric assemblages in the contemporary academy. *The Sociological Review,* 60(2), 355–72.

Calamity Jane. 2011. [Untitled comment]. Grayling cries freedom, by F. Furedi. *Times Higher Education* [Online, 16 June] Available at: http://www.timeshighereducation.co.uk/story.asp?sectioncode=26&storycode=416521&c=1 [accessed: 2 September 2011].

Camporesi, P. 1989. The consecrated host: a wondrous excess, in *Fragments for a History of the Human Body: Part One,* edited by M. Feher with R. Naddaff and N. Tazi. New York: Zone, 220–37.

Castle, R. 2008. Foreword, in *The RED Report: Recognition, Enhancement, Development. The Contribution of Sessional Teachers to Higher Education,* by Alisa Percy et al. Strawberry Hills, NSW: Australian Learning and Teaching Council.

C-Dog 2009. Sprung. [Online, 12 November] Available at: http://seadogblog.blogspot.com.au/2009/11/sprung.html [accessed: 21 March 2012].

Charman-Anderson, S. 2008. Email becomes a dangerous distraction. [Online, 9 September] Available at: http://www.smh.com.au/news/biztech/youve-got-interruptions/2008/09/08/1220857455459.html?page=fullpage [accessed: 21 February 2012].

Chen, R.T.-H., Bennett, S. and Maton, K. 2008. The adaptation of Chinese international students to online flexible learning: two case studies. *Distance Education,* 29(3), 307–23.

Christakis, N. and Fowler, J.H. 2010. *Connected: The Amazing Power of Social Networks and How They Shape our Lives.* London: HarperPress.

Clarke, C. 2003. *Charles Clarke's Statement to the Commons.* [Online, 22 January] Available at: http://www.guardian.co.uk/education/2003/jan/22/highereducation.accesstouniversity/ [accessed: 14 October 2011].

Clegg, S. 2003. Problematising ourselves: continuing professional development in higher education. *International Journal for Academic Development,* 8(1), 37–50.

Coates, H. et al. 2009. Australia's casual approach to its academic teaching workforce. *People and Place,* 17(4), 47–54.

Coates, H. 2011. *Working on a Dream: Educational Returns from Off-Campus Paid Work.* Australasian Survey of Student Engagement (AUSSE) Research Briefing, 8 (March). Camberwell, Vic: Australian Council for Educational Research. [Available at: http://research.acer.edu.au/ausse].

Cockcroft, K., Grasko, D., and Fridjhon, P. 2006. On counting sheep: the self-medication and coping strategies of university students suffering from primary insomnia. *South African Journal of Higher Education,* 20(5), 627–38.

Collins, T. 2009. Jobs threat as University of Birmingham plans to close department. *Birmingham Mail* [Online, 12 November] Available at: http://www.birminghammail.net/news/birmingham-news/2009/11/12/jobs-threat-as-university-of-birmingham-plans-to-close-department-65233-25150280/ [accessed: 9 June 2011].

Committee on Higher Education. 1963. *Higher Education Report of the Committee Appointed by the Prime Minister under the Chairmanship of Lord Robbins 1961–63 [The Robbins Report].* HMSO.

Commonwealth of Australia [John Dawkins] 1988. *Higher Education: A Policy Statement.* Canberra: Australian Government Publishing Service.

Connolly, W.E. 2009. Speed, concentric cultures, and cosmopolitanism, in *High-Speed Society: Social Acceleration, Power, and Modernity,* edited by H. Rosa and W.E. Scheuerman. University Park, PA: The Pennsylvania State University Press, 261–85.

Coser, L.A. 1971. *Masters of Sociological Thought: Ideas in Historical and Social Context.* New York: Harcourt Brace Jovanovich.

Cox, C. 1996. The (end of the) end of history, in *The Ends of Theory,* edited by J. Herron et al. Detroit: Wayne State University Press, 120–34.

Cox, W. and Pavletich, H. 2011. *7th Annual Demographia International Housing Affordability Survey: 2011.* [Online] Available at: http://www.demographia.com/dhi.pdf [accessed: 6 June 2011].

Craik, J. 1994. *The Face of Fashion: Cultural Studies in Fashion.* London: Routledge.

Cummins, A.M. 2002. 'The road to hell is paved with good intentions': quality assurance as a social defence against anxiety. *Organisational & Social Dynamics,* 2(1), 99–119.

DaCosta, C. 1997. Towards mass higher education: transforming the university through modularisation and semesterisation, in *Usable Knowledges as the Goal of University Education: Innovations in the Academic Enterprise Culture*, edited by K.M. Gokulsing and C. DaCosta. Lewiston: E. Mellen Press, 155–79.

Davies, B. 2003. Death to critique and dissent? The policies and practices of new managerialism and of 'evidence-based practice'. *Gender and Education*, 15(1), 91–103.

Davies, B. and Bansel, P. 2005. The time of their lives? academics in neoliberal time(s). *Health Sociology Review*, 14(1), 47–58.

Davies, L. 2012. General staff donate $200 million to employers. *Advocate: Journal of the National Tertiary Education Union*, 19(3), 11.

Dawfbunny. 2012. [Untitled comment]. *Disappearing Jobs at Sydney University*. The Drum Opinion, ABC News site [online, 10 February] Available at: http://www.abc.net.au/unleashed/3822688.html [accessed: 28 March 2012].

de la Fuente, R. 2002. Academic freedom and social responsibility. *Higher Education Policy*, 15(4), 337–39.

Deneen, P.J. 1999. The politics of hope and optimism: Rorty, Havel, and the democratic faith of John Dewey. *Social Research*, 66(2), 577–609.

Department of Industry, Innovation, Science, Research and Tertiary Education 2011. *Student 2011 Full Year: Selected Higher Education Statistics Publication*. Available at: http://www.innovation.gov.au/HigherEducation/HigherEducationStatistics/StatisticsPublications/Pages/default.aspx [accessed: 13 February 2013].

Dessaix, R. 1998. Showing your colours, in *(and so forth)*, by R. Dessaix. Sydney: Pan Macmillan/Picador, 121–33.

Dewey, J. 1933. *How We Think: A Restatement of the Relation of Reflective Thinking to the Educative Process*. Boston: D.C. Heath and Company.

Ditton, M.J. 2009. How social relationships influence academic health in the 'enterprise university': an insight into productivity of knowledge workers. *Higher Education Research and Development*, 28(2), 151–64.

Drake, J. 1996. *The Alexander Technique in Everyday Life*. Hammersmith, London: Thorsons.

Dunbabin, J. 1999. Universities c.1150–c.1350, in *The Idea of a University*, edited by D. Smith and A.K. Langslow. London: Jessica Kingsley Publishers, 30–47.

During, S. 2006. Is Cultural Studies a discipline? And does it make any political difference? *Cultural Politics*, 2(3), 265–81.

Eagleton, T. 1981. *Walter Benjamin or Towards a Revolutionary Criticism*. London: New Left Books.

Eagleton, T. 1990. *The Significance of Theory*. Oxford: Blackwell.

Eagleton, T. 2000. *The Idea of Culture*. Oxford: Blackwell.

Eby, F. and Arrowood, C.F. 1940. *The History and Philosophy of Education: Ancient and Medieval*. Englewood Cliffs, N.J.: Prentice-Hall.

Edwards, D., Bexley, E. and Richardson, S. 2011. *Regenerating the Academic Workforce: The Careers, Intentions and Motivations of Higher Degree Research Students in Australia: Findings of the National Research Student Survey (NRSS)*. [Online: Australian Council for Educational Research]. Available at: http://works.bepress.com/sarah_richardson1/ [accessed: 6 February 2012].

Edwards, M. 2008. Phones, laptops welcome at new exam. *The World Today*. ABC Local Radio, 20 August. Transcript available at: http://www.abc.net.au/worldtoday/content/2008/s2341549.htm [accessed: 10 November 2008].

Ehrenreich, B. 2009. *Bright-Sided: How Positive Thinking is Undermining America*. New York: Picador.

Elias, P. and Purcell, K. 2004. Is mass higher education working? Evidence from the labour market experiences of recent graduates. *National Institute Economic Review*, 190, 60–74.

Elshtain, J.B. 1999. Limits and hope: Christopher Lasch and political theory. *Social Research*, 66(2), 531–43.

Enders, J. 2000. Academic staff in Europe: changing employment and working conditions, in *Academic Work and Life: What it is to be an Academic, and How this is Changing*, edited by M. Tight. Amsterdam: JAI/Elsevier Science, 7–32.

Escobar, M. et al. (eds). 1994. *Paulo Freire on Higher Education: A Dialogue at the National University of Mexico*. Albany: State University of New York Press.

Fisher, M. 2011. The privatisation of stress. *Soundings: A Journal of Politics and Culture*, 48, 123–33.

Floud, R. 2001. Universities are sinking under inspection load. *Times Higher Education* [Online, 23 March] Available at: http://www.timeshighereducation.co.uk/story.asp?storyCode=158318&sectioncode=26 [accessed: 29 March 2012].

Foucault, M. 1977. *Discipline and Punish: The Birth of the Prison*. London: Allen Lane.

Four Corners. 2005. Interview: Dr Brendan Nelson. ABC Television. 27 June.

Freire, P. 1970. *Pedagogy of the Oppressed*. New York: Herder and Herder.

Freire, P. 1994 [1992]. *Pedagogy of Hope: Reliving Pedagogy of the Oppressed*. New York: Continuum.

Friedman, M. and R.D. Friedman. 1998. *Two Lucky People: Memoirs*. Chicago: University of Chicago Press.

Frow, J. and Morris, M. 1993. Introduction, in *Australian Cultural Studies: A Reader*, edited by J. Frow and M. Morris. St Leonards, NSW: Allen & Unwin, vii–xxxii.

Furedi, F. 2003. Afterword: the downsizing of intellectual authority. *Critical Review of International Social and Political Philosophy*, 6(4), 172–8.

Furedi, F. 2011. Grayling cries freedom. *Times Higher Education* [Online, 16 June] Available at: http://www.timeshighereducation.co.uk/story.asp?sectioncode=26&storycode=416521&c=1 [accessed: 2 September 2011].

Gallop, J. 2002. *Anecdotal Theory*. Durham: Duke University Press.

Game, A. and Metcalfe, A. 1996. *Passionate Sociology*. London: Sage Publications.

Gardiner, L. (dir.) 2011. Cashing in on degrees. *Dispatches*. Vera Productions: Channel 4, 4 April.

Garfinkel, H. 1967. *Studies in Ethnomethodology*. Englewood Cliffs, N.J.: Prentice-Hall.

Gaultney, J.F. 2010. The prevalence of sleep disorders in college students: impact on academic performance. *Journal of American College Health*, 59(2), 91–7.

Geertz, C. 1973. Ideology as a cultural system, in *The Interpretation of Cultures: Selected Essays*. New York: Basic Books: 193–233.

Gillard, J. 2009. [Untitled speech]. *Universities Australia Conference*, Canberra, 4 March.

Giroux, H.A. 2000. *Impure Acts: The Practical Politics of Cultural Studies*. New York: Routledge.

Giroux, H.A. 2002. The corporate war against higher education. *Workplace: A Journal of Academic Labor* [Online], 5(1), Available at: http://louisville.edu/journal/workplace/issue5p1/giroux.html [accessed: 14 October 2011].

Gittins, R. 2011. Invest in children of knowledge revolution. *Sydney Morning Herald* [Online, 31 August] Available at: http://newsstore.smh.com.au/apps [accessed: 8 September 2011].

Glasson. B.J. 2012. The intellectual outside: anti-intellectualism and the subject of populist discourses in Australian newspapers. *Continuum: Journal of Media & Cultural Studies*, 26(1), 101–14.

Goffman, E. 1959. *The Presentation of Self in Everyday Life*. New York: Anchor Books.

Gornitzka, Å. Kyvik, S. and Larsen, I.M. 1998. The bureaucratisation of universities. *Minerva*, 36(1), 21–47.

Graff, G. 1994. Other voices, other rooms…, in *Bridging the Gap: Literary Theory in the Classroom*, edited by J.M.Q. Davies. West Cornwall, CT: Locust Hill Press, 15–39.

Green, V.H.H. 1974. *A History of Oxford University*. London: BT Batsford Ltd.

Gregg, M. 2006. *Cultural Studies' Affective Voices*. Basingstoke: Palgrave Macmillan.

Gregg, M. 2009. Learning to (love) labour: production cultures and the affective turn. Communication and Critical/Cultural Studies, 6(2), 209–14.

Gregg, M. 2011. *Work's Intimacy*. Cambridge: Polity.

Grossman, F.K., Kruger, L.-M. and Moore, R.P. 1999. Reflections on a feminist research project: subjectivity and the wish for intimacy and equality. *Psychology of Women Quarterly*, 23(1), 117–35.

Groves, J. and Clark, L. 2010. The stay at home students: university fees rise will force middle classes to live with their parents. *The Daily Mail* [Online, 13 October] Available at: http://www.dailymail.co.uk/news/article-1320027/Vince-Cable-Tuition-fees-force-middle-class-students-live-parents.html# [accessed: 7 July 2011].

Hage, G. 1998. On 'having' ethnography: mimic me ... if you can. *Australian Journal of Anthropology*, 9(3), 285–90.

Hage, G. 2011. [Untitled presentation]. *Academia: A Scholarly Life* conference, Parramatta, University of Western Sydney, 22 July.

Hair, A., Renaud, K.V. and Ramsay, J. 2007. The influence of self-esteem and locus of control on perceived email-related stress. *Computers in Human Behavior*, 23(6), 2791–803.

Hall, G. 2002. *Culture in Bits: The Monstrous Future of Theory*. London: Continuum.

Hall, S. 1992. Cultural studies and its theoretical legacies, in *Cultural Studies*, edited by L. Grossberg, C. Nelson and P.A. Treichler. New York: Routledge, 277–94.

Harnad, S. 2007. UK research evaluation framework: validate metrics against panel rankings. [Online: Open Access Archivangelism, 22 November] Available at: http://openaccess.eprints.org/index.php?/archives/333-UK-Research-Evaluation-Framework-Validate-Metrics-Against-Panel-Rankings.html [accessed: 11 April 2012].

Hartman, Y. and Darab, S. 2012. A call for slow scholarship: a case study on the intensification of academic life and its implications for pedagogy. *The Review of Education, Pedagogy, and Cultural Studies*, 34, 49–60.

Hatton, T.J. and Chapman, B.J. 1987. *Post-School Training in Australia in 1900–1980*. Canberra: Conference on Human Resources, Department of Economic History, Australian National University. Working Paper No. 94.

Hay, L.L. 1987. *You Can Heal Your Life*. Concord: Specialist Printing.

Herz, L. and Herz, A. 2007. *Beyond Balance: How to Cultivate Work-Life Synergy in the Law*. [Online]. Available at: www.legalsanity.com [accessed: 13 April 2012].

Hey, V. 2002. 'Not as nice as she was supposed to be': schoolgirls' friendships, in *Ethnographic Research: A Reader*, edited by S. Taylor. London: Sage Publications/Open University, 67–90.

Hicks, D. 1996. Envisioning the future: the challenge for environmental educators. *Environmental Education Research*, 2, 101–08.

Hicks, D. 1998. Stories of hope: a response to the 'psychology of despair'. *Environmental Education Research*, 4(2), 165–76.

Hicks, D. and Holden, C. 1995. *Visions of the Future: Why We Need to Teach for Tomorrow*. Stoke-on-Trent: Trentham Books.

Higgins, J. 1999. *Raymond Williams: Literature, Marxism and Cultural Materialism*. Milton Park, Oxon: Routledge.

Hodge, B. 1995. Monstrous knowledge: doing PhDs in the New Humanities. *Australian Universities' Review*, 2, 35–9.

Homer. 1951. *The Iliad of Homer*. Chicago: University of Chicago Press.

Hope, C. 2011. £9,000 tuition fees will be the exception, promises Higher Education minister. *The Telegraph*. [Online, 21 February]. Available at: http://www.telegraph.co.uk/education/educationnews/8336685/9000-tuition-fees-will-be-the-exception-promises-Higher-Education-minister.html [accessed: 16 April 2011].

Horin, A. 1995. Jobs and families: how mums cope. *Sydney Morning Herald*, 24 August, 1 & 8.

Horsley, M., Martin, G. and Woodburne, G. 2005. Salary relativities and the academic labour market. [Broadway, N.S.W.]: Oval Research Centre, University of Technology, Sydney.

Hough, A. 2010. Students 'are a burden on taxpayers', new universities minister believes. *The Telegraph* [UK] [Online, 7 February]. Available at: http://www.telegraph.co.uk/education/educationnews/7815956/Students-are-a-burden-on-taxpayers-new-universities-minister-believes.html [accessed: 7 February 2012].

Houston, D., Meyer, L., and Paewei, S. 2006. Academic staff workloads and job satisfaction: expectations and values in academe. *Journal of Higher Education Policy and Management*, 28(1), 17–30.

Howard, J., Hayden, B. and Shaw, J. 2000. The Prime Minister opens the new *Quadrant* office [Edited versions of speeches given at the opening of the new *Quadrant* office on 4 August 2000]. *Quadrant*, 44(9), 2–4.

Howe, L.W. and Howe, M.M. 1975. *Personalizing Education: Values Clarification and Beyond*, New York: Hart Pub. Co.

Hugo, G. 2005. Demographic trends in Australia's academic workforce. *Journal of Higher Education Policy and Management*, 27(3), 327–43.

Hugo, G. 2011. [Untitled speech]. *Academia: A Scholarly Life* conference. Parramatta: University of Western Sydney, 21 July.

Hunter, I. 1992. Aesthetics and cultural studies, in *Cultural Studies*, edited by L. Grossberg, C. Nelson and P.A. Treichler. New York: Routledge, 347–72.

Jackson, R. 1999. The universities, government and society, in *The Idea of a University*, edited by D. Smith and A.K. Langslow. London: Jessica Kingsley Publishers, 91–105.

Jackson, T., Dawson, R. and Wilson, D. 2001. The cost of email interruption. *Journal of Systems and Information Technology*, 5(1), 81–92.

James, R., Krause, K.-L. and Jennings, C. 2010. *The First Year Experience in Australian Universities: Findings from 1994 to 2009*. Centre for the Study of Higher Education: University of Melbourne.

Jaschik, S. 2010. Salaries fell for 32.6% of faculty. [Online, 8 March] Available at: http://www.insidehighered.com/news/2010/03/08/facsalaries [accessed: 25 January 2012].

Jensen, A. L. and Morgan, K. 2009. *Overload: The Role of Work-Volume Escalation and Micro-Management of Academic Work Patterns in Loss of Morale and Collegiality at UWS; The Way Forward*. South Melbourne, Vic: National Tertiary Education Union.

Kanpol, B. 1998. Critical pedagogy for beginning teachers: the movement from despair to hope. [Online] Available at: http://users.monash. edu.au/~dzyngier/Critical%20Pedagogy%20For%20Beginning%20 Teachers%20Barry%20Kanpol.htm [accessed: 10 August 2012].

Kearney, M. (pres.) 2006. *The Idea of a University*. UK: BBC Radio 4. 7 September.

Keohane, N.O. 1999. The American campus: from colonial seminary to global multiversity, in *The Idea of a University*, edited by D. Smith and A.K. Langslow. London: Jessica Kingsley Publishers, 48–67.

Ker, I. 1999. Newman's *Idea of a University*: a guide for the contemporary university?, in *The Idea of a University*, edited by D. Smith and A.K. Langslow. London: Jessica Kingsley Publishers, 11–29.

Khawaja, N.G. and Dempsey, J. 2007. Psychological distress in international university students: an Australian study. *Australian Journal of Guidance & Counselling*, 17(1), 13–27.

Kilcullen, R.J. 1996. Max Weber: on bureaucracy. Available at: http://www. humanities.mq.edu.au/Ockham/y64l09.html [accessed: 29 February 2012].

Kiley, M. 2009. Rethinking the Australian doctoral examination process. *Australian Universities Review*, 51(2), 32–41.

Kimber, M. 2003. The tenured 'core' and the tenuous 'periphery': the casualisation of academic work in Australian universities. *Journal of Higher Education Policy and Management*, 25(1), 41–50.

Kingsbury, R. 1974. *The Realities of University Life*. London: University Tutorial Press.

Klocker, N. and Drozdewski, D. Commentary. *Environment and Planning A*, 44(6): 1271–77.

Kohlberg, L. 1973. The claim to moral adequacy of a highest stage of moral judgment. *The Journal of Philosophy*, 70(18), 630–46.

Kolodny, A. 1980. Dancing through the minefield: practice and politics of a feminist literary criticism. *Feminist Studies*, 6(1), 1–25.

Lakoff, G. and Johnson, M. 1980. *Metaphors We Live By*. Chicago: University of Chicago Press.

Ligota, C. and Quantin, J.L. 2006. Introduction to *History of Scholarship: A Selection of Papers from the Seminar on the History of Scholarship Held Annually at the Warburg Institute*. Oxford: Oxford University Press, 1–38.

Lindsay, R., Breen, R. and Paton-Saltzberg, R. 2002. Pedagogic research and evidence-based management. *Psychology Teaching Review*, 10(1), 20–30.

Lippard, L.R. 1999. Foreword: looking on, in *The Tourist: A New Theory of the Leisure Class*, by D. MacCannell. Berkeley: University of California Press, ix–xiii.

Lipsett, A. 2009. 6,000 lecturers facing redundancy, says universities union. *The Guardian* [Online, 16 July] Available at: http://www.guardian.co.uk/

education/2009/jul/16/lecturers-redundancy-recession   [accessed: 25 January 2012].

Locker, P. 2009. Conclusion – The learning landscape: views with endless possibilities, in *The Future of Higher Education: Policy, Pedagogy and the Student Experience*, edited by L. Bell, M. Neary and H. Stevenson. London: Continuum, 139–47.

Löfgren, O. 2003. The new economy: a cultural history. *Global Networks*, 3(3), 239–54.

Low, R. 2013. *Schooling Faith: Religious Education and Neo-Liberal Hegemony in Neo-Calivinist 'Parent-Controlled' Schooling*. PhD thesis, University of Sydney.

Luedicke, M.K. and Giesler, M. 2007. Brand communities and their social antagonists: insights from the Hummer case, in *Consumer Tribes*, edited by B. Cova, R.V. Kozinets and A. Shankar. Amsterdam: Elsevier, 275–95.

Lunt, P.K. and Livingstone, S.M. 1992. *Mass Consumption and Personal Identity: Everyday Economic Experience*. Buckingham: Open University Press.

Lusty, N. 2009. Every kind of everyday. *Cultural Studies Review*, 15(1), 199–206.

Lynch, K. 2006. Neo-liberalism and marketisation: the implications for higher education. *European Educational Research Journal*, 5(1), 1–17.

Lyotard, J-F. 1984. *The Postmodern Condition: A Report on Knowledge*. Minneapolis: University of Minnesota Press.

MacDermott, K. 2008. *Whatever Happened to Frank and Fearless? The Impact of the New Public Management on the Australian Public Service*. Canberra: ANU E Press.

MacDonald, E. 2011. HECS hit for science, maths students. *The Canberra Times* [Online, 30 November] Available at: http://www.canberratimes. com.au/news/national/national/sport/hecs-hit-for-science-maths-students/2375446.aspx?storypage=0 [accessed: 1 February 2012].

Mander, J. 1992. *In the Absence of the Sacred: The Failure of Technology and the Survival of the Indian Nations*. San Francisco: Sierra Club Books.

Marginson, S. 2002. Nation-building universities in a global environment: the case of Australia. *Higher Education*, 43(3/4), 409–28.

Marks, G. et al. 2000. Patterns of participation in year 12 and higher education in Australia: trends and issues. *LSAY Research Reports*, 17. Available at: http:// research.acer.edu.au/lsay_research/66 [accessed: 13 February 2013].

Martin, W. 1996. Introduction: The Ends of Theory, in *The Ends of Theory*, edited by J. Herron et al. Detroit: Wayne State University Press, 14–34.

Marulanda-Carter, L. and Jackson, T.W. 2012. Effects of e-mail addiction and interruptions on employees. *Journal of Systems and Information Technology*, 14(1), 82–94.

Maskell, D. and Robinson, I. 2002. *The New Idea of a University*. Thorverton, UK: Imprint Academic.

Massey, D. 1994. *Space, Place and Gender*. Oxford: Polity Press.

Maton, K. 2009. Cumulative and segmented learning: exploring the role of curriculum structures in knowledge-building. *British Journal of Sociology*, 30(1), 43–57.

Maton, K. 2012. Heretical knowledge: how knowledge-blindness in educational research obstructs progress. Paper presented to the Department of Social and Political Sciences seminar series, University of Sydney, 26 April.

Mauss, M. 1990 [1923]. *The Gift: The Form and Reason for Exchange in Archaic Societies*. London: Routledge.

May, R. et al. 2011. The casual approach to university teaching; time for a re-think? *Research and Development in Higher Education: Reshaping Higher Education*. Refereed papers from the 34th HERDSA Annual International Conference, (Gold Coast, Australia, 4–7 July 2011), edited by K. Krause et al. Milperra, NSW: Higher Education Research and Development Society of Australasia, Inc, 188–97.

McInnis, C. 2000. Changing academic work roles: the everyday realities challenging quality teaching. *Quality in Higher Education*, 6(2), 143–52.

McInnis, C., Hartley, R. and Anderson, M. 2000. *What Did You Do With Your Science Degree? A National Study of Employment Outcomes for Science Degree Holders 1990–2000*. Prepared for the Australian Council of Deans of Science (ACDS). Available at: http://www.acds.edu.au/whydoa.html [accessed: 1 February 2012].

McKenna, D. 1994. Trade union perspective on occupational stress. Paper presented at *Stress and Wellbeing*, the National Occupational Stress Conference, Gold Coast, June.

McLaren, P. L. 1994. Foreword, in *Paulo Freire on Higher Education: A Dialogue at the National University of Mexico*, by M. Escobar et al. Albany: State University of New York Press, ix–xxxiii.

McQueen, H. 2001. *The Essence of Capitalism: The Origins of Our Future*. Sydney, N.S.W.: Hodder Headline Australia.

McQuillan, M. et al. (eds). 1999. *Post-Theory: New Directions in Criticism*. Edinburgh: Edinburgh University Press.

McRobbie, A. 1982. The politics of feminist research: between talk, text and action. *Feminist Review*, 12, 46–57.

Menzies, R.G. 1959. Foreword, in *The Humanities in Australia: A Survey with Special Reference to the Universities*, by A. Grenfell Price. Sydney: Angus & Robertson for the Australian Humanities Research Council.

Miller, S. 1995. Post-modernism and its influence on the Humanities, in *Re-Inventing the Humanities: International Perspectives*, edited by D. Myers. Kew, Vic: Australian Scholarly Publishing, 54–60.

Moberly, S.W. 1949. *The Crisis in the University*. London: SCM Press.

Morey, A.I. 2004. Globalization and the emergence of for-profit higher education. *Higher Education*, 48(1), 131–50.

Morgan, W.J. 1987. The pedagogical politics of Antonio Gramsci – 'pessimism of the intellect, optimism of the will'. *International Journal of Lifelong Education,* 6(4), 295–308.

Morris, H. 2000. The origins, forms and effects of modularisation and semesterisation in ten UK-based business schools. *Higher Education Quarterly,* 54(3), 239–58.

Morris, M. 2006. *Identity Anecdotes: Translation and Media Culture.* London: Sage.

Morris, M. 2011. Commentary: coping with cynicism. *Cultural Studies,* 25(1), 123–7.

Myers, D. 1995. Revolution and Renewal in the Humanities: The Necessary Politicization of the Ivory Tower, in *Re-Inventing the Humanities: International Perspectives,* edited by D. Myers. Kew, Vic: Australian Scholarly Publishing, 27–43.

Myers, D.G. 1994. On the teaching of literary theory, in *Bridging the Gap: Literary Theory in the Classroom,* edited by J.M.Q. Davies. West Cornwall, CT: Locust Hill Press, 3–13.

Myss, C. and Shealy, C.N. 1993. *The Creation of Health: The Emotional, Psychological, and Spiritual Responses that Promote Health and Healing.* New York: Three Rivers Press.

National Committee of Inquiry into Higher Education 1997. *Higher Education in the Learning Society [The Dearing Report].* [London]: HMSO.

Neil. 2011. [Untitled comment]. *Disappearing Jobs at Sydney University.* The Drum Opinion, ABC News site [Online, 10 February] Available at: http://www.abc.net.au/unleashed/3822688.html [accessed: 28 March 2012].

Newman, J.H. 1976. *The Idea of a University: Defined and Illustrated.* Oxford: Clarendon Press.

OFistFullOfDollars. 2011. [Untitled comment]. *Disappearing Jobs at Sydney University.* The Drum Opinion, ABC News site [Online, 10 February] Available at: http://www.abc.net.au/unleashed/3822688.html [accessed: 28 March 2012].

OxCHEPS [Oxford Centre for Higher Education Policy Studies]. 2006. Statistics on higher education: academic salaries. Available at: http://oxcheps.new.ox.ac.uk/new/statistics/salaries.html [accessed: 4 November 2011].

Pacheco, I. and Rumbley, L.E. 2008. Exploring academic salaries in a comparative context. *International Higher Education,* 52(Summer), 6–7.

Parker, R.S. 1989. The administrative vocation. *Australian Journal of Public Administration,* 48(4), 336–45.

Patty, A. 2008. Phone a friend in exams. *Sydney Morning Herald,* 20 August, 1, & 4.

Peale, N.V. 1952. *The Power of Positive Thinking.* New York: Ballantine Books.

Pelias, R.J. 2004. *A Methodology of the Heart: Evoking Academic and Daily Life.* Walnut Creek, CA: AltaMira Press.

Pettinger, L. 2004. Brand culture and branded workers: service work and aesthetic labour in fashion retail. *Consumption Markets & Culture*, 7(2), 165–84.

Power, M. 1997. *The Audit Society: Rituals of Verification*. Oxford: Oxford University Press.

Power, S. and Whitty, G. 1999. New Labour's education policy: first, second or third way? *Journal of Education Policy*, 14(5), 535–46.

Pratt, J. 1997. *The Polytechnic Experiment: 1965–1992*. Buckingham: The Society for Research into Higher Education and Open University Press.

Prensky, M. 2008. Using cell phones for exams: op-ed submission to the *Sydney Morning Herald*. Available at: http://www.marcprensky.com/writing/Prensky-UsingCellPhonesForExams-OpEd-Australia.pdf [accessed: 10 November 2008].

Probyn, E. 2005. *Blush: Faces of Shame*. Sydney: University of NSW Press.

ProfPTJ 2009. The academic vocation. [Online, 1 June]. Available at: http://duckofminerva.blogspot.com.au/2009/06/academic-vocation.html [accessed: 16 February 2012].

Psacharopoulos, G. 2006. World Bank policy on education: a personal account. *International Journal of Educational Development*, 26(3), 329–38.

Readings, B. 1996. *The University in Ruins*. Cambridge, MA: Harvard University Press.

Redden, G. 2008. From RAE to ERA: research evaluation at work in the corporate university. *Australian Humanities Review*, 45(Nov.), 7–26.

Reger, J. 2001. Emotions, objectivity and voice: an analysis of a 'failed' participant observation. *Women's Studies International Forum*, 24(5), 605–16.

Rhodes, R.A.W. 1994. The hollowing out of the state: the changing nature of the public service in Britain. *The Political Quarterly*, 65(2), 138–51.

Rich, A. 2002. Notes towards a politics of location, in *Arts of the Possible: Essays and Conversations*. New York: W.W. Norton & Co, 62–82.

Richardson, J.L. 2001. *Contending Liberalisms in World Politics: Ideology and Power* Boulder, CO: Lynne Rienner Publications.

Ritzer, G. 1993. *The McDonaldization of Society: An Investigation into the Changing Character of Contemporary Social Life*. Newbury Park, CA: Pine Forge Press.

Roberts, K.L. and Turnbull, B.J. 2002. From apprentices to academics: are nurses catching up? *Collegian*, 9(1), 24–30.

Roberts, K.L. and Turnbull, B.J. 2004. Nurse-academics' scholarly productivity: perceived frames and facilitators. *Contemporary Nurse*, 17(3), 282–92.

Romanin, S. and Over, R. 1993. Australian academics: career patterns, work roles, and family life-cycle commitments of men and women. *Higher Education*, 26(4), 411–29.

Rorty, R. 1998. *Achieving our Country: Leftist Thought in Twentieth-Century America* Cambridge, MA: Harvard University Press.

Rosa, H. and Scheuerman, W.E. 2009. Introduction, in *High-Speed Society: Social Acceleration, Power, and Modernity*, edited by H. Rosa and W.E. Scheuerman. University Park, PA: The Pennsylvania State University Press, 1–29.

Rosen, C. 2008. The myth of multitasking. *The New Atlantis: A Journal of Technology and Society*, 20(Spring), 105–10.

Ross, A. 2004. *Low Pay, High Profile: The Global Push for Fair Labor*. New York: The New Press.

Rutherford, J. 2005. Cultural Studies in the corporate university. *Cultural Studies*, 19(3), 297–317.

Ruthven, K.K. 1992. *Beyond the Disciplines: The New Humanities*. Canberra: Australian Academy of the Humanities.

Ryan, D. 1998. The Thatcher government's attack on higher education in historical perspective. *New Left Review*, 227(Jan./Feb.), 3–32.

Ryle, M. 1999. 'Relevant provision': the usefulness of cultural studies, in *Teaching Culture: The Long Revolution in Cultural Studies*, edited by N. Aldred and M. Ryle. Leicester: National Institute of Adult Education, 39–52.

Sayer, J. 1999. Linking universities across Europe: principles, practicalities and perspectives, in *The Idea of a University*, edited by D. Smith and A.K. Langslow. London: Jessica Kingsley Publishers, 68–90.

Schudson, M. 1999. You've got mail: a few observations on hope. *Social Research*, 66(2), 625–8.

Secretary of State for Science and Education. 1985. *The Development of Higher Education into the 1990s* [*The Joseph Report*] (Cmnd. 9524), London: HMSO.

Sedgwick, E.K. 2003. Paranoid reading and reparative reading, or, you're so paranoid, you probably think this essay is about you, in *Touching Feeling: Affect, Pedagogy, Performativity*. Durham: Duke University Press, 123–51.

Seligman, Martin E.P. 1992. *Learned Optimism*. Milsons Point, N.S.W.: Random House Australia.

Seligman, Martin E.P. 2002. *Authentic Happiness: Using the New Positive Psychology to Realize Your Potential for Lasting Fulfilment*. Milsons Point, NSW: Random House Australia.

Shattock, M. 2001. The academic profession in Britain: a study in the failure to adapt to change. *Higher Education*, 41(1), 27–47.

Shepherd, J. 2010. Browne review: universities warned to expect £4.2bn cuts. *The Guardian* [Online, 15 October]. Available at: http://www.guardian.co.uk/education/2010/oct/15/browne-review-universities-cuts [accessed: 1 February 2012].

Shore, C. and Wright, S. 2004. Whose accountability? Governmentality and the auditing of universities. *Parallax*, 10(2), 100–16.

Shutkin, W.A. 2000. *The Land That Could Be: Environmentalism and Democracy in the Twenty-First Century*. Cambridge, MA: MIT Press.

Sidhedevil 2010. Response to 'Is-outing-panic-disorder-academic-suicide?'. Metafilter, December 12. Available at: http://ask.metafilter.com/172936/ [accessed: 16 May 2011].

Sidhu, R.K. 2006. *Universities and Globalization: To Market, To Market*. Mahwah, NJ: Lawrence Erlbaum Associates.

Simon, B. 1991. *Education and the Social Order 1940–1990*. London: Lawrence & Wishart.

Skeggs, B. 1995. Theorising, ethics and representation in feminist ethnography, in *Feminist Cultural Theory: Process and Production*, edited by B. Skeggs. Manchester: Manchester University Press, 190–206.

Slaughter, S. 1998. National higher education policies in a global economy, in *Universities and Globalization: Critical Persepctives*, edited by J. Currie and J. Newson. London: Sage, 45–70.

Sloman, A. 2008. Research Evaluation/Excellence Framework (REF)? or Research Monitoring Framework (RMF)? [Online, 2 March]. Available at: http://www.cs.bham.ac.uk/research/projects/cogaff/misc/research-evaluation.html [accessed: 23 May 2012].

Smith, B. and Frankland, M. 2000. Marketisation and the new quality agenda: postgraduate coursework at the crossroads. *Australian Universities Review* 2, 7–16.

Smith, D. 1999. The changing idea of a university, in *The Idea of a University*, edited by D. Smith and A.K. Langslow. London: Jessica Kingsley Publishers, 148–74.

Snyder, S. 1965. The left hand of God: despair in medieval and renaissance tradition. *Studies in the Renaissance*, 12, 18–59.

Sparkes, A.C. 2007. Embodiment, academics, and the audit culture: a story seeking consideration. *Qualitative Research*, 7(4), 521–50.

Stallybrass, P. and White, A. 1986. *The Politics and Poetics of Transgression*. Ithaca: Cornell University Press.

Standing, G. 2011. *The Precariat: The New Dangerous Class*. London: Bloomsbury Academic.

Stevens, P.A. 2004. Academic salaries in the UK and US. *National Institute Economic Review*, 190, 104–13.

Stewart, W.A.C. 1989. *Higher Education in Postwar Britain*. Houndmills, Basingstoke: Macmillan.

Stoner, J.A.F. et al. 1994. *Management*. 2nd Edition. Sydney: Prentice Hall Australia.

Stuhr, J. 1995. The Humanities Inc.: taking care of business, in *Re-Inventing the Humanities: International Perspectives*, edited by D. Myers. Kew, Vic: Australian Scholarly Publishing, 3–10.

Swain, H. 2011. Classicist, musician, axeman: interview with Malcolm Gillies. *The Guardian*, 3 May, EducationGuardian 7.

Tallis, R. 1999. *Enemies of Hope: A Critique of Contemporary Pessimism*. Houndmills, Basingstoke: Macmillan.

Taylor, J. 1990. Determining the subject balance in higher education: how should this be done? *Higher Education*, 19(2), 239–57.

TBear. 2012. [Untitled comment]. *Disappearing Jobs at Sydney University*. [Online: *The Drum Opinion*, ABC News site, 10 February] Available at: http://www.abc.net.au/unleashed/3822688.html [accessed: 28 March 2012].

Thatcher, M. 1987a. *Speech to Conservative Party Conference*. Winter Gardens, Blackpool, 9 October. Thatcher Archive: CCOPR 664/87. Available at: http://www.margaretthatcher.org/document/106941 [accessed: 2 September 2011].

Thatcher, M. 1987b. Interview for *Woman's Own* ('no such thing as society'). 23 September. Thatcher Archive: COI transcript. Available at: http://www.margaretthatcher.org/document/106689 [accessed: 1 June 2012].

Tiger, L. 1999. Hope springs internal. *Social Research*, 66(2), 611–23.

Tight, M. 2009. *The Development of Higher Education in the United Kingdom since 1945*. Maidenhead: Open University Press.

Torres, C.A. 1994. Introduction, in *Paulo Freire on Higher Education: A Dialogue at the National University of Mexico*, by M. Escobar et al. Albany: State University of New York Press, 1–25.

Tory Boy. [Untitled comment]. 2011. *Disappearing Jobs at Sydney University*. [Online: *The Drum Opinion*, ABC News site, 10 February] Available at: http://www.abc.net.au/unleashed/3822688.html [accessed: 28 March 2012].

Treadgold, R. 1999. Transcendent vocations: their relationship to stress, depression, and clarity of self-concept. *Journal of Humanistic Psychology*, 39(1), 81–105.

Trow, M. 1996. Continuities and change in American higher education, in *Goals and Purposes of Higher Education in the 21st Century*, edited by A. Burgen. London: Jessica Kingsley Publisher, 24–36.

Turner, G. 2012. *What's Become of Cultural Studies?* London: Sage.

UAC 2011. Course costs. [Online: Universities Admissions Centre]. Available at: http://www.uac.edu.au/undergraduate/fees/costs.shtml [accessed: 9 November 2011].

University of Buckingham n.d.[a] History of the university. [Online] Available at: http://www.buckingham.ac.uk/about/history [accessed: 15 December 2011].

University of Buckingham n.d.[b] Independence. [Online] Available at: http://www.buckingham.ac.uk/about/independence [accessed: 15 December 2011].

UWS 2011. Academia: a scholarly life. [Online: University of Western Sydney]. Available at: http://www.uws.edu.au/academia_a_scholarly_life/academia_a_scholarly_life_conference [accessed 6 June 2011].

Urry, J. 2009. Speeding up and slowing down, in *High-Speed Society: Social Acceleration, Power, and Modernity*, edited by H. Rosa and W.E. Scheuerman. University Park, PA: The Pennsylvania State University Press, 179–98.

Virilio, P. 1986 [1977]. *Speed and Politics: An Essay on Dromology*. New York: Semiotext(e).

Wark, M. 1993. Homage to catatonia: culture, politics and Midnight Oil, in *Australian Cultural Studies: A Reader*, edited by J. Frow and M. Morris. St Leonards, NSW: Allen & Unwin, 105–16.

Watson, D. 2009. *The Question of Morale: Managing Happiness and Unhappiness in University Life*. Maidenhead, Berkshire: Open University Press.

Watson, D. and Bowden, R. 1999. Why did they do it?: The Conservatives and mass higher education, 1979–1997. *Journal of Education Policy*, 14(3), 243–56.

Weber, M. 1948a. Bureaucracy, in *From Max Weber: Essays in Sociology*, edited by H.H. Gerth and C.W. Mills. London: Routledge & Kegan Paul: 196–252.

Weber, M. 1948b. Science as a vocation, in *From Max Weber: Essays in Sociology*, edited by H.H. Gerth and C.W. Mills. London: Routledge & Kegan Paul: Gerth and Mills, 129–56.

Weber, M. 1949. Objectivity in social science and social policy, in *The Methodology of the Social Sciences*, edited by E.A. Shils and H.A. Finch. New York: Free Press, 49–112.

Weller, A.C. 2000. Editorial peer review for electronic journals: current issues and emerging models. *Journal of the American Society for Information Science*, 51(14), 1328–33.

Weller, P. 1989. Politicisation and the Australian public service. *Australian Journal of Public Administration*, 48(4), 369–81.

Wells, K. and Wells, S. 1995. An Asian perspective: a pragmatic approach, in *Re-Inventing the Humanities: International Perspectives*, edited by D. Myers. Kew, Vic: Australian Scholarly Publishing, 82–6.

White, P. 1996. *Civic Virtues and Public Schooling: Educating Citizens for a Democratic Society*. New York: Teachers College Press.

Whyte, W.H. 1960. *The Organization Man*. Harmondsworth: Penguin.

Wickham, G. 2005. Ethics, morality and the formation of cultural studies intellectuals. *Cultural Studies Review*, 11(1), 71–86.

Wilkinson, R. and Marmot, M. 2003. *Social Determinants of Health: The Solid Facts*. [Copenhagen]: World Health Organization.

Willetts, J. et al. 2012. Creative tensions: negotiating the multiple dimensions of a transdisciplinary doctorate, in *Reshaping Doctoral Education: International Approaches and Pedagogies*, edited by A. Lee and S. Danby. Abingdon: Routledge, 128–43.

Williams, L. 2004. Rage and hope. [Online]. Available at: http://www.perfectfit.org/CT/index2.htmls [accessed: 6 September 2012].

Williams, R. 1979. *Modern Tragedy*. London: Verso Editions.

Williams, R. 1988. *Keywords: A Vocabulary of Culture and Society*. Revised Edition. London: Fontana.

Williamson, J. 1986. The problems of being popular. *New Socialist*, 41(Sept.), 14–15.

Winefield, A.H. et al. 2003. Occupational stress in Australian university staff: results from a national survey. *International Journal of Stress Management*, 10(1), 51–63.

Winter, R., Taylor, T., and Sarros, J. 2000. Trouble at mill: quality of academic worklife issues within a comprehensive Australian university. *Studies in Higher Education*, 25, 279–94.

Wolf, A. 2002. *Does Education Matter? Myths about Education and Economic Growth*. London: Penguin.

Woodward, W. and White, M. 2003. Poor students will pay more in 'market-based system'. *The Guardian* [Online, 21 January]. Available at: http://www.guardian.co.uk/uk/2003/jan/21/tuitionfees.highereducation [accessed: 28 October, 2011].

Worrall-Carter, L. and Snell, R. 2003–04. Nurse academics meeting the challenges of scholarship and research. *Contemporary Nurse*, 16(1–2), 40–50.

young aco 2012. [Untitled comment]. *Disappearing Jobs at Sydney University*. The Drum Opinion, ABC News site [online, 10 February] Available at: http://www.abc.net.au/unleashed/3822688.html [accessed: 28 March 2012].

Zournazi, M. 2002. *Hope: New Philosophies for Change*. Annandale, NSW: Pluto Press.

Appendix

Peer Learning Exercise: Addressing a Research/Writing Problem

Aims:

- To provide you with concrete assistance in working through an obstacle, dilemma or problem in your thesis.
- To help you develop a peer support process or network.
- To encourage you to learn about and reflect on peer-assisted learning (PAL).
- To develop 'metalearning' skills – that is, to increase your understanding about your own learning styles, strengths and weaknesses.

Task:

Step 1: Thinking

Identify a potential choice, dilemma, problem, block or obstacle that you are facing (or expect to face) in your thesis. It may be an actual problem that is hindering or complicating your progress, or it may simply be a choice that you will have to make at some point and would like to discuss with a peer. It might be something you face right now, or it might be an issue to ponder on a longer timeframe. Your issue/problem might be:

- Topic-related: a question of focus, or scope, or limits.
- Approach related: a question of your angle.
- Literature/reading: maybe you want some concrete suggestions for readings.
- Methodological.
- Ethical: for example, perhaps you are doing a cyber-ethnography and you're not sure whether to participate openly, participate covertly or just to 'lurk'.
- Conceptual: you might currently be thinking through or wrestling with an idea or set of ideas.
- Writing/style/tone.
- Audience: you might be thinking through questions of disciplinarity.

Note 1: Often these categories will overlap: a methodological decision will have a lot to do with practical questions like funding and timelines; to help think through an ethical issue you might need suggestions on good readings on research ethics; the question of writing style has a lot to do with audience, and so on.

Note 2: Don't pick 'supervision' as your problem. Although problems with supervision arise and are important and legitimate, this is not the forum to raise them. Of course, it is allowable for you to *mention* supervision issues in your reflection, but don't make them the focus or allow the analysis to drift into complaint. An example of how you might legitimately discuss supervision for the purpose of this assignment is if, for example, you are still determining your topic, its limits and your approach. In the context of a discussion of such issues it would be pertinent to note in a neutral fashion that your choices might have an impact on supervision, in terms of relevant expertise and so on.

If you are having difficulties with supervision you should approach the Postgraduate Convenor in your department and/or SUPRA.

Step 2: Pairing (or Grouping) Up

Organise yourself into a pair (or a group of 3) with another student/s. You can do this in person, or you might like to use the 'meet-up space' discussion board within the assignment folder as a place to sound out possible partners. In so doing, make clear the nature of your 'problem' or issue and the type of help that you are hoping to get.

In choosing a partner, bear in mind that there are advantages to working with someone from your discipline or who knows your topic area well, but there are also advantages in having input from someone outside the field. It depends in part on logistical questions (who is available) but also on the type of help you are seeking. If you want help with readings or concepts, then it might be best to try to find someone from within your field. On the other hand, if you are wanting other types of help (e.g. methodological, writing style, structural, or even topic-related) then an outsider can be very useful. Often they can shed fresh light on things.

If you really want to, I will consider allowing you to use someone from outside the unit as your peer. But I discourage that, since such people are *already* available to you as a sounding board; choosing someone from inside the unit allows you to gain new assistance. You may well be surprised how useful it is to have someone you don't know and/or who isn't from your discipline as a peer.

Once you have partnered or teamed up, whether in person or online, you need to solidify the arrangement by signing up using the online sign-up sheet. Both the 'meet-up space' discussion board and the sign-up sheet are accessed by clicking on the 'Assignments' link and then opening the 'Peer-Learning Exercise 1' folder.

Step 3: Meetings

Arrange a meeting. Make sure that at this first meeting you set up a crystal clear arrangement – ideally in writing. Things to consider at your first contact are:

Dates and times of meetings: How many? When?
Nature of the contact: Face to face? By email? Online? By phone?
Timelines: When are you both/all intending to submit the assignment?
Expectations: What type of help are you likely to be wanting? General help or specific help? Do you want your partner/s to read some of your work? If so, will it be in advance of the meetings?

At your first substantive meeting (which may or may not be the same meeting as the one in which you organise the logistics), you will start the actual discussion of your issue

Step 4: Writing Up

Your assignment should contain the following four components:

a) An account of your problem/issue/dilemma: This should be reasonably elaborate. Don't just baldly state what your dilemma is/was. You need to flesh it out by articulating why it was a dilemma, what some of your options are/were, why you feel you were stuck on it, the implications of different ways of resolving it, and so on.

b) A short, neutral, account of the process (the number of meetings you had, with how many people etc).

c) An account of the progress of your thinking regarding the issue or problem. What ideas did it give you? What pathway will you pursue? Have you resolved the issue? If not, have you eliminated certain possibilities?

d) A short critical reflection about the process of peer-assisted learning. This account should make use of at least one of the recommended readings. It doesn't matter (in terms of your mark) how useful the process was or how successfully the problem was resolved. What matters is the quality of your analysis: why did/n't it work well? If it did work well, why? What does PAL have to offer students? If it didn't work well, what does that make you think about the supposed benefits of PAL? Did you just have bad luck or is the idea fundamentally flawed? Under what circumstances do you think it is likely to work well or not?

It is up to you how you weight these four components in terms of relative word length. Just make sure that a), c) and d) are more elaborate than b).

Further Reading

This is of use in two ways: if you read it before the process, it will enhance the process itself. It will also be of use in augmenting and enriching your critical reflection. Much of the literature refers to secondary schooling, and you will need to pick your way through it a bit, but there is relevant material in the following:

Sampson, Jane et al. *Reciprocal Peer Learning: A Guide for Staff and Students*. Sydney: Faculty of Education, University of Technology, 1999.
Topping, Keith J. *Peer Assisted Learning: A Practical Guide for Teachers*. Cambridge, MA: Brookline Books, 2001.
Topping, Keith & Stewart Ehly, eds. *Peer-Assisted Learning*. Mahwah, N.J.: L. Erlbaum Associates, 1998.

Assessment Criteria

- Ability to work well as a partnership, as evidenced by the successful negotiation of and compliance with timelines and by mutual satisfaction with the process, as evidenced in the critical reflections.
- Quality of the critical reflection, including: insightfulness, capacity to develop observations into analysis; ability to situate this experience within a wider analytical frame including, potentially, the academic literature on peer-assisted learning.
- Note: a successful process and outcome, while it will be taken into account, is not an absolute pre-requisite for a good mark. A 'useful failure', when well reflected upon, can also gain a good mark.

Index

Cambridge University, 1–2, 32n2, 43–4, 55n19, 56, 75, 204

Cameron, David, 23

casualization, 2, 6, 8–11, 71, 87, 93, 113–14, 123–4, 132, 134, 164, 199–203, 217
    and precarity, 69, 114, 123–4, 130, 203, 217

Catholic University of Ireland, 1, 50, 56

Colleges of Advanced Education (CAEs), 38, 49, 57, 82, 107

coping, 8, 131, 195

creativity, 45, 52, 59–60, 62, 68, 79, 80–1, 100, 117–19, 130, 137, 214, 218

critical theory, 17, 27, 141–70, 206, 208

critical thinking, 50–2, 59–60, 209–10

Crosland, Anthony, 35, 57

culture, 5, 19–20, 24, 26–9, 49, 51, 53n18, 54, 61, 64, 67, 73–4, 76, 90, 157–8, 160, 179–80, 183–7 *passim*, 190, 206, 210

curriculum, 127, 159–69, 197, 206

Cultural Studies, 18–19, 26–30, 53, 74, 137, 141–70, 171–90, 194, 197, 210, 216

Dawkins, John, 21, 38, 48–9, 51, 57

Dearing Report, 47–8, 54

Derrida, Jacques, 145–6, 152, 163, 176

Dewey, John, 207, 213

disciplines, competition between, 28–9, 64, 202 (*see also* Arts and Humanities; Cultural Studies; transdisciplinarity)

economic rationalism, 23, 25, 62–4

efficiency, 13, 32, 33, 36, 41, 47, 53, 75, 79, 84–5, 96, 103, 108, 110, 116–17, 122–3, 134–5, 174–5, 218

email, 70, 84, 100, 109, 116, 119–21, 135, 205

emotions, 15–18, 119–20, 129, 146, 147n4, 206–7
    anxiety, 99–101, 103–4, 120–1, 131–2
    fraudulence, 191–216
    hope, 26, 30, 141–70, 217
    shame, 14, 16, 188, 206–8, 212, 215–16

entrepreneurialism, 6, 13, 38, 43n12, 46–7, 49, 81, 89, 90, 91, 128, 173–4

excellence, 27–8, 68, 82–3, 96–7, 101, 179–80, 190, 210

feminism, 16–19, 23, 40n9, 192–3, 206–7, 213

Foucault, Michel, 54, 99, 154, 163–4 *passim*, 176

Freire, Paolo, 51, 143–4, 147, 170

Furedi, Frank, 45, 51–2, 173

Giroux, Henry, 51–3, 144, 150

globalization, 20, 33, 163n12, 198 (*see also* universities, internationalization of; students, international)

HECS (*see* tuition fees)

hope (*see* emotions)

Howard, John, 22, 38, 39, 49, 67, 172, 175–6, 180

illness, 98, 105, 128–33, 148, 205–6

instrumentalism, 15, 19, 23, 24–5, 29, 45, 52, 57, 77, 96

For Product Safety Concerns and Information please contact our
EU representative GPSR@taylorandfrancis.com, Taylor & Francis
Verlag GmbH, Kaufingerstraße 24, 80331 München, Germany